THE
BLESSED
ABYSS

THE BLESSED ABYSS

Inmate #6582 in
Ravensbrück Concentration Camp
for Women

Nanda Herbermann

Translated by Hester Baer
Edited by Hester Baer and Elizabeth R. Baer

WAYNE STATE UNIVERSITY PRESS   DETROIT

Library of Congress Cataloging-in-Publication Data

Herbermann, Nanda, 1903–1979.
[Gesegnete Abgrund. English]
The blessed abyss : inmate #6582 in Ravensbrück concentration camp for women / Nanda
Herbermann ; translated by Hester Baer ; edited by Hester Baer and Elizabeth R. Baer.
p.   cm.
Includes bibliographical references and index.
ISBN 0-8143-2904-7 (alk. paper)—ISBN 0-8143-2920-9 (pbk. : alk. paper)
1. Ravensbrück (Concentration camp)   2. Herbermann, Nanda,
1903–1979.   3. Women political prisoners—Germany—Biography.
I. Baer, Hester.   II. Baer, Elizabeth Roberts.   III. Title.
D805.G3 H438 2000
940.53'1743157—dc21
00-032068

ISBN 0-8143-2904-7 (alk. paper)
ISBN 0-8143-2920-9 (pbk : alk. paper)

Contents

NANDA HERBERMANN

DER GESEGNETE ABGRUND

Preface

As work on this book progressed during the last four years, we were often asked how we had discovered the memoir by Nanda Herbermann, which we present here in its first English edition. Here is the story. In 1996, while looking through some family documents in German, Hester discovered a reference to a distant relative who had written a book about her experiences in a concentration camp. Elizabeth was at that time teaching a course on the Holocaust at Gustavus Adolphus College and Hester was completing her coursework for a doctorate in German. We had never heard of Nanda Herbermann, but our curiosity was piqued, and we quickly ordered a copy of her book through interlibrary loan.

Hester began to translate the 1946 edition of the memoir during the summer of 1996. The project originated as a rough translation for family members, but as more people asked to read the book, Hester revised the translation. Together, we determined that the book contained information about, and insights into, the Third Reich and the experiences of women in the camps that would be of interest to a wider audience. We thus began to investigate the life of Nanda Herbermann and to research the history of Ravensbrück, the concentration camp in which she was imprisoned.

As we learned more about Herbermann and the historical background out of which her memoir emerged, our understanding of the memoir and our analysis of it moved through a number of stages. Central to our thinking about the book was the question of its relationship to other narratives written by victims of Nazi persecution. Is it a Holocaust memoir, a concentration camp memoir, or is it better understood within the context of memoirs written by German women about their experiences in the Third Reich? *The Blessed Abyss* does not seem to fit comfortably within any of these categories, though the scholarship generated by historians and literary critics about all three types of memoirs sheds light on Herbermann's memoir in different ways.

Certainly, Herbermann was explicitly victimized by the Nazis through her incarceration in police prisons and in Ravensbrück, an experience that set her apart from most "Aryan" German women during the Third Reich. Nonetheless, her avowed German patriotism and her chauvinistic adherence to German values even in the face of her own victimization present parallels to memoirs by other German women, as does—in a different vein—her gradual understanding of the connections between fascism and patriarchy.

The Blessed Abyss is, of course, a concentration camp memoir, presenting as it does Herbermann's memories of her experiences in Ravensbrück. Yet her memoir differs in striking ways from the majority of non-Jewish women's writings about Ravensbrück and other camps. Most of these memoirs were written by women who were imprisoned for their roles in the Communist or Socialist antifascist resistance movements; their experiences and representations of the camps were of course highly influenced by their political backgrounds.

It would be problematic in many ways to label Nanda Herbermann's book a Holocaust memoir, not least because of her own anti-Semitism and lack of consciousness of the Holocaust and genocide. Indeed, Herbermann experienced all kinds of privileges because she was "Aryan," including her ultimate release from Ravensbrück at the direct order of Heinrich Himmler. Yet many thematic, historical, and psychological parallels can be found between Herbermann's memoir and memoirs by Jewish women. Many such parallels can also be found between *The Blessed Abyss* and Charlotte Delbo's memoirs: both memoirs were written by non-Jewish women arrested for work in resistance; both memoirs recount experiences at Ravensbrück and were written immediately after the war; and both were intended to serve the purpose of witnessing the horrors of the Third Reich in order to educate readers. Though Delbo is not Jewish, her books have entered the canon of women's Holocaust memoirs, further complicating the issue of what constitutes a "Holocaust" memoir. In addition, scholarship on women, gender, and the Holocaust, which has developed primarily in reference to Jewish women, is particularly applicable and useful in an attempt to understand *The Blessed Abyss*.

Ultimately, the question of how to categorize Herbermann's memoir is perhaps the wrong way to approach the book. *The Blessed Abyss* is a complex and ambivalent memoir that often stands in tension with and provides a counterpoint to other representations of the Third Reich, the Holocaust, and the concentration camps, while also having much in common with other memoirs. To our minds, this tension and ambivalence make Herbermann's book particularly compelling and an important contribution toward an understanding of the totality of the Nazi apparatus. The book provides new insight into the workings of the Holocaust in the Ravensbrück camp, into the experiences of women during the Third Reich and in the concentration camps, and about the Gestapo's procedures in regard to activist Catholics. The book also proves interesting as an early document of German remembrance.

We have not abridged Nanda Herbermann's memoir in any way. We have included here the front matter of the original 1946 edition of the book; the only items to be excluded are two drawings—one of Jesus and one of women prisoners in Ravensbrück—that were gifts to Herbermann, drawn by a fellow camp inmate. Herbermann included in the 1946 edition this note about the identities of those individuals she mentions in her text: "The names of the inmates, with the exception of those about whom I had only positive things to report, have all been changed. The names of the commandants, the remaining administration of the concentration camp, and the overseers, insofar as they are mentioned, have been retained."

Many people contributed substantially to our research and thinking about this book, and to them we wish to extend our heartfelt thanks. The staff at the library of the United States Holocaust Memorial Museum aided our early research on Ravensbrück and helped us clarify some of Herbermann's references to individuals, to camp routines, and other particulars of the Nazi time. We would especially like to thank librarian Ron Kurpiers, whose unfailing support during the week we did research there made this a better book. Christa Schulz and Sigrid Jacobeit of the Mahn- und Gedenkstätte Ravensbrück provided encouragement about the project and assistance in research at Ravensbrück. Christa Schulz took the time to give us a personal tour of the Ravensbrück memorial site in January 1998 and to provide us with much useful information on the history of the camp during Herbermann's imprisonment and during the period in which the camp was under GDR (German Democratic Republic) control. Elisabeth Prégardier, editor of the new German edition of *The Blessed Abyss*, provided enormously important materials and references about Nanda Herbermann. Special thanks to her for giving us our own copy of the long out-of-print original edition of *The Blessed Abyss*. We also thank Jennifer Backer, formerly of Wayne State University Press, who was an early and enthusiastic advocate for the manuscript and whose superb editing greatly strengthened the final book. We are very grateful to Arthur Evans, director of the press, and Kristin Harpster, our editor, who have both been supportive, prompt, and responsive throughout the process of bringing the book to reality.

Several members of the Herbermann family have also guided us during the work on this project. Hans-Günther Herbermann opened his home to us in Münster and shared his memories of his aunt with us, which helped us develop a much more personal impression of Nanda Herbermann.

Nanda's niece, Joan Hundhausen, daughter of Nanda's twin sister and a resident of Boulder, Colorado, also generously shared personal memories, important historical information, and pictures of her aunt. Thanks also to Bernie Herbermann, of Omaha, Nebraska, for the pictures and memories he provided of Nanda. Most important, thanks to Emmie Herbermann Roberts, who was instrumental in our discovery of the original edition, helped us contact these family members, and provided us with a helpful family tree.

Closer to home, a number of people gave us ongoing assistance, advice, and support for which we are grateful. Jed Mayer and Nathaniel Baer read the manuscript of the translation in various drafts and offered valuable editorial advice. Special thanks to Jed for moral and intellectual support throughout the many stages of this project. Thanks to Clint Baer, for always believing we could do it. Colleagues at Gustavus Adolphus College, most particularly the Women's Studies reading group, Explorations, and Eric Carlson, associate professor of history, read the introduction at various points and offered advice for revisions. Special thanks to President Axel Steuer for granting Elizabeth a five-month sabbatical during which the manuscript was completed, and to Jean Jacobi, who collaborated in the production of the text from its inception, always cheerfully and competently. Other colleagues whose advice we have heeded include John Conway, Stephen Feinstein, Myrna Goldenberg, Lou Roberts, and Simon Sibelman. Audiences at the Annual Scholars' Conference on the Holocaust and the Churches, at the Center for Advanced Feminist Studies at the University of Minnesota, and at the Women's Worlds Conference in Tromsø, Norway, offered valuable comments and inspiration for our continued partnership on the project. Thanks, too, to Vladka and Ben Meed for providing Elizabeth with a foundation for understanding the Holocaust.

We owe a great debt of gratitude to Atina Grossmann, one of the readers of the manuscript, who generously agreed to work directly with us. Not only did she provide incredibly detailed comments, which contributed significantly to our introduction, but she also (unwittingly) assisted our collaboration by becoming a kind of ideal reader through whom we were able to synthesize our sometimes antithetical thoughts about *The Blessed Abyss*. Finally, we wish to thank each other for mentoring and encouragement in both directions. Working together on this book has been a rewarding new aspect of an already rich relationship between us.

Introduction

On February 4, 1941, Nanda Herbermann, a thirty-eight-year-old Catholic German who worked as a freelance writer and editor, was arrested by the Gestapo in Münster, Germany. Accused of collaboration with the Catholic resistance, Herbermann was subsequently held in a number of police prisons before she was deported to Ravensbrück Concentration Camp for Women in July 1941.[1] On March 19, 1943, Herbermann was released from Ravensbrück upon direct orders by the Reichsführer of the SS, Heinrich Himmler himself. Nanda's brother Heinz Herbermann, one of her five brothers who served in the German army during World War II, had petitioned Himmler directly for her release.

Privileged to return home to Münster in the midst of the war, but under strict orders from the Gestapo not to reveal any information about the concentration camp, Nanda Herbermann soon began to record her memories of her experiences there on paper. As the war ended, Herbermann set about preparing her manuscript for publication. One of the first concentration camp memoirs to appear in print, *The Blessed Abyss: Inmate #6582 in Ravensbrück Concentration Camp for Women* was originally published as *Der Gesegnete Abgrund: Schutzhäftling #6582 im Frauenkonzentrationslager Ravensbrück* under the imprint of the Allied occupying forces by the Catholic press Glock und Lutz in Nuremberg in 1946.[2]

Herbermann constructed her memoir as a morality tale for middle-class Germans in the immediate postwar period. In publishing *The Blessed Abyss*, she hoped to contribute to the rehabilitation of the German nation by demonstrating to her audience that the Nazis were an "un-German" force. Presenting herself as both a member of the collective German nation and as a victim of Nazi crimes, Herbermann sought to show her readers that the Nazis were evil by proving to them that even "good Germans" (such as herself) were persecuted during the Third Reich. Consistently setting herself apart from the other women whom she came to know in Ravensbrück,

Herbermann portrayed herself as morally superior to, but also as sympathetic with, these other victims. Only by collectively atoning for the "sins" of the Nazis against all victims, Herbermann ultimately argued in her memoir, could the German nation cleanse itself of these sins and embark on the path toward reconstruction.

Herbermann's experience working for the Catholic press in Germany, in particular as a writer and editor for the journal *Der Gral* (The grail), undoubtedly shaped her sense of narrative and audience. Prior to the Nazi seizure of power, Herbermann had worked as an editorial assistant for *Der Gral,* and as secretary to its editor, Father Friedrich Muckermann. An outspoken anti-Nazi, Muckermann persisted in publishing veiled critiques of the Third Reich in the journal even after 1933. In 1934, he was forced to flee to Holland as a result of Nazi objections to his writings and political activities. In his absence, Herbermann took over as editor. During 1934 and 1935, she made several trips to Holland to visit Muckermann, to bring him books and clothing he had been forced to leave behind, and to consult with him about the operation of the journal. These trips to Holland constituted the basis of the Nazis' accusations against Herbermann that resulted in her arrest and ultimate imprisonment in Ravensbrück.[3]

In writing her memoir, Herbermann sought to provide a detailed portrait of life in Ravensbrück. She presents a great deal of invaluable historical information about the daily operations in the camp, the largest concentration camp for women. At the same time, she was cognizant of contributing to the project of shaping German memory about the Third Reich and the "Final Solution" through the presentation of her own narrative, which reveals her efforts to reconstruct her personal identity in the aftermath of her experiences in the camp. Defined by the Nazis as a political prisoner because of her work with anti-Nazi Catholics, Herbermann was forced to question both her religious identity and her national identity as a result of her arrest and imprisonment. Grouped together with women of all social backgrounds in the camp, she began to revise her assumptions about class and gender identity as well. Although her self-aggrandizing tone vis-à-vis other victims and her valorization of an essentially "good" German identity make Herbermann's book problematic, it is the ambivalence at the heart of her narrative—about her competing identities and her victim status—that make her memoir compelling and informative. Her early release from Ravensbrück impelled her to recognize her privilege, for only one in thousands was allowed to walk away from the camp. It was perhaps out of the crucible of this tension, as well as the genuine emotional attachment Herbermann developed for those whom she met in Ravensbrück, that she learned through her experiences that others imprisoned in the camp did not deserve to be there either.

Women and the Holocaust

Despite the fact that Holocaust studies is now a mature field, with the creation of centers for Holocaust and genocide studies in many national and international locations and dozens of scholarly studies being published annually, the topic of women and the Holocaust remains, at best, in its infancy. Although it is true that many memoirs by women survivors are in print, relatively little gendered analysis of these memoirs, or of women's experiences in the Holocaust overall, has been published.[4] Sybil Milton, Joan Ringelheim, and Myrna Goldenberg were the first to do research in this field in the late 1970s and early 1980s. Their pioneering books laid the groundwork for a gendered analysis of the Holocaust, but progress in the field has been slow in coming; until recently, only a few essays had been published on this topic.[5] In the late 1990s, however, the field has begun to come into its own with a number of new studies.[6]

Despite this recent spate of publications, the extant books on the subject of gender and the Holocaust make up a very small percentage of publications in the prolific field of Holocaust studies. Why, one might ask, a full fifty-four years after liberation and thirty years since women's studies emerged as a field of study have so few books been published about women, gender, and the Holocaust? Many speculations and explanations are possible. One of the most compelling is that feminist analysis has been almost taboo in Holocaust studies, perhaps because it seemed to imply that one victimhood (female) was more acute than another (male). Similarly, scholars have feared that an analysis of gender might dilute the severity and seriousness of anti-Semitism as the overriding cause of the Holocaust. Finally, several critics have suggested that Jewish women have been alternately ignored or mythologized in Jewish history and that scholarship on the Holocaust has been shaped by this tendency. Such, of course, has been the fate of women in historical studies in general until the past few decades.

Yet, as Myrna Goldenberg has trenchantly observed, in Holocaust studies "we study each concentration camp as a separate entity because each differed from the next; we track the experiences of Jews according to their country of origin . . . we examine the behavior and attitudes of religious and secular Jews, of urban and rural Jews, of heterosexuals and homosexuals, and of Jews and non-Jews. In the same way, we are obligated to examine, separately, the lives of women and of men to determine the differences and the similarities in the way they were treated as well as in the way they responded."[7] We must recognize that in studying *difference* we come to understand the Holocaust more fully. Marlene Heinemann called for such gendered analysis in her 1986 study; more than a decade later, we have made little progress toward this goal.

To be sure, there are encouraging signs of late that gendered analysis of the Holocaust has at last begun to receive appropriate attention. The oldest Holocaust conference, the Annual Scholars' Conference on the Holocaust and the Churches, which has taken place for a quarter of a century, now regularly features at least one or two panels on the topic of women in the Holocaust. The Association of Holocaust Organizations devoted its 1999 conference exclusively to this topic.[8]

And yet, as such gendered analysis gains strength, the signs of a backlash have already emerged. Gabriel Schoenfeld, senior editor of *Commentary* magazine, published a by now infamous article in that journal in June 1998 titled "Auschwitz and the Professors." In the context of this article, which excoriates much of the effort to study and teach the Holocaust, Schoenfeld saves his most caustic comments for the efforts under way to study gender and the Holocaust. Predictably, he opines that much of the scholarship is in the service of a "naked ideological 'agenda.' "[9] A condensed version of his article appearing in the May 21, 1998, issue of the *Wall Street Journal* provoked letters of response from Ringelheim, Weitzman and Ofer, and survivor Nechama Tec, defending the use of gender as a category of analysis.

It is revealing to learn that it is not only contemporary feminists who have argued that studying the difference in experiences of men and women in the Holocaust is a worthwhile enterprise. Indeed, none other than the historian of the Warsaw Ghetto, Emmanuel Ringelblum, recognized that such study would be necessary, even while the war was still in full force: "The future historian would have to dedicate a proper page to the Jewish woman during this war. She will capture an important part in this Jewish history for her courage and ability to survive. Because of her, many families were able to get over the terror of those days."[10] Survivor Primo Levi made a similar observation about the plight of women in Auschwitz: "For a variety of reasons, the women's situation was a good deal worse than that of the men: first, less physical endurance, coupled with work more arduous and degrading than the labors imposed on the men; the agonies of disrupted families; and above all the haunting presence of the crematoria, located right in the middle of the women's camp, inescapable, undeniable, their ungodly smoke rising from the chimneys to contaminate every day and every night, every moment of respite or illusion, every dream and timorous hope."[11]

As one might expect, studies of women and the Holocaust by feminist historians and literary critics in the 1980s and early 1990s reflect the state of theoretical approaches available to scholars at that time. What we might term "essentialist" approaches dominated the field even after critiques of essentialism became commonplace in feminist theory. So, for example, some scholars pointed to the particular ways in which women were vulnerable: to rape; to the onset of infertility; to instant death on arrival at death camps if pregnancy was detected or if women were accompanied by small children. These studies focused on women as victims of Nazism, a victimization that targeted their femaleness.[12]

Other studies took the opposite approach: searching out ways in which women's unique strengths or socialization aided their survival. For example, studies were done of the natural tendency of women to bond and connect, in order to demonstrate that such friendships encouraged sharing of food, skills, and support, and thus improved women's chances of survival. A persuasive study in this category is Judith Baumel's "Social Interaction among Jewish Women in Crisis during the Holocaust," in which she recounts the story of the Zehnerschaft, a group of ten women who survived as a unit through two years and three camps.[13] Similarly, other studies looked at the ways in which the domestic skills women had acquired—sewing, cooking, nursing—could be used to their advantage in ghettos and camps, which were almost always segregated by sex. Ellen Fine's "Women Writers and the Holocaust: Strategies for Survival" is emblematic of this approach.[14]

Many of these early studies took autobiographies and memoirs written by survivors as objective truth; that is to say, the analyses of these texts treated them as reflections of reality, rather than as constructs profoundly affected by both the author and the reader. Joan Ringelheim, one of the pioneers of feminist scholarship on the Holocaust, makes an interesting case in this regard. Ringelheim called the first conference on women and the Holocaust in 1983 and has continued to publish important articles on the topic since. Three of these articles have the same title: Ringelheim has been holding a kind of intertextual dialogue with herself as her own understanding of the issues has deepened and as other scholars have posed new theoretical approaches to textual study.[15] Clearly, much work of just this nature remains to be done, bringing into the discourse of Holocaust studies the insights of more recent feminist theory and gender studies.

Nanda Herbermann's memoir can be fully understood only within the framework of such a theoretical and feminist approach to the text. At the same time, her book will contribute a new perspective to be considered by scholars who have thus far focused their research into women's memories of the Nazi concentration camps primarily on Jewish Holocaust memoirs and antifascist resistance memoirs. Herbermann's memoir does not fit comfortably into any of the "traditional" categories of women's Holocaust and concentration camp memoirs. Precisely this fact makes the book difficult and provocative, but also significant in terms of broadening our understanding of the persecution of women in the Third Reich.

In what follows, we have endeavored to provide for readers historical information and textual analysis that will contextualize the reading experience and highlight the ways in which Herbermann's identity as a woman, a Catholic, and a German profoundly affected her construction of her memoir. To that end, we discuss her family background and life prior to the Nazi seizure of power, the milieu of Catholicism in which she was raised, and Ravensbrück, a camp unique in many ways within the Nazi camp universe. Finally, we turn to an analysis of Herbermann's memoir that seeks to locate it within this complex set of historical discourses and experiences.

Nanda Herbermann

Know the memoirist before knowing the memoir.
—JAMES YOUNG

Nanda Herbermann was born into a middle-class Catholic family in Münster in 1903. Maria Ferdinanda Herbermann, nicknamed Nanda, and her twin sister, Anna Helene, were named for their parents, Helene and Ferdinand Herbermann, a tax collector. Their mother was their father's second wife and the blended family numbered a dozen children. Nanda attended a high school for girls in Münster but was unable to graduate when a serious illness forced her to leave school. After her recovery, she did a three-year apprenticeship at the well-regarded Stenderhoff Bookstore in Münster.

Helene immigrated to America in 1923 at the age of nineteen. Though she spoke no English, she responded to a call for immigrants willing to serve as housekeepers and childcare providers. The economic situation in Germany was dismal and, locating a sponsor in Pittsburgh, Helene first became a nanny and later trained to be a nurse.

Nanda, a petite woman about 5'5" and 120 pounds, remained behind in Germany. Through her work in the bookstore, she was introduced to the intellectual and artistic circles of Münster, as well as to many prominent Catholics. Through these contacts, Herbermann was invited to audition for the theater. As a result, she studied to be an actress and worked in various capacities in the theater throughout the 1920s, even playing the role of Gretchen in Goethe's *Faust* in a production in Münster. According to family members, Herbermann had a dramatic flair and enjoyed being the center of attention throughout her life.

The contacts Herbermann made in the bookstore also eventually led her to a new position in 1928, as editorial assistant to Father Friedrich Muckermann, an activist priest who was considered something of an enfant terrible in Catholic circles. Though he was an outspoken opponent of

Bolshevism, a topic on which he published widely, Muckermann was kn⌐
to live a bohemian lifestyle, trafficking with "film people, freemasons, Jews,
Bolsheviks" and participating in activities seen as questionable for a priest,
such as an international dance congress.[16] Strongly committed to "political
Catholicism," Muckermann was a prolific writer on cultural and political
issues in the Catholic press and served as publisher and editor of the Catholic
journal *Der Gral.*[17] *Der Gral,* which was subtitled "A Monthly on Literature
and Life," was an important journal that regularly contained articles by
prominent German Catholics on subjects such as philosophy and theology,
the plastic arts, social issues, and politics. In addition, the journal published
new poetry, short fiction, and reviews of a diverse range of books. One
commentator described the journal as "on the Catholic side, the test point
that went furthest out on a limb in considering all intellectual and spiritual,
literary and artistic, cultural and political experiments of the decade [the
1920s]."[18] Herbermann began as an assistant to Muckermann, but was soon
writing regular reviews of children's books and books for women.

In June 1934, Muckermann wrote an editorial for *Der Gral,* titled
"Pompa diaboli," which was a thinly veiled attack on Hitler and Nazi politics.
Muckermann began by bemoaning the contemporary state of affairs, in
which "even" Catholics seemed to have lost their instinct for differentiating
between good and evil: "Observe the conduct of devout people in relation
to the most important phenomena of the times. Listen to the judgments
of educated people, who have received the sacrament of baptism, about
movements and books. Judgments are made and hopes are expressed which
make one's hair stand on end. They can no longer distinguish the good
apples from the bad, or wolves from lambs. . . . Something is missing which
one can observe often enough in a child: the instinct for good and evil in
people."[19] Muckermann went on to discuss this lack of instinct in terms
that make his article an evident metaphor for the Catholic reaction to the
contemporary political situation in Germany, referring for example to the
saying that "only the dumbest calves choose their butchers themselves." In
explicating the title of his editorial, translated from Latin to German as
"the pomp or splendor of the devil," Muckermann recalled how, in early
Christianity, baptism was a ritual through which the one being christened
broke free from the triumphal procession of Satan, the prince of the world.
Quoting an article that traced the etymology of the word "pompa" in a
theological context, Muckermann pointed out that in the Roman world,
"pompa" referred to the triumphal processions of generals, which had a
uniquely "sacral-militaristic" character. Baptism into Christianity, however,
constituted a decision between two worlds, a rejection of pomp—of the false
appearances and fraudulence of the triumphal procession—in favor of an
acceptance of Christ and the humility of the cross. Muckermann urged his

readers to reconsider their own baptism in this regard, thus rather blatantly suggesting that they would do well to reject the pomp of the devil Hitler and the militaristic splendor of National Socialism.

Muckermann continued to write for *Der Gral* until September 1934, when the journal ran the following "Announcement to our readers": "Certain difficulties have arisen which led to the confiscation of the June issue. The publisher and editorial staff have decided to undertake several changes in personnel in order to relieve the situation of the *Grail* in the current times. The fundamental stance of the *Grail* is not affected by this alteration. Thus we ask our readers to remain true to us in their established fashion."[20] In fact, the Nazis had confiscated the June issue because of Muckermann's editorial. Muckermann himself, whose editorial was only his latest transgression against the Nazis, was forced to flee to Holland during the summer of 1934 in order to escape arrest. There, he began a new journal, *Der Deutsche Weg* (The German way), which provided him with a base from which to criticize the Third Reich.[21] Herbermann acknowledges in her memoir that she wrote unsigned articles for this journal. Copies of the journal were smuggled into Nazi Germany, as were underground Catholic publications from Switzerland, France, and Poland.[22]

With the September 1934 issue of *Der Gral,* the masthead of the journal changed to reflect Nanda Herbermann's new role as leader of the editorial staff. Herbermann also continued to write for the journal, taking on greater tasks such as explicating the artwork that was chosen for each issue and writing short articles on social or literary themes. By 1936, she was writing not only reviews of children's books and literature for women but a substantial percentage of all short book reviews published in the journal.

Herbermann's role as editor and her writing in the journal shed light in several ways on her subsequent experiences and stand in tension with the ways in which she represents them in *The Blessed Abyss.* It is evident that Muckermann's open opposition to the Third Reich was a highly political act, and the role that Herbermann took on in assisting Muckermann and in continuing to operate the journal in his absence was thus politicized as well. It is striking that Herbermann is at pains in her memoir to dispel this idea: she portrays her work for Muckermann and for the journal as a work of devotion to her faith and to the priest Muckermann, rather than as a work of devotion to higher ideals in a political sense. Clearly, Herbermann was something of a New Woman during the 1920s: an actress and chain-smoker, she did not marry, worked in various white-collar jobs, gained entry into the intellectual circles of the city in which she lived, and ultimately became a respected writer and editor in her own right.[23] In the 1930s, despite constant surveillance by the Gestapo and periodic raids, she operated and edited an important journal almost single-handedly. Yet by the time she wrote her memoir in 1946, after

Germany's defeat and the collapse of the Nazi regime, she sought to cover up this identity in many ways.

In her writings in *Der Gral* from the 1930s, too, Herbermann expressed a consciousness of women's issues and an interest in female artists and writers that squared with her identity as a New Woman. Her articles are all written in a serious journalistic style that is quite at odds with the trite, sentimental tone of *The Blessed Abyss.* In the October 1934 issue of *Der Gral,* for example, the second issue under Herbermann's control, she chose a painting by German painter Paula Modersohn-Becker as a frontispiece.[24] In a short article about the painting and Modersohn-Becker herself, Herbermann wrote, "Through her 'Letters and Journals,' which appeared in book form many years ago, Paula Modersohn-Becker became known to wide circles of people. These letters are the testimony of a great woman and a mature, divinely inspired painter. In regard to her talent and disposition, she herself once wrote: 'In myself I feel it like a soft weaving, a vibrating, a beating of wings, a trembling restfulness, a holding of breath: if, one day, I can paint, I shall paint that.' That is the voice of a humble, creative woman, who must obey the voice of her innermost being and cannot do otherwise."[25] Herbermann portrays Modersohn-Becker as possessing essentially "female" traits and as being a driven artist at the same time; her "divine inspiration" functions as a rationale for her art.

In all of her reviews of books for children and young people, Herbermann consistently urged parents to consider the importance of reading literature in the moral and creative education of young minds. She suggested biblical stories for children and books about faith, but she also warned parents not to neglect providing their children with fairy tales and myths, which would awaken their fantasy life and their creativity. In her recommendations of books for both children and women, Herbermann emphasized the importance of art in strengthening character and in confirming faith.

In a review article from December 1935 about recent books for and about women, Herbermann took the opportunity to meditate briefly on the feminine ideal, great art, and women's particular receptivity to religion: "It is occasionally good, before discussing specific books which give particular prominence to female figures, to say something of the ideal which we have in mind in this area. If all serious literature should present the image of the eternal, then the particular symbolism of the woman must come to the fore in the female figure, or at least appear in the background. The woman is, precisely in her eternal figure, in the eternal-feminine, in her solemn mystery, the readiness to conceive of the divine."[26] After further musings on this topic, Herbermann went on to recommend books as diverse as German Catholic author Henriette Brey's homeland novel *The Deep Fountain;* Norwegian author Barbara Ring's *Anne Karine Corvin* (which Herbermann described as "almost hard in a masculine sense" and filled with "strong humor"); a biography of the agricultural scientist Margarethe von Wrangell ("It leaves behind the strong impression that she was not just a woman, but also a strong-willed fighter who remained true to her idea until her death"); and a new biography of Greta Garbo.

Though it would be a stretch to term her writings in *Der Gral* feminist, Herbermann consistently wrote about women, art and literature in ways that show her awareness of prejudice against women and their secondary status in society. Her writings are grounded in a conception of women as essentially pious; yet she is able to utilize this conception as a justification for women as producers and critics of art and literature. Despite her lack of higher education, Herbermann's articles also show that she possessed considerable knowledge of the German literary tradition and of theological and philosophical issues, as well as a well-formed and critical aesthetic judgment.

The Catholic Church and National Socialism

Nanda Herbermann's commitment to working in the service of her faith was clearly grounded in her family. One of Nanda's sisters became a nun and a brother became a priest who served as a missionary in New Guinea. An American relative, Charles G. Herbermann, son of a German immigrant, served as the first editor-in-chief of *The Catholic Encyclopedia* after its founding in 1902. Not only was her home environment one that inculcated religious values, but the town in which Herbermann grew up, Münster, was a stronghold of Catholicism. During the Nazi period, Münster was the seat of Bishop Clemens August Count von Galen (1878–1946), often credited with being one of the most outspoken anti-Nazi Catholic bishops. Herbermann would have had the opportunity in the late 1930s to hear his many sermons and pastoral letters, spoken from the pulpits in the St. Lamberti Church and the Münster Cathedral. We know that Nanda Herbermann attended mass at this cathedral, as she recounts in her memoir that it was there that she first spotted the three men who subsequently arrested her in February 1941. In fact, her connection to the cathedral may have contributed to her arrest; she comments in chapter 6 that the "Gestapo certainly wanted to finger me as the 'middle man' between Father Muckermann and the Bishop of Münster with whom [the Gestapo thought] I was 'in close contact' (which was not at all the case, but pure speculation on the part of these awful men)."

Precisely because the family and cultural environment in which Herbermann was raised was heavily Catholic, it is crucial for the purpose of understanding *The Blessed Abyss* to map out what this Catholicism meant to her. James Young has reminded us that the "significance and meaning of events created in these texts [Holocaust narratives] often reflect the kind of understanding of events by victims at the time." He goes on to say that "it was not 'the facts' in and of themselves that determined actions taken by the victims of the Holocaust—or by the killers themselves; but it was the structural, mythological, and figurative apprehension of these facts that led to action taken on their behalf."[27] Herbermann's apprehension of the events that befell her clearly had this sort of effect on her memoir. Her identity as a German, a Catholic, and a woman shaped not only her experiences in the camp but also her subsequent recounting of them. The intertwined mythoi of nationalism and Catholicism constituted a powerful, perhaps ineluctable, combination that provided Herbermann with a sacral and patriotic worldview, one that rendered her—at least at the outset of her imprisonment—certain of what was right and what was wrong.

The Blessed Abyss contains visible markers of this sacral worldview: the invocations and epigrams from religious writers at the beginning of many chapters; the comparison between her imprisonment and the stations of the cross; and the recollection of the strength Herbermann found in spirituality and prayer. The impress of her Catholic upbringing is also present in less explicit ways as well: Herbermann casts herself as saint and martyr, and, initially, espouses Catholic views on such issues as lesbianism.

In her study of Nazi treatment of lesbians, *Days of Masquerade: Life Stories of Lesbians during the Third Reich,* Claudia Schoppmann delineates the various forces within German society that openly condemned homosexuality and counts among these the Catholic Church: "There were clubs dedicated to combating the existence of homosexual organizations. Among these were . . . the Catholic Association to Protect the People (*Volkswartbund*) [which] . . . published the *Volkswart,* a monthly journal dedicated to fighting public immorality."[28] The homophobia Herbermann demonstrates was clearly part of Church and Nazi teachings, whose belief systems comfortably reinforced each other in this instance.

Christian anti-Judaism is another example of the way in which the belief systems of the Church and Nazism reinforced each other.[29] Indeed, in a conversation with two Catholic bishops of Germany in April 1933, Hitler spoke "of the Jewish question, stressing the fundamental agreement between National Socialism and Catholicism, point[ing] out that the Church always had regarded the Jews as parasites and had banished them into the ghetto."[30] Traces of the Catholic Church's influence on Herbermann can be found in her attitudes toward Jews in *The Blessed Abyss.* To be sure, there were many Christians involved in rescuing Jews.[31] But the long history of expulsion and ghettoization of Jews, of endeavors to "convert" them to Christianity, of accusations that Jews were "Christ killers," and other Christian acts of anti-Judaism must be acknowledged, as must the fact that the vast majority of Christians during the Holocaust were either perpetrators or bystanders. As Michael Dobkowski has stated in a recent article, "The silence of the Christian hierarchy, both Catholic and Protestant, during the years of Nazi domination of Europe, is a vexing and painful issue. . . . Nazi anti-Semitism would not have been as extreme and toxic as it was if the Catholic Church had not had an integral role in the centuries-long demonizing of Jews."[32]

The Catholic Church in Germany had had a somewhat troubled relationship with the state in the seventy-five years preceding Hitler's seizure of power. Most notable was Chancellor Otto von Bismarck's Kulturkampf, initiated in the 1870s, which marked German Catholics as a potential threat to the newly unified state. A series of laws were enacted that severely circumscribed the role of clergy in political life, and Jesuits were expelled from the country. Though this effort was abandoned by Bismarck within a decade, it continued to affect the identity and role of German Catholics within political circles. Catholics felt themselves defined as "outsiders" within their own land.

The Center Party, a largely Catholic political party with a history dating back to the nineteenth century, remained a force with which to be reckoned, due to the large Catholic population in Germany, and was the wellspring of "political Catholicism."[33] Karl-Egon Lönne has indicated, "There can be no doubt as to the atmosphere of mutual hostility which existed between the Center Party–BVP [Bavarian People's Party] and the NSDAP [the Nazi Party]."[34] Yet, as Guenter Lewy points out, there were many points of convergence between the Catholic Church and the ideology of the Nazis, including anticommunism, anti-Semitism, support for nationalism, and opposition to liberalism and pacifism.[35]

In July 1933, the Third Reich and the Vatican signed an agreement, called the Concordat, which was supposed to usher in a period of harmony between Catholics and the state. The Concordat purported to offer safeguards for the freedom of the Catholic press, Catholic property, Catholic education for the young, and Catholic involvement in charitable, professional, and youth organizations. In turn, the Church agreed to the prohibition of political Catholicism: banned were political activity and party membership on the part of clergy and religious orders, as well as Catholic trade unions and political organizations.[36] On June 30, 1934, the date of the so-called Night of Long Knives, several Catholic leaders, including Dr. Eric Klausener, the general secretary of Catholic Action, and Dr. Fritz Gerlich, the editor of an anti-Nazi Catholic weekly journal, *Der Gerade Weg*, were murdered by the Nazis in order to discourage any further political action on the part of Catholic organizations.

The arm of the Third Reich created specifically for dealing with Catholic individuals and organizations seen as threatening to the state was called the Unit for Political Catholicism. It was to this office in Münster

Herbermann was brought for interrogation after her arrest and to which she returned, with haughty triumphalism, after her release from Ravensbrück. According to John Steward, the Nazis used the existence of political Catholicism as an excuse to wage war against the Catholic Church in general. The Gestapo's Unit for Political Catholicism was active throughout Germany (especially the largely Catholic regions in southern Germany) and kept extensive files on Catholics from all walks of life whom they suspected of resistance of various kinds.[37]

Despite the real threat the Nazis posed to some outspoken Catholics, subsequent historians have had good reason to call the Concordat into question, as it raises important concerns about the extent of the Catholic Church's collaboration with the Nazi regime.[38] Because of their Church's formal agreement with the Third Reich, many Catholics looked favorably on enlisting in Nazi organizations and pledging fidelity to Hitler and the state.

However, it was less than three years after the signing of the Concordat that Bishop von Galen publicly decried the impunity with which the Nazis violated the agreement: "How many Catholics, priests and laymen, have been attacked and insulted in the papers and at public meetings, without judicial sentence being passed! . . . There are fresh graves in German soil in which are lying the ashes of those whom the Catholic people regard as martyrs for the faith, since their lives gave witness to their most dutiful and loyal devotion to God and the Fatherland, to the nations and the Church, while the dark secrecy which surrounds their deaths is most carefully preserved."[39] This early outcry by von Galen set the tone for his subsequent public anti-Nazi statements. Like other outspoken anti-Nazi Catholics, von Galen focused his criticisms exclusively on the negative impact of the Third Reich on Catholics and fundamental Catholic beliefs; he ignored all other victims of the fascist regime.

In the summer of 1941, von Galen sparred with the Nazis about the confiscation of Church property and delivered an attack from his pulpit on the euthanasia program. This attack, outlining the details of secret transportation, cremation, and the deception of relatives, led Martin Bormann, private secretary to Hitler and the most rabid anti-cleric of the Nazi inner circle, to declare that the bishop deserved the death sentence. A speech given by Hitler in a Munich beer hall in November 1941 alludes to von Galen, and seven months later, Hitler threatened to "extract retribution to the last farthing" from von Galen after the war was won.[40] Contemporaneous accounts of von Galen's writing and delivery of these sermons make clear his genuine fear that he would be immediately arrested by the Gestapo, a well-founded fear given the arrests of clergy that had already occurred.[41]

Von Galen's anti-Nazi sermons were published in leaflet form and distributed throughout Germany. Excerpts from many of his sermons and letters were also published in the United States in 1942, in a book titled *The Persecution of the Catholic Church in the Third Reich: Facts and Documents.* Translated from the German, the book was published anonymously with the avowed purpose of demonstrating, while the war was yet in progress, "that the word 'persecution' is applicable in its most exact sense to the treatment meted out by the National Socialists to the Catholic Church in Germany."[42] Of course, more recent scholarship makes such characterization questionable. Nonetheless, this view of the Church's persecution, contemporaneous with Herbermann's arrest, provides us with insight into the environment in which she lived and worked.

Bishop von Galen himself has been touted by both the postwar West German government and by scholars for his work in the resistance. The comments of Gordon Zahn are typical: "Few names will outrank that of Clement [*sic*] August von Galen, the Bishop of Münster, in any roll of honor registering the names of opponents of Hitler and his national Socialist regime."[43] Certainly, von Galen was more daring in his opposition to the Nazis than many other powerful Germans, albeit only in regard to specific issues, mostly relating to or inspired by Catholic doctrine. As John Conway has suggested, "The significance of Bishop Galen's challenge should neither be exaggerated nor minimized."[44]

In this vein, a recently completed dissertation by Beth A. Griech-Polelle has called into question Bishop von Galen's heroism, pointing out that his focus was almost exclusively on saving Catholics and Catholic prerogatives; indeed, careful study of the full texts of some of his sermons reveals significant anti-Judaism. Griech-Polelle has brought to light a little known and rarely cited passage from the conclusion of von Galen's most famous sermon, the third sermon from the summer of 1941, which focused on euthanasia. Having dwelt on the commandment "Thou shalt not kill" in delivering his critique of the Nazi practice of killing the handicapped and mentally ill, von Galen went on to say, "Is the people of Israel the only people whom God has encompassed and protected with a father's care and a mother's love, has drawn to himself? . . . The only [people] that rejected God's truth, that threw off God's laws and so condemned itself to ruin?"[45] Von Galen's comments reflected the widespread anti-Judaism within the Catholic Church to which Nanda Herbermann was certainly exposed throughout her life. Though Herbermann was already imprisoned in Ravensbrück by the time von Galen delivered this particular sermon, her memoir must be understood in the context of her upbringing in the Catholic Church, when even a Bishop recognized as one of the more outspoken opponents of Nazism folds such comments into his sermons.

The memoir that Nanda Herbermann published in 1946, an account of one German Catholic woman's struggle to come to terms with the conflicting and sometimes intersecting ideologies of the Catholic Church and the German state under Nazism, provides a compelling test case for research into the complex relationship between both institutions. A concise and balanced view of the issues at stake in the debate over the role of Catholicism in the Third Reich can be found in an essay by John Conway. Noting that the posture of German Catholic historians has been a largely defensive one since 1945, Conway argues for a "wider perspective," one that would enable us to see the connections among the persecution of Jews, Catholics, and Protestants. Such connections are illuminated by the recognition that the Nazis opposed the entire Judeo-Christian spectrum in their efforts to "remodel society along totalitarian and racial lines."[46] Of course, any such comparative analysis of Nazi persecution of people for their religious beliefs must highlight the fact that only Jews were targeted for the "Final Solution."

Ravensbrück

Within the Nazi concentration camp universe, made up of death camps, concentration camps, and labor camps located throughout western and eastern Europe and numbering in the hundreds, Ravensbrück was the largest camp built exclusively for women prisoners. Though initially intended as a prison to be used for those who had transgressed laws of the Third Reich, it eventually housed a gas chamber and crematorium; many inmates were transported elsewhere for execution before the gas chamber was put into operation in 1945.

Ravensbrück has not been the subject of extensive historical study, in part because of its location in what became the GDR.[47] Under Communist rule, the camp served as a military base for Soviet soldiers, who evacuated the site only in 1994. In the building that had served as the cell block, a modest staff ran a small museum and a summer program for East German youth. Circumscribed tours were available to visitors and scholars. The museum was linked to a large and active international association of survivors of the camp, who held regular meetings there. These *Lagergemeinschaften*, or camp organizations, had ties to the Socialist Unity Party (SED, the state party of the GDR) and other Communist parties, and were dominated by survivors who had been imprisoned for their work in the German Communist Party (KPD).[48] In accordance with official GDR ideology about the Holocaust, the camp was interpreted primarily as a site where heroic "antifascists" had been imprisoned. Although many women were indeed imprisoned in Ravensbrück for their political beliefs and their work in Communist or Socialist resistance groups, the GDR celebrated these women while only paying lip service to other persecuted groups or refusing to recognize them at all. Research on such topics as prostitution and lesbian inmates, for example, was strictly forbidden.

Since the fall of the wall, the museum and memorial site at Ravensbrück have been newly reconfigured as part of the Foundation of Brandenburg Memorials.[49] The camp's archives have once again become accessible to scholars of the Holocaust, and one of the primary objectives of the new museum and memorial site, and of its director Sigrid Jacobeit, is to expand our understanding of gender and the Holocaust and of the persecution of groups such as "asocials," Gypsies (Roma or Sinti), and political and religious prisoners of conscience. Indeed, a number of recent publications (primarily in German) point to the significance of the camp for studies of these victims and of gender and the Holocaust.[50] Ravensbrück and its archives present new resources for understanding the role of gender for persecutors and inmates. A large-scale project is now under way to reconstruct the day-by-day history of Ravensbrück, which will provide an invaluable resource for researchers into the camp itself, as well as such gender-related topics as prostitution, lesbianism, so-called asocials, female inmates in the camp hierarchy, and female guards and overseers.[51] Researchers have also begun to investigate Jewish women in the camp, who have been neglected until now, in part because they were in the minority at Ravensbrück for much of the camp's existence. Many Jewish women did pass through the camp for temporary stays on their way to other camps or to forced-labor sites.[52] Reconstruction of the history of the camp is particularly important though made difficult by the fact that its function within the Nazi camp universe changed often.

Construction of Ravensbrück began in the fall of 1938, when five hundred male prisoners from Sachsenhausen concentration camp outside Berlin were sent to the scenic site of meadows and woods beside the Schwedt See, a small lake near the town of Fürstenberg. These prisoners built fourteen wooden barracks, two barracks to be used as an infirmary, which subsequently was called the *Revier* (sick bay), a kitchen, a shower building, grounds for roll call, a cell block, and a brick wall several feet high surrounding these buildings. Outside the wall, the commandant's headquarters and homes for the Nazi officers and guards were constructed.

On May 18, 1939, the first 867 prisoners—all women—were transferred from the prison at Lichtenburg Castle, which had become severely overcrowded, to Ravensbrück. It is estimated that 132,000 prisoners entered the camp during its six-year history. The early prisoners were primarily German women arrested for resistance work, religious beliefs, or political activities in opposition to Nazi ideology, or as so-called asocials—criminals (often accused of "crimes" such as having physical contact with men considered enemies or "racial inferiors") and prostitutes. In 1941, the year Nanda Herbermann was deported to the camp, 3,100 women were sent there, bringing the inmate total to 5,900, including 300 men who had been transported from Dachau to Ravensbrück in June 1941 to construct a number of new buildings. In December 1941, a commission of doctors arrived from Berlin to select the first transport to be sent to the gas chambers. All Jewish prisoners were selected for this transport, as were any inmates who were very sick or weak.[53] By the end of the war, women from twenty European countries had been imprisoned in the camp: 36.8 percent from Poland; 21.2 percent others from the Soviet Union; 18.2 percent from Germany/Austria; 7.5 percent from Hungary; 6 percent from France; 3.2 percent from Czechoslovakia; and 2.2 percent from Yugoslavia.[54] It is estimated that 15 percent of the prisoners were Jewish.[55]

Arriving in the camp as a prisoner in the early years, a woman would be told to undress, have her body cavities inspected for hidden jewels, have her head shaved to prevent lice, given a shower, and issued a camp uniform, which consisted of a striped dress, or skirt and blouse, underwear, an apron, a kerchief, and clogs. In the waning years of the Third Reich, camp uniforms were no longer available, and new prisoners were issued "civilian" clothing on which an enormous "X" had been either sewn or painted; this marked them clearly as inmates, in the event an escape was attempted. Some survivors tell of being issued fancy cocktail dresses and other absurd costumes, unsuited for camp life. Following these rituals, the newcomers were marched to the quarantine block where they resided from three to six weeks. This was a period of relative inactivity; their initiation into work squads came only after they were reassigned to more permanent barracks.

Work in Ravensbrück was of three kinds: labor that sustained the camp itself, such as kitchen work, work in the hospital, the painting squad, etc.; work that furthered the war effort and the industrial goals of the Third Reich, such as assignment to labor in the nearby Siemens factory; and, finally, work that seemed to have no purpose other than to exhaust and eventually kill the laborers, such as the work detail that endlessly moved sand from one pile to another. Prisoners labored twelve-hour days, winter and summer, indoors and out, almost always under the scrutiny of their SS guards; they were subject to meeting quotas of enormous measure and to the vicious attacks of the guards' dogs if they did anything to displease.

Food was meager at best and became increasingly worse as the war dragged on. Generally, a day's rations consisted of ersatz coffee before sunrise, a thin soup of turnips and potatoes for lunch, and another soup for dinner, with bread. Some prisoners report cheese and a piece of sausage on Sundays, but this disappeared in later years. Efforts to "organize" (that is, take illicitly) food were constant among prisoners; often, this was the only means of survival. Thus, work assignments that put one in contact with food, or something that could be bartered for food, were highly prized.

The block, or barracks, to which a prisoner was assigned could make a tremendous difference in the experience she had in the camp. Several narratives describe in relatively favorable terms the block that housed the Jehovah's Witnesses or the "Bible Students," as they were referred to in German and in camp parlance. They were clean, quiet, earnest, and studious. By contrast, every account of Block II, the infamous asocials' block, describes it as filthy, chaotic, noisy, and full of inmates who were often ill and given to stealing and various forms of violence. This is the block to which Nanda Herbermann was assigned shortly after her arrival, first as barracks elder (supervisor of one side of the block) and then as block elder (supervisor of the whole block and the two barracks elders). Most of the inmates in Block II were prostitutes, arrested because the Nazis considered them morally degenerate; some of these women were also lesbians.

Herbermann provides detailed and historically valuable documentation of daily life in the camp. In the chapters titled "The sick among us," "Clothing and laundry problems," and "The lice plague," she reveals how women were particularly physically vulnerable in the camp and how this often led to an increased emotional vulnerability as well. Female inmates in Ravensbrück who were forced to have their heads shaved in connection with lice plagues, for example, often experienced the loss of their hair as much more degrading than it would have been for their male counterparts. Herbermann discusses the impossibility of keeping clean (and thus avoiding lice) in unsanitary conditions where the possession of a comb was a luxury and no one was ever able to wash her hair. Similarly, she documents the struggle among women in each block to keep their clothing clean and to obtain a reasonable pair of stockings each winter. Forced to wear skirts, women without proper stockings would be doubly exposed to cold and bad weather.

More serious still was the particular brutality to which female inmates were vulnerable on the basis of their sex and reproductive capacity. In her chapter "The sick among us," Herbermann reports, "Newly born children of young mothers, who had been taken into custody during their pregnancy, were killed or the fetuses were aborted before birth. In the sick bay I myself heard such a small being crying, who was murdered fifteen minutes later. I knew German and foreign inmates who confessed to me after their delivery to the concentration camp that they were pregnant and hoped that they would be released in time. But they were not released, nor did they bear a child."

Here and in the chapter "Sick transports," Herbermann further attests to the so-called medical experiments to which Ravensbrück inmates were subjected. For example, Nazi doctors routinely sterilized women in the camp, primarily the Gypsy inmates. Carl Clauberg was the primary perpetrator of these operations. In August 1942, Nazi doctors initiated a series of surgeries on perfectly healthy women, almost all of whom were Polish. Approximately seventy-five women were subjected to incisions in their legs, which were then filled with gravel, glass, germs, and other matter that might simulate war wounds. Sulfur drugs were then tested for efficacy on these women. Other prisoners had sections of bone and muscle removed, legs fractured, or bone, muscle, and nerve transplants done. Herbermann mentions the particularly visible effects of skin transplants, incisions, and experiments on bones that she saw on the women who returned from such experiments. Given the primitive conditions, and their already compromised health, many of these victims died; others were permanently crippled and disfigured. When these secret surgeries were made known to other camp inmates, there was a systematic effort to hide the victims, often referred to in camp terminology as "rabbits," as it was feared that the Nazis would take their lives to hide the evidence. Some fifty of these women did survive the war and some have written accounts of their suffering.[56] Ample photo documentation of the leg wounds exists as well; when prisoner Germaine Tillion was freed in April 1945, she carried with her a roll of undeveloped film showing the results of surgeries.

While many aspects of Herbermann's memoir point to the unique ways in which women in Ravensbrück were vulnerable and victimized on the basis of their sex, she also discusses certain kinds of resistance she sees as unique to women, certain aspects of their experience as women that helped them survive in camp, or at least allowed them a "dignified ending." Maternity or "mothering," whether between biological mothers and daughters, older and younger women, or healthy and sick women, is one of these experiences. In several instances, Herbermann reports maternal feelings for "her prostitutes" and for others, such as the young Gypsy girl to whom she devotes a chapter. These maternal feelings (which for Herbermann are often linked to religion) become the basis for small acts of resistance. In her chapter "Dignified endings," Herbermann recounts a striking story in which she utilized her "red armband," which allowed her to move freely around the camp, to reunite a Polish mother and daughter briefly before the mother, who had been sentenced to death that morning, was taken off to be shot. Though, as she points out, she herself could have been severely punished had she been caught, she and other women in the camp did all they could to facilitate such resistance in order to restore each other's human dignity. Quoting the poet Stefan George, she concludes her story, "Stefan George speaks in one of his books of 'many endings without dignity.' In these months [that is, at the time of Herbermann's writing, in the last days of the war or immediately after the war], I must use these words again and again in reference to the criminal men of the Third Reich.

But an ending in the concentration camp was often full of dignity, more dignified than that of the men who initiated and were guilty of and ordered the endings."

Prostitution in Nazi Concentration Camps

One particularly valuable aspect of Nanda Herbermann's memoir is her confirmation of several important details about forced prostitution and the bordellos established by the SS in a number of concentration camps in the mid-1940s. In her chapters "As 'barracks elder' with the prostitutes," "Alone no more!" and "Block elder over four hundred prostitutes," Herbermann discusses the histories of a number of prostitutes she came to know in Ravensbrück to illustrate how the horrible social conditions in which many of them grew up led them to prostitution and how society, which had failed them to begin with, now persecuted them uniquely: they were victims twice-over to the two-faced morality of the Nazi state. Discussing the SS bordellos at Mauthausen and other concentration camps for men in which women from her block were sent to work, Herbermann asserts in the chapter "Alone no more!": "It is a horrible fact that people who had been imprisoned for their depravity and for 'endangering human society' were now commanded by the state, which held them for this precise reason, to be depraved again."

The subject of forced prostitution and camp bordellos has remained largely taboo in Holocaust studies and histories of National Socialism until recently, when two important publications in German broke the silence and began to address these topics. Christa Schulz's article "Weibliche Häftlinge aus Ravensbrück in Bordellen der Männerkonzentrationslager" (Female inmates from Ravensbrück in bordellos at concentration camps for men) appeared in 1994, shortly before the publication that same year of Christa Paul's *Zwangsprostitution. Staatlich errichtete Bordelle im Nationalsozialismus* (Forced prostitution: bordellos established by the national socialist state). Nanda Herbermann's memoir is an important source for both Schulz and Paul.

Herbermann's discussion of camp bordellos in chapter 20 is regrettably brief; nonetheless, by simply mentioning their existence she provides more information than do most eyewitnesses. Paul points out how unfortunate it is that Herbermann limits herself to the comment, "What I heard from these inmates who returned from [bordellos in] Mauthausen and other KZ's was gruesome. I will leave it up to others to report of this in more detail."[57] Very few others did report about their experiences in more detail, for the obvious reason that most survivors who were forced to work as prostitutes in camp bordellos found their experiences too painful to report about and feared being socially stigmatized or discriminated against in their postwar lives as a result of these experiences.

As block elder in the "prostitute's block," Herbermann was in a position to know about and report on the bordellos without feeling that she would implicate herself by doing so. Though she does not discuss the bordellos in great detail, Herbermann does confirm that prostitutes were regularly selected and recruited from her block to work at the bordellos at Mauthausen and other camps. She also notes that these women would generally be sent back approximately every three months to be "exchanged" for new prostitutes. While the SS wooed women into "volunteering" to work in bordellos with promises of an early release and better living conditions, Herbermann reports that at least one woman she knew, "Frieda," did not survive the violence she was subjected to there and never returned from Mauthausen. The use of Ravensbrück inmates as prostitutes for Mauthausen is described in this passage in Margarete Buber-Neumann's memoir:

> In 1942 a "Commission" of the S.S. officers arrived from Mauthausen. They inspected the human flesh available in Block 2 [this was Nanda's block from late 1941 until late fall 1942; Buber-Neumann had served as block elder in Block II for two months in late fall 1940] and made a preliminary choice. All the women picked out were then led off to the wash-room, where they had to strip and be examined by the "Commission." Those with firm breasts, sound limbs and general physical attractions were short-listed, so to speak, and from their "re-education" in the camp they were sent to replenish the S.S. brothel in Mauthausen. After six months of this activity they were promised their freedom—to return to the world of free citizens "re-educated" and cleansed.[58]

In the early 1990s Christa Paul sought out several survivors who had worked in bordellos for concentration camp inmates or in bordellos for SS officers. Despite their reluctance, she was able to interview them. Both Schulz and Paul base many of their conclusions on this valuable oral testimony, in combination with some limited testimony of certain privileged male inmates who knew of the existence of the bordellos or visited them and a number of letters and other historical materials that also document the existence of the bordellos. Although much information about forced prostitution and camp bordellos remains sketchy, some solid conclusions can be drawn.

As both Schulz and Paul show, the SS began to establish bordellos for the use of male inmates of concentration camps in summer 1942, about one year after Heinrich Himmler initially gave the order for them to do so; by the end of 1944 at least eleven such bordellos had been built in

Buchenwald, Dachau, Mauthausen, Gusen, Auschwitz, Monowitz, Birkenau, Flossenbürg, Neuengamme, Sachsenhausen, and Dora-Mittelbau.[59] According to Paul, women from Ravensbrück were forced into prostitution at all of these bordellos except for the three at Auschwitz and its satellites, where female inmates from Auschwitz were forced to work.[60] It is important to note here that although Herbermann and others consistently report that women could "volunteer themselves of their own free will" for work in these bordellos, it is impossible to speak of "free will" when considering the circumstances under which inmates of concentration camps were forced to make such a decision.[61] In combination with other bordellos established by the Nazi state (for the soldiers in the Wehrmacht, for SS officers, and for foreign and forced laborers working in the German Reich), concentration camp bordellos formed part of an extensive system in which, Paul estimates, a minimum of 34,140 women were forced to work as prostitutes during the Third Reich.[62]

Camp bordellos were established for a number of reasons. Among these were the Nazi effort to prevent homosexual relationships among male inmates and the effort to divert inmates from attempts at resistance or political organization. According to both Schulz and Paul, however, the primary purpose of the bordellos was to provide an incentive to inmates to work harder. Himmler ordered the establishment of the bordellos as part of a new incentive system that paid inmates small amounts of "camp money" when they produced at higher rates or fulfilled certain quotas; with this money they could purchase hard-to-obtain items such as cigarettes or various food products—or they could visit the bordello, which otherwise was only to be had for a price of RM2.[63]

Conditions in the bordellos varied from camp to camp. In general, the female inmates working as prostitutes in the bordellos were forced to fulfill a quota of eight men per day. These men would be subject to a hygienic inspection before and after their visit to the prostitute; according to some accounts they were given shots. The female inmates were also required to wash after each visit. It does not appear, however, that they were provided with any method of birth control, though some of the women did undergo forced sterilizations prior to being put into service as prostitutes. Paul quotes several accounts of pregnancies and forced abortions, some resulting in death for the women involved.

Gender, History, and Representation

The extremely significant historical research conducted by both Schulz and Paul reveals again the very real sense in which biology did become destiny

34

for many women in the Holocaust. In addition, the difficulty sc\
exploring such unresearched topics as forced prostitution points
to how invaluable survivor testimony is in reconstructing the m
history of the Holocaust. Yet just as such historical research into
experiences during the Holocaust and the Third Reich must continue in an
attempt to establish facts, new theoretical approaches must be considered
that assist in the interpretation and representation of these facts. This is
especially essential at a moment in time when it will soon no longer be
possible to question survivors directly, and we will instead have to work
primarily with the memories they have left behind in the form of personal
narratives and recorded interviews.

Pascale Bos, in an essay titled "Women and the Holocaust: Analyzing Gender Differences," calls for a move beyond the essentialist analyses
that characterized previous feminist approaches to the study of the Holocaust. Bos provides a framework for future gendered analysis that shifts the
emphasis from the tricky claim that women's experiences of the Holocaust
were "better" or "worse" than those of men to the premise that we must
look at how these experiences were perceived by women, remembered by
women, and written or spoken about by women. Bos suggests that we begin
to study the sense in which experience, memory, and expression were shaped
by gender socialization, what she calls the "lens of gender." As she argues,
survivor testimony, particularly texts written by survivor-authors, does not
provide unmediated access to "historical reality." Rather, these texts are
highly mediated by language and by individual positionalities that shape
the way memories are reconstructed as part of subjectivity and in the process
of constructing a written text. Scholars have been too quick to attribute an
unmediated truth value to the memories of survivors rather than understanding them as complex constructs, which at times stand in tension with other
versions of history, and as such can shed light on the competing discourses
within history and experience. Bos suggests that gender must be one of
the primary categories through which we begin to analyze these competing
discourses and constructions of memory. As she argues, "[W]e need to
look more carefully into the effects of men's and women's different prewar socialization and their ensuing ways of acting in, looking at, describing
and experiencing the world."[64]

Utilizing a similar framework of gendered analysis, Karen Remmler
goes one step further in suggesting that gender identities not only shaped the
construction of survivors' memories, but were in fact integral in survivors'
attempts to reconstruct their own subjectivity after having been utterly
dehumanized. Remmler argues that "we can read texts on the Holocaust not
as universal examples of suffering, but as examples of how, even in moments
of utter destruction and dehumanization, Holocaust survivors reclaim agency

through a gendered recollection of painful memories."[65] In a comparative reading of Mali Fritz's memoir of her experiences in Auschwitz, *Essig gegen den Durst: 565 Tage in Auschwitz-Birkenau*, published in 1986, and a 1989 novel by Polish writer Marie Nurowska about the post-Holocaust identity of a contemporary Polish woman, *Postscriptum für Anna und Miriam*, Remmler reads the female body in both texts as a site of remembrance through which female subjectivity is posited "as an identity that exists within the continuum of history rather than in a metaphor of femaleness."[66] As Remmler argues, the body functions in both texts to ground human suffering in the particular historical and social context of the Holocaust and its legacy for survivors. At the same time, in representing the victimization of the female body in particular, both texts demonstrate the specificity of gender in shaping the remembrance of the Holocaust.

As James Young has incisively argued, "The fictiveness in testimony does not involve disputes about facts, but the inevitable variance in perceiving and representing these facts, witness by witness, language by language, culture by culture."[67] The work of Bos and Remmler shows that just as individual experience, linguistic and cultural background shape the perception and representation of events, so too does gender. In order to understand the specificity of remembrance and representation of the Holocaust, it is thus imperative that gender be taken into account as a category of textual analysis in readings of all survivors' texts. But it is also essential that the texts of women writers, often neglected in Holocaust scholarship, be given greater consideration. As Bos concludes, "My analysis of the inevitably gendered nature of experience, memory, and narrative suggests that texts by female authors need to be as widely read as texts by men, by male as well as female scholars, students and the general audience, because they provide a perspective which differs from that of men."[68]

Nanda Herbermann's memoir is one such text, which offers a clear example of how and why gender did matter both to the Nazi tormentors in their treatment of inmates and especially to the way inmates such as Herbermann perceived and represented their experiences of the camps. Herbermann's book provides a great deal of information about the particularity of tortures and punishments devised for women in Ravensbrück, and her consistent focus on the body throughout the text functions to ground the narrative contextually. At the same time, her gender identity, what Bos calls "prewar gender socialization"—along with her religious, class, and national identities—accounts for many lacunae in her memory and representation of camp life and for the ambivalences that mark her text.

Any attempt to understand life in concentration camps touches on taboos, precisely because of the impossibility of coming to terms with the inhumanity and terror inflicted there. Yet despite the commonality of torment to which all inmates were subjected, there was indeed a plurality of experiences of the camps and, indeed, a hierarchy of persecution according to the status of inmates. As an "Aryan" and a political prisoner who was not a Communist or a Socialist, Nanda Herbermann was at the top of this hierarchy: she was privileged to be assigned various positions that allowed her a certain level of freedom of movement within the camp, a certain level of power over other inmates, and an ability to speak to and occasionally negotiate with guards. Ultimately, Herbermann was released from the camp. None of these privileges were available to Jewish women, and it is unlikely that so-called asocials were granted such privileges either.

Herbermann herself had a very ambivalent reaction to these privileges. She saw her assignment to Block II as a unique punishment devised to torment her in particular: as a pious, bourgeois woman, she feels compelled to comment over and over again about the lack of cleanliness in the block and the—to her mind—outrageous and sometimes perverse behavior of the women in the block. When she is moved to the camp office to do clerical work, Herbermann is torn between the desire to commit small acts of resistance by allowing certain files to disappear and the compulsion to maintain the order that is so ingrained in her. Outraged by her own mistreatment, Herbermann often fails to recognize her privilege. She shows no awareness of Holocaust or genocide and wears her internalized values (which often square with Nazi values) on her sleeve, never hesitating to give voice to anti-Semitic comments. The consistent self-aggrandizing tone of her book reflects her belief that her readers will share her value system and the assumption that Germans have been victimized and must now be redeemed.

All of these factors make Herbermann's book difficult to read at times. Despite, and even because of, these difficulties, however, *The Blessed Abyss* both augments our understanding of Nazi Germany and the concentration camps and provides insight into the context of German remembrance in the immediate postwar period.

The Blessed Abyss

> The only concrete history that can be retrieved remains that carried by personal stories.
> —SAUL FRIEDLÄNDER

When Nanda Herbermann arrived in Ravensbrück in July 1941, she stepped into what she would later come to call the "blessed abyss," a kind of proving ground for her faith. That her camp experience reinforced her faith in God to the extent that she was able to perceive and represent it in many ways as a "positive" tribulation points again to how privileged that experience in fact was. As the title of the book reflects, Herbermann's memoir records her imprisonment as a process of personal growth and enlightenment amid the most abysmal circumstances imaginable. As such, Herbermann's aim in writing her memoir was fourfold: to provide an inspirational narrative of her own spiritual journey; to utilize that narrative in the attempt to educate postwar Germans about Nazi crimes and compel them to "atone"; to plead for sympathy and understanding from the Allied occupation forces and from the outside world for German suffering in the immediate postwar period; and, finally, to provide historical documentation of Ravensbrück.

As a native German Catholic imprisoned in Ravensbrück for resistance work, Herbermann's "victimhood" certainly differed from that of Jewish inmates imprisoned in death camps. Her narrative thus sheds light on a different set of experiences and perceptions of the concentration camps, which led Herbermann to remember and represent different aspects of camp life. Nanda Herbermann was in many ways a product of the same cultural context that spawned National Socialism. She subscribed to a certain extent to a perpetrator mentality; nonetheless, she perceived herself as a victim of the same ideologies to which she had originally subscribed. As a result, she began to question these ideologies, albeit still within the context of her own cultural background. Indeed, her memoir often reflects the tensions between her identification with both perpetrators and victims, tensions that result in representational ambivalences and gaps in remembrance. Yet it is precisely these tensions that, Herbermann felt, made her uniquely suited to address postwar Germans about the immediate past and their need to atone for it; as such, her book is particularly interesting as a foundational document of German remembrance.[69]

One of the earliest concentration camp memoirs to appear in print, *The Blessed Abyss* was published before generic conventions surrounding the representation of memories of National Socialism or the Holocaust had taken hold.[70] Though little is known of the genesis of the manuscript, it can be assumed that Herbermann would not have had the opportunity to read many (if any) other memoirs of concentration camp experiences. What is immediately striking about the book's style is Herbermann's use of prosaic—even trite—language. Contrary to our contemporary expectations, which have been shaped by the pared-down, minimalist prose of many later Holocaust narratives, Herbermann's book is marked by a colloquial style. Shifting between chatty and scolding tones, Herbermann filled her text with exclamation marks and second-person address to her former "comrades." The translation has remained as true to the original tone of the book and its stylistic oddities as possible.

Since Herbermann was a professional writer and editor, she must have been conscious of her prose, and it is interesting to speculate on her motivations for choosing such a colloquial tone. The style of *The Blessed Abyss* stands in stark contrast to the much more professional tone of Herbermann's reviews and articles written for *Der Gral* in the 1930s. Of course, it is possible that she found her experiences in Ravensbrück too painful to deliberate meticulously over every word and simply wanted to get them down on paper as quickly as possible. It is also conceivable that she felt that such a tone would appeal to her potential readers—a German public in large part composed of bystanders and perpetrators—drawing them in through its accessibility. Herbermann was certainly very conscious of her prospective reading public, whom she addresses at certain intervals and to whom she appeals directly in the final chapter of her book. Perhaps her acquaintance with women of various social and economic backgrounds in Ravensbrück also led her to reject the style of an elite journal in favor of a more colloquial tone. In addition, it is likely that she had an additional audience in mind: the Allied occupation government and other foreign readers, whom she perhaps hoped to impress into sympathy with the German plight through the pathos of her prose.

As a German Catholic, Herbermann struggled to come to terms with the effects her imprisonment in the camp had on her understanding of the discourses that had shaped her personal identity. In this sense, the memoir reflects Herbermann's growing ambivalence about the Roman Catholic Church, the German nation, and her role as a woman in the resistance. Over the course of her imprisonment and through the process of writing her memoir, Herbermann thus began to think in new ways about her religious identity, her national identity, and her gender identity. While *The Blessed Abyss* is on one level a concentration camp narrative, it is also, like many autobiographies, an attempt to sort out conflicting ideologies and make sense of fragmented subjectivities.

Elaine Martin has provided a framework for thinking about writings by non-Jewish, German women about the Holocaust and National Socialism. Noting "the interrelationship of racism, sexism, and fascism within the German patriarchal social structure," she points out that "Most of women's writings about the Third Reich are autobiographical, either directly in autobiographies, diaries, and memoirs, or indirectly in autobiographical novels, short stories, and poetry. Despite the genre differences among the works, several common themes emerge that are not generally characteristic of men's works about the era. Perhaps the most salient difference is the connection drawn—either overtly or implicitly—by many women writers between patriarchy and fascism."[71]

As early as 1946, Herbermann, too, drew this implicit connection in *The Blessed Abyss*. In contrast to her unquestioning acceptance of Catholic and Nazi intolerance of lesbians and Jews, Herbermann began to question the overlapping ideologies of the Catholic Church and the National Socialist state in their mutual oppression of women. When Herbermann was assigned as barracks elder and then block elder in Block II, she was at first horrified by the conditions in the block and particularly by the conduct of the women who were imprisoned there. However, Herbermann soon came to empathize with and learn from these women, whom she called "her" prostitutes. As a devout Catholic, Herbermann began to question the Church's condemnation of the "immorality" of prostitution, realizing through her contact with the prostitutes that their "downfall" was a social problem, not a moral one. "This must be a task of the new state and also of the Church in the future," she writes in her chapter "Block elder over four hundred prostitutes," "to give these children who are outcasts from human society a chance to refine and better themselves in an environment not ruled by whips and rubber truncheons, but rather by goodness, understanding, and patience. Under the terrorism of the SS and Gestapo, under that constant mistreatment, these people could by their natures only get worse."

Galvanized by her encounters with prostitutes in the camp, Herbermann published a novel in 1949 titled *Was Liebe Erträgt* (What love must endure), which incorporates many of the stories she was told by "her" prostitutes in Ravensbrück. This protofeminist novel constitutes a lengthier attempt by Herbermann to situate prostitution as a question of social welfare rather than morality and to provoke social change through providing the public with an "insider's look" at the social conditions that lead to prostitution. As she writes in the introduction, "They [prostitutes] can only find their way back if we who call ourselves 'respectable' Christians don't keep throwing stones at them, but instead use these stones to pave the way for them, so that they can no longer sink into the mire of vice, of sin, of injustice that we as brother and sister have often enough inflicted upon them in our arrogance."[72]

Yet despite her ultimate sympathy for her fellow inmates, Herbermann's representation of the women in Block II remains deeply ambivalent. She begins chapter 20, her account of life in Block II, with a description of how unbearable existence was there, a fact she attributes in large part to the inmates themselves. Portraying herself as the martyr vainly attempting to maintain sanitary conditions, she repeatedly remarks on the lack of standards of hygiene in the block and what she sees as the wretched, corrupt, and dirty behavior of the women forced to live there, made worse for her by their lack of moral rectitude. As the chapter continues, however, Herbermann goes on to address nine of these women in the second person, telling their horrifying individual stories while expressing her sympathy to them through direct address. Similarly, in her chapter "The lice plague," Herbermann refers to the inmates as "little pigs," placing the blame for the lice infestation on them, rather than on the unsanitary and cramped conditions imposed on the women by their Nazi tormentors. At the same time, she expresses "deep sympathy for the women who were robbed of their often beautiful hair" when the Nazis shaved their heads after a lice inspection, articulating regret that she could do nothing to protect the women from this horrible invasion.

Herbermann's German values of hygiene, cleanliness, and order, which compelled her to find the women in her block repugnant, thus consistently conflicted with her human sympathy for them. This extensive and conflicted discourse of hygiene that runs through the entire memoir is striking in several ways. Clearly, cleanliness plays a strong role in Herbermann's attempts to redefine her own subjectivity after Ravensbrück—she literally attempts to cleanse herself of the experience of the camp through representing herself as a crusader for good hygiene and sanitation. At the same time, cleanliness functions as one of the primary metaphors through which she is able to distinguish herself from the other inmates of the camp and thus represent herself as a "good German" in her appeal to her reading public. As a proponent of cleanliness (one of the primary bourgeois German values), she could situate herself in a position from which to critique certain aspects of Church doctrine (such as the immorality of prostitution) without implicating herself. Herbermann's ultimate acceptance of the prostitutes, and the fact that she went so far as to write a book that was meant to crusade on their behalf (and against Church teachings on this point), is one aspect of the tension in her book surrounding her perception and representation of female bodies—her own and others.

Also representative of this tension is one of the more curious lacunae in Herbermann's memoir: her infrequent mention of food. As more critical attention has been given to gender distinctions in Holocaust memoirs, several scholars have noted the prevalence of references to hunger, organizing food and fantasizing about recipes in women's memoirs.[73] Survivor Susan E. Cernyak-Spatz has said that inmates discussed food so often at Terezin that there was a camp expression for it: "We called it 'cooking with the mouth.'"[74] Sybil Milton suggests that women's food preparation skills, part of their prewar socialization, and their willingness to swap recipes and methods of extending scarce food rations within the camps became a means of their survival.[75]

It is interesting to speculate about the reasons for Herbermann's reticence in this regard compared to other female memoirists. Scholars have made the connection between the centrality of food in the lives of Jewish women, particularly at the high holidays, and the centrality of food in their memoirs, creating the basis for a sense of community.[76] In Catholicism, on the other hand, fasting and asceticism often dominate attitudes toward food.

Herbermann refuses to eat the piece of bread offered her by a concerned guard on her first night in prison (chapter 5); similarly, she gives away her ration of food as she arrives at the admittance block of Ravensbrück and comments that she "often gave [her] piece of bread or potatoes" to her table mates (chapter 17). She expresses revulsion at the food and her surroundings; perhaps giving away her food was also part of her "self-sacrifice" to God. In this sense, this particular gap in Herbermann's memoir can again be read as part of her attempt to represent herself as a martyr. Within her own cultural context, rejecting food—and deemphasizing it in her recollections of the camp, where hunger certainly must have plagued her as much as it did others—may also have been part of her attempt to retain control over her body, or reassert that control in the aftermath of her release.[77]

Herbermann's understanding of bodies—her own and those of others—underwent a dramatic change as a result of her imprisonment in Ravensbrück. In a sense, her attempt to reclaim her own body and her own subjectivity after her release from the camp was inextricably linked not only to the experience of her own body in conditions of deep humiliation, torment, and pain (particularly during her confinement in the cell block for a minor infraction of rules, an experience she writes about in chapter 22), but also to her new experience of other women's bodies. Through her relationships with the prostitutes in her block, she came to accept to a certain extent "sinful" and "dirty" bodies, understanding for the first time that it was not always by choice or evil intention that women became "sinful" and "unclean." Of course, Herbermann accepts these women always with the hope of leading them toward redemption. Nonetheless, her descriptions of the women belie a certain fascination for the very different ways they inhabit their bodies and express their sexuality, albeit a fascination she feels compelled to couch in condemning language. This fascination can be detected in Herbermann's descriptions of "her prostitutes" and the lives they led prior to their camp experience. Even her condemnatory veiled reference to lesbian sex in her block evidences this ambivalent interest to a certain extent. "Many of my wards were completely morally ruined in this environment," she writes in chapter 21. "They performed the most depraved acts with each other, since sexuality was the only thing left for them." Religion is Herbermann's salvation in the camp, and she observes that sex fills a similar role for other women—again, one that she clearly condemns. Herbermann is consistently at pains to represent herself as a saintly, nunlike woman, never tempted by the "sins of the flesh"—indeed, she mentions on several occasions in the early chapters of the book the marked offense she took at the Gestapo's "lewd" suggestion that she and Father Muckermann had been having an affair. Although there is nothing to suggest that such an affair took place, Herbermann's aggressive expressions of shock over sex in her book do seem somewhat forcedly naive, given the milieu in which she lived and worked during the 1920s and early 1930s. Not only were the circles in which Muckermann traveled known to be "bohemian," but Herbermann herself had been a stage actress and had traveled primarily in literary and artistic circles during the Weimar period. Any attempt to reconstruct the changes in Herbermann's mindset and self-representation must remain speculative, but the tensions her biography suggests may be instructive in reading her memoir.

Herbermann's representation of femininity and ideals of womanhood in her memoir is also contradictory and ambivalent. At the beginning of *The Blessed Abyss*, Herbermann is extremely self-effacing, representing herself as a servile woman simply carrying out her secretarial duties to Father Muckermann, admitting little knowledge of the dangers of her activities. As she writes in chapter 6 ("'You have power!'") of the repeated interrogations she underwent at the hands of the Gestapo, however, she begins to see her actions as daring and idealistic nonetheless. "You can't pretend to us that you took these dangerous journeys upon yourself out of pure idealism to your cause. Women don't do that!" the Gestapo interrogator says to her, and she replies: "Oh, my dear gentlemen, a woman can do much more!" As she begins to think of herself as truly part of the resistance, capable of resistance, Herbermann is empowered to defy the Gestapo and, once in the camp, to engage in further small acts of resistance. Nonetheless, it remains somewhat surprising that she continues to downplay the political aspects of her work to such a great extent.

Because women's resistance work was often "domesticated" or "normalized"—that is, it consisted of typical "women's work" such as typing or feeding people and thus merged into the continuum of women's pre- and post-resistance lives—women such as Herbermann often did not perceive their work in the resistance as strongly political or heroic in any way. Indeed, Herbermann refers repeatedly to the fact that she was arrested for literally attempting to clothe her employer by bringing garments to him in Holland. Of course, the extent of Herbermann's work in the resistance, writing and publishing anti-Hitler articles and magazines, was much greater than this "crime" suggests; nonetheless the fact that such a "normal" activity ultimately led to her arrest in part explains her lack of stress on her political engagement. At the same time, however, her deemphasizing her own political agency can again be read as part of her attempt to appeal to a postwar German audience composed primarily of Hitler-sympathizers. By situating herself as a mostly apolitical and ingratiatingly servile woman, Herbermann again positioned herself as a "good German." She also further distanced herself from the

Communists, with whom political resistance to the Nazis had become closely associated in the immediate postwar period.[78]

As we have suggested, Herbermann utilized this position to articulate her ideas about German guilt and the new German nation. It is interesting that she does not renounce her patriotism but is compelled to defend the majority of Germans. She consistently delineates a dichotomy in her memoir between what she sees as the innocent and unknowing German people and the monstrous, criminal, and, to her mind, truly sick and evil perpetrators of the Nazi regime, thus rejecting the doctrine of collective guilt that structured the early Allied policy of denazification (the attempt to eradicate Nazi ideology among Germans) in postwar Germany.

In 1945, Catholic archbishop Conrad Gröber of Freiburg spoke out against the idea of collective guilt, arguing that significant portions of the German population (in particular many Catholics) had not willingly submitted to the fascist dictatorship. Subsequently, the rejection of the idea of collective guilt and the critique of denazification became central to the Church's response to Allied policy. Through rejecting this aspect of Allied policy, the Church affirmed its own image as an institution untainted by collaboration with Nazism. At the same time, through articulating this critique "in the interest of Germans," the Church won respect from the population, thus strengthening its renewed position of authority in postwar society. Because the Allies recognized the churches as the only institutions to emerge from the Third Reich relatively intact and with a moral authority that to some extent "transcended" politics, it was possible for the churches to articulate such critiques.

Herbermann was clearly influenced by Church policy on the doctrine of collective guilt, but her antipathy to the idea went deeper. Many anti-Nazi Germans from all sides of the political spectrum disagreed with the Allies' characterization of all Germans as guilty because it seemed to undermine their own acts of resistance against the Third Reich, as well as their deeply ingrained nationalism and belief in the humanist tradition of Germany that they saw Hitler as having perverted. In reference to the concentration camps, for example, Herbermann writes in chapter 17, "I simply could not come to terms with the thought, with the fact, that something so horrible could be carried out against people by other people, and especially by German people. I felt as if I should always be apologizing to the foreigners [in the camps] and telling them: What goes on here is not German, most German people know nothing of this! These concentration camps are wholly monstrous creations of the criminal dictators of the Third Reich, and certainly not of the German people." By the final chapter of the memoir, Herbermann goes so far as to indicate that her book is meant as a defense of the German people:

Why am I now publishing this book, which is truly written with my lifeblood? I mean to portray the life demanded of an inmate of the Geheime Staatspolizei and the SS during the Third Reich in prisons and concentration camps so objectively and in a manner true to life that the reader can gain a clear picture of this life in hell. But I have a second and more essential goal in mind with the publication of these remarks: the entire German people is now being held responsible by many parties for the horrible and abominable things that occurred in the concentration camps. This is not right. . . . Those who do not have blood on their hands might use whatever strength is still available to them to work along with us, who have experienced and suffered this horror on our own bodies and in our own souls, so that our Germany may be revived with honor, and we may finally take shelter and be at home there again, so that a fatherland may exist for us again, for us who have wandered around for the last twelve years, homeless and constantly persecuted and spied upon in our own fatherland. And we will try to make amends for the horror and depravity, for the murder and atrocious injustice committed by Germans unto Germans and unto hundreds of thousands of innocent foreigners. We, the survivors, have this holy obligation, as well as the obligation to atone before God and the world. One thing remains true, and the world will also learn to understand it after our time of atonement: the German people may not and cannot be simply equated with these Nazi criminals.

Allied efforts at denazification were never particularly successful, due to political opposition on the part of the public and to the bureaucratic difficulties of examining the personal histories of an entire nation's population. Indeed, the doctrine of collective guilt opposed by Herbermann was soon shelved by the Allies because of the demands of the emergent cold war, and has remained controversial into the present day. Neither, however, did the German public, whether they had blood on their hands or not, voluntarily confront or atone for their nation's past in the immediate postwar period, as Herbermann had hoped. It was, arguably, not until the year of Herbermann's death, 1979, that a national discussion of the Holocaust and German guilt truly began in the Federal Republic.[79]

After the war, Herbermann received support from the state in reparation for the injuries to her health suffered in Ravensbrück. She took up residence in an apartment on a pleasant promenade in Münster and devoted the rest of her life to literary pursuits. In addition to *The Blessed Abyss* and her novel about prostitution, she wrote a biography of Father Friedrich Muckermann. She also published frequently in magazines and newspapers, in particular in the *Westfälische Nachrichten* in Münster, which sometimes printed her sketches as well. In addition to her literary activities, Herbermann served as the chair of the Münster Committee for the Recognition of

People Persecuted for Political, Racial, or Religious Reasons. Despite her work in this regard, Herbermann does not appear to have maintained close contact with her former fellow prisoners or ever visited the camp site again, a fact that is unsurprising given the former camp's location in the GDR. Nanda Herbermann was one of the first women to receive the Bundesverdienstkreuz, a West German medal of honor, which was presented to her by the president of the Federal Republic, Theodor Heuss. Herbermann committed much of her time to involvement in Catholic activities and maintained a wide circle of friends. She never married, and all of her siblings are now deceased. Herbermann died in a nursing home in Münster in 1979.

Notes

1. In his article, "Catholic Resistance in the Third Reich," Dietrich offers this definition: "The resistance of the Catholic Church may be understood in essence as a religious concern for defense against totalitarian claims to sovereignty." He goes on to detail the forms that this resistance took, including antifascist publications, opposition to the regime's euthanasia program, the offering of religion classes, help extended to individual Jews by "average Catholics," and anti-Nazi sermons and pastoral letters read from the pulpit. Dietrich's conclusion is that such resistance was largely individual and local: "The institutional Church did not lead an organized resistance movement" (171–86).
2. The book went through three editions, but has been long out of print in German. A new German edition is forthcoming: Herbermann, *Der Gesegnete Abgrund.*
3. In his study *The Gestapo and German Society,* Gellately notes that "the preoc- cupations of the local Gestapo varied according to local circumstances," and he goes on to enumerate his findings of such specific activities in Düsseldorf Gestapo files: "In Düsseldorf . . . Catholicism and policing the pulpit were . . . of great importance, and countless priests were hauled in for minor infractions." These files also reveal that "before 1939 there were efforts underway to stop the smuggling of money over the border into Holland" (49).
4. Some of these memoirs by women have reached a semi-canonical status: these include works by Charlotte Delbo, a non-Jewish member of the French resistance whose three memoirs have been published in English in one volume, *Auschwitz and After;* by Austrian Jewish survivor Ruth Klüger, whose memoir is *Weiter leben. eine Jugend;* and by Charlotte Salomon, a Jewish refugee in France who died in Auschwitz and whose life has been told through her paintings in a biography by Felstiner: *To Paint Her Life.*
5. These include two anthologies of primary sources, survivor Vera Laska's *Women in the Resistance and in the Holocaust,* and the more recent *Different Voices,* ed. Rittner and Roth, which includes many previously published secondary sources as well. *When Biology Became Destiny,* ed. Bridenthal, Grossmann, and Kaplan, and Koonz's *Mothers in the Fatherland* are books by historians of German women's history that focus on women in the Third Reich. Finally, Heinemann's feminist analysis *Gender and Destiny,* and Brenner's *Writing as Resistance* are works of literary criticism.

6. *Women in the Holocaust,* ed. Ofer and Weitzman, is an anthology of essays devoted to the experiences of Jewish women and principally written by historians. Gurewitsch has contributed new primary sources with her *Mothers, Sisters, Resisters.* Fuchs's *Women and the Holocaust* is a collection of essays on specific texts, specific women, and topics such as lesbians in the Holocaust, reproduction, resistance, and filmic representation. Baumel has published *Double Jeopardy,* a collection of her own previous writings on the subject with a focus on Orthodox Jewish women. Finally, Kremer's *Women's Holocaust Writing* analyzes the work of seven émigré and American women writers who explore the representations of women's Holocaust experiences in fiction.

7. Goldenberg, "Different Horrors, Same Hell," 152.

8. An additional indication of the growing acceptance of and interest in gendered analysis of the Holocaust is found in the brisk sales of Ofer and Weitzman's anthology, *Women in the Holocaust,* which exceeded 3,500 copies in hardback by May 1999.

9. Schoenfeld, "Auschwitz and the Professors," 45.

10. Quoted in Ofer and Weitzman, *Women in the Holocaust,* 14.

11. Levi, foreword, 14.

12. Much of Heinemann's *Gender and Destiny* is devoted to such analysis.

13. Baumel, "Social Interaction among Jewish Women in Crisis during the Holocaust," 64–84.

14. See Fine, "Women Writers and the Holocaust."

15. See Ringelheim, "Women and the Holocaust," all three versions.

16. Quoted in Kaufman, "Ein 'Warner gegen die Mächte der Finsternis,'" 14. This and all other translations from the German are by Hester Baer, unless otherwise noted.

17. We use the term "political Catholicism" here in the sense that it is used by Tom Buchanan and Martin Conway in their illuminating anthology *Political Catholicism in Europe, 1918–1965:* "Political Catholicism does not mean Catholics who were active in politics but political action which was Catholic in inspiration" (2).

18. Quoted in Kaufman, "Ein 'Warner gegen die Mächte der Finsternis,'" 14.

19. Muckermann, "Pompa diaboli," 385.

20. See *Der Gral* 12.28 (September 1934): 576.

21. Lewy, *The Catholic Church and Nazi Germany,* 143.

22. Ibid., 211.

23. The "New Woman" of Weimar Germany has been the subject of much interesting scholarship in the past decade or so. For two good overviews, see Grossmann, "The New Woman and the Rationalization of Sexuality in Weimar Germany," and Frevert, *Women in German History.* Analyses of representations of the New Woman in film and literature can be found in Huyssen, "Mass Culture as Woman," and Petro, *Joyless Streets.* More specific historical analyses of the New Woman in regard to sexual politics are provided by Grossmann in her *Reforming Sex.* See also several essays on the New Woman in *When Biology Became Destiny.*

24. Paula Modersohn-Becker (1876–1907) was a painter who belonged to the Worpswede School of German artists. A good friend of the poet Rainer Maria Rilke, she was known for a particular sensibility for nature expressed in her art. Dissatisfied by the sentimentalism that characterized the style of the Worpswede artists, Modersohn-Becker sought a simplicity of form in her work. This, in combination with her attempts at expressing her own subjective vision in her paintings, earned her a subsequent reputation as a major precursor of German

expressionism. Modersohn-Becker died at the age of thirty-one, after giving birth to her first child.

25. Herbermann, "Zu unserem Kunstwerk," 41–42.
26. Herbermann, "Frauenliteratur," 135.
27. Young, *Writing and Rewriting the Holocaust,* 3, 4.
28. Schoppmann, *Days of Masquerade,* 6.
29. The painful history of Christian anti-Semitism, or anti-Judaism as it is sometimes termed, has been amply documented in such works as Wistrich's *Antisemitism,* Roth and Rubenstein's *Approaches to Auschwitz,* and Weiss's *Ideology of Death.*
30. Lewy, *The Catholic Church and Nazi Germany,* 51.
31. Over twelve thousand "Righteous Gentiles" have been recognized by Yad Vashem in Jerusalem for their daring actions on behalf of Jews targeted for extermination by the Nazis. A study by survivor Nechama Tec (who survived the war by passing as a Catholic) provides moving testimony of these individuals. See Tec, *When Light Pierced the Darkness.*
32. Dobkowski, "A Deafening Silence," 23–24.
33. Lewy gives the following figures: "[T]he Catholic Church by the end of the twenties numbered over 20,000 priests for 20-million Catholics, as against 16,000 pastors for 40-million Protestants" (*The Catholic Church and Nazi Germany,* 4).
34. Karl-Egon Lönne, "Germany," in Buchanan and Conway, *Political Catholicism in Europe, 1918–1965,* 168.
35. Lewy, *The Catholic Church and Nazi Germany,* 18. Dietrich has made a similar observation in his "Catholic Resistance to Racist Eugenics," 138.
36. Scholder, in his two-volume study *The Churches and the Third Reich,* quotes Father Muckermann as having reported a passing remark Hitler made about himself: " 'Bismarck was Protestant and therefore unable to conduct his *Kulturkampf* with the necessary expertise; but he himself, as a Catholic, understood the matter better' " (1:381). Scholder, in characterizing Hitler's political astuteness regarding the Concordat, concludes that this remark of Hitler's "hits the nail on the head."
37. See Steward, *Sieg des Glaubens.*
38. In their book *Cries in the Night,* a study of seven Catholic women who devoted themselves to the rescue of the Jews, Phayer and Fleischner hint at the obstruction by the Catholic Church of efforts to rescue Jews and the complicity of the Church with the Third Reich. Borrowing terminology from French historian Jules Isaac, they call the "tradition" of anti-Semitism within Christianity the Teaching of Contempt: "The Teaching of Contempt, found in liturgy, preaching, catechesis and theology, has for nearly two thousand years presented the Jewish people as spiritually dead: cursed, punished and cast aside by God because they had rejected the Messiah" (xvii).
39. Quoted in Mariaux, *Persecution of the Catholic Church in the Third Reich,* 19.
40. Conway, *Nazi Persecution of the Churches,* 276–84.
41. Estimates vary as to the numbers of clergy imprisoned; Conway points out that, in general, these imprisonments were intended as deterrents and were rarely of long duration. See ibid., 175, 429nn. 10, 11.
42. Mariaux, *Persecution of the Catholic Church in the Third Reich,* v. Subsequent to the war, W. Mariaux was identified as the author of this work.
43. Zahn, *German Catholics and Hitler's Wars,* 82. Other writers who have characterized von Galen in this positive light include Doris Bergen, Peter Hoffmann, and Guenter Lewy. See Bergen, *Twisted Cross,* 41; Hoffmann, *German Resistance to Hitler,* 58; and Lewy, *The Catholic Church and Nazi Germany,* 265–66.

44. Conway, *Nazi Persecution of the Churches*, 283.
45. Griech-Polelle, "A Pure Conscience Is Good Enough," 119.
46. Conway, "Between Cross and Swastika," 180.
47. Perhaps in part because of the camp's thus marginalized status, very few memoirs of Ravensbrück have been published in English. For a survey of those memoirs that do exist, see pages 253–60.
48. For more information on the camp organizations, including a fascinating account of a meeting between one survivor organization and a group of feminist social scientists from West Berlin, see Atina Grossmann, "Zwei Erfahrungen im Kontext des Themas 'Gender und Holocaust,'" in *Forschungsschwerpunkt Ravensbrück*, ed. Jacobeit and Philipp, 136–46.
49. For a more detailed description of the geography of the camp and the contemporary museum and memorial site, see pages 249–51.
50. Sigrid Jacobeit herself has edited several of these books, including *"Ich grüße Euch als freier Mensch,"* an anthology that primarily documents the liberation of the camp by the Red Army and includes many documents and pictures, and *Ravensbrückerinnen*, which presents the biographies of twenty-seven women (including photos or drawings of these women) who were imprisoned in the camp and is based on an exhibition held at the museum. For a more explicit scholarly focus on gender issues, see Jacobeit and Philipp, *Forschungsschwerpunkt Ravensbrück*. Several other recent publications focus on gender issues and Ravensbrück. A detailed anthology with histories of the camps and individual articles on numerous topics, including one on prostitutes in Ravensbrück that cites Nanda Herbermann, is presented by Füllberg-Stolberg et al., *Frauen in Konzentrationslagern Bergen-Belsen, Ravensbrück*. Paul's *Zwangsprostitution* focuses on prostitution during the Nazi period, particularly on Ravensbrück women who were subjected to forced prostitution in camps and SS bordellos. Finally, Klier gives a detailed account of medical experiments in the camp in her *Die Kaninchen von Ravensbrück*.
51. See Grit Philipp, "Personen, Ereignisse, Zusammenhänge. Erste Ergebnisse des Forschungsprojektes 'Kalendarium der Ereignisse im Frauen-Konzentrationslager Ravensbrück 1939 bis 1945,'" in *Forschungsschwerpunkt Ravensbrück*, ed. Jacobeit and Philipp, 115–23.
52. See two reports about a joint Israeli-German research project to investigate the history of Jewish women in the camp: Judith Buber Agassi, "Opfer und Überlebende. Jüdische Häftlinge im KZ Ravensbrück," 71–78, and Linde Apel and Sabine Kittel, "Annäherungen an die Geschichte jüdischer Frauen. Bermerkungen zu einer Werkstattausstellung," 79–85, both in *Forschungsschwerpunkt Ravensbrück*, ed. Jacobeit and Philipp.
53. Zörner, *Frauen-KZ Ravensbrück*, 228–29.
54. Litschke, "National Memorial of Ravensbrück—Museum," 2.
55. Milton, "Women and the Holocaust," 223.
56. See Poltawska, *And I Am Afraid of My Dreams*, and Symonowicz, *Beyond Human Endurance*.
57. Paul, *Zwangsprostitution*, 75.
58. Buber-Neumann, *Under Two Dictators*, 199.
59. See Schulz, "Weibliche Häftlinge aus Ravensbrück."
60. Paul, *Zwangsprostitution*, 26.
61. Ibid., 23–26.
62. Ibid., 135.

63. See Schulz, "Weibliche Häftlinge aus Ravensbrück."
64. Bos, "Women and the Holocaust."
65. Remmler, "Gender Identities and the Remembrance of the Holocaust," 167–68.
66. Ibid., 172.
67. Young, *Writing and Rewriting the Holocaust,* 32.
68. Bos, "Women and the Holocaust."
69. In her article "The Hour of the Woman," Heineman explores "the universal-ization, in West German collective memory, of crucial aspects of the stereo-typically female experience of Germany at the end of the war and during the immediate postwar years" (355). The three "stereotypically female experiences" she discusses include female victimhood resulting from bombings, flight, and rape by Soviet soldiers; the Trümmerfrau, the heroic "Woman of the Rubble"; and the sexually promiscuous woman who fraternized with occupying soldiers. Heineman's analysis provides a useful context for understanding the conflicting constructions Herbermann reveals about herself in *The Blessed Abyss.* "The notion that ordinary Germans were innocent victims of forces beyond their control was a familiar motif in postwar representations of the Third Reich" (359) asserts Heineman, and certainly this is *one* of Herbermann's notions of self, although her victimhood occurred in a different fashion. But Heineman also demonstrates that the conflicting selves experienced by Herbermann were typical of the post-war era: "Refugees and evacuees from the eastern portions of the old Reich, Christians, those who had been adversely affected by denazification, those who felt themselves to be victims of Communism, veterans, former prisoners of war, women—all offered histories that claimed simultaneously to explain their unique situations and to represent, in some way, an experience that was characteristically German" (357).
70. Other very early memoirs are quite different from Herbermann's. The most well known of these is Eugen Kogon's *Der SS-Staat. Das System der deutschen Konzen-trationslager,* ed. Verlag der Frankfurter Hefte (Berlin: Verlag des Druckhauses Tempelhof, 1946). Kogon was a prisoner in Buchenwald. When the Allied forces liberated the camp, the U.S. Army enlisted Kogon to assist in interviews with prisoners about the camp and to help compile data that would ultimately become part of an extensive report on Buchenwald. Kogon utilized this data in writing his book, which is an objective, scientific account of the camps with little emphasis on Kogon's own personal history or memories. The book was published as part of an "everyman's library" series to make it accessible to the widest possible audience, and it was widely read in Germany in the late 1940s and 1950s.
71. Martin, *Gender, Patriarchy and Fascism in the Third Reich,* 16–17.
72. Herbermann, *Was Liebe Erträgt,* 7.
73. See, for example, two publications about Terezin that document this obsession. Schwertfeger, *Women of Theresienstadt,* states that virtually all women's memoirs from Terezin include mention of "food, memories of it, missing it, craving it, dreaming of it" (38). DeSilva has edited a cookbook produced by female prisoners in the camp titled *In Memory's Kitchen.* This preoccupation is also very evident in Gurewitsch, *Mothers, Sisters, Resisters,* in which many of the survivors' interviews dwell on food.
74. Quoted in DeSilva, *In Memory's Kitchen,* xxix.
75. Milton, "Women and the Holocaust," 312.
76. See Baumel, "Social Interaction among Jewish Women in Crisis during the Holocaust," 71; Ruth Bondy, "Women in Theresienstadt and the Family Camp

in Birkenau," in *Women in the Holocaust,* ed. Ofer and Weitzman, 310–26; and Goldenberg, "Food Talk."

77. In her groundbreaking study of food and fasting in the religious practices of medieval Catholic women, *Holy Feast and Holy Fast,* Bynum is careful to state explicitly that her conclusions cannot be generalized to the twentieth century (299). Nonetheless, her chapters "Food as Control of Self" and "Food as Control of Circumstance" provide a history of the tradition of fasting and "inedia" to achieve piety and identification with the body of Christ. It is likely that Nanda Herbermann would have been aware of this tradition through her Catholic upbringing and would have noted its prevalence among medieval women specifically. In her epilogue, Bynum refers briefly to Simone Weil and Theresa Neumann of Bavaria, twentieth-century women whose abstinence Bynum likens to "the female piety that emerged in thirteenth- and fourteenth-century Europe" (297).

78. A fascinating memoir of the war years, Andreas-Friedrich's *Berlin Underground, 1938–1945* and its sequel about the postwar period, *Battleground Berlin: Diaries, 1945–1948,* bear comparison to Herbermann's memoir on several scores. Andreas-Friedrich was a non-Jew involved in resistance work of a "domestic" nature and, also like Herbermann, published the first volume of her memoirs (a version of a diary kept during those years) shortly after the war ended. Again like Herbermann, she was concerned in both volumes to demonstrate to readers that not all Germans were Nazis during the Nazi era and that there were indeed "good" Germans. There are significant differences in the memoirs as well: Andreas-Friedrich was working to support Jews in hiding; her tone is definitely more "jaunty" than that of Herbermann; and she more overtly narrates her work in resistance.

79. It was in this year that the American television miniseries "Holocaust" was aired on German television, introducing the word "Holocaust" into the mainstream for the first time and inaugurating a widespread public discussion of genocide, German history, guilt, and responsibility for "coming to terms with the past." For an analysis of the implications and history of this event, see Huyssen, "The Politics of Identification," *After the Great Divide,* 94–114, and the essays in Rabinbach and Zipes, *Germans and Jews since the Holocaust.*

THE
BLESSED
ABYSS

NANDA HERBERMANN

DER
GESEGNETE
ABGRUND

Schutzhäftling Nr. 6582
im Frauenkonzentrations-
lager Ravensbrück

GLOCK UND LUTZ VERLAG
NÜRNBERG · BAMBERG · PASSAU

Dedicated to my fellow prisoners!

And this is the victory
that has overcome the world—our faith.
—1 John 5:4

Contents to *The Blessed Abyss*

Chapter 1

Under persecution by the Gestapo

"Are you the secretary of Father Friedrich Muckermann?"[1]

"Lead me to the editorial rooms of *The Grail*."[2]

The small, stocky man with the angry, flashing eyes who spoke to me in this way pulled a metal badge out of his pocket with his left hand and held it up quickly with the words: "Geheime Staatspolizei, secret police."

Yes, I was the secretary of Father Muckermann, and this encounter with the Gestapo in the year 1934 was the beginning of a chain of persecution and hounding by its agents.

For many years I had held the position of secretary with Father Muckermann. I was the managing director of his monthly magazine of literature and life, *The Grail*, and later I also served as editor of the various newspaper articles he published.

Long before the seizure of power, Father Muckermann had pointed to the true nature of National Socialism in speeches and writings everywhere and had openly warned of its dangers and the consequences that would necessarily arise from it for Germany and the entire German people. This had earned him the glowing hatred of party followers. Then, in 1934, when he left Germany overnight as a result of constant attacks and open threats by the National Socialist newspapers and, at the instigation of his friends, crossed the Dutch border, the entire directorship of the editorial operation was transferred to me. I dedicated myself to this assignment with the assistance of a few remaining faithful followers and was restlessly busy, often late into

---

1. Father Friedrich Muckermann (1883–1946) was a publisher, Jesuit priest, and founder of the Catholic periodical *Stimmen der Zeit* (Voices of the times). In 1933, Muckermann was banned by the Nazis from publishing and from speaking in public. In 1934, he fled to the Netherlands, where he became the editor of the resistance journal *Der Deutsche Weg* (The German way). In 1936 he emigrated to Italy, and in 1937 he fled Italy to Paris via Vienna. He eventually settled in Switzerland in 1943. Muckermann died in 1946.

2. *Der Gral* was a Catholic literary monthly founded in 1906 by Eichert and Kralik, edited by Father Muckermann in Münster and published in Essen.

the night. A number of employees left us out of fear of persecution; we who remained, however, held together until the year 1938, full of energy but with our teeth clenched. At that time, the Gestapo appeared in the editorial building, forbade all further work, confiscated all editorial property, and threw us out on the street, naturally without any grounds or explanation. This was the order of the day in the Third Reich. All the furnishings of *The Grail* editorial offices (seven rooms, as well as the press-agency office and all furniture and valuable office machines) were taken out on trucks, never to be seen again.

The large and valuable library of Father Muckermann was thrown out of the second-floor windows into the trucks below—this wonderful special collection that had been brought together through years of intensive work. I myself was unoccupied and unemployed from then on (1938). For three years I had to fend for myself by working as a freelance writer, through thick and thin, more often than not going hungry, until I was arrested on February 4, 1941.

Why was I arrested by the Gestapo three years after the dissolution of *The Grail* and seven years after the departure of Father Muckermann from Germany?

When Father Muckermann left Germany in 1934 against his will, but in response to the urgent advice of benevolent people, and escaped to safety outside the country, he had, in great haste, brought nothing more with him than the most necessary toiletries and whatever he was wearing at the time. It was lucky that he escaped the hostility and persecution in good time, for shortly after his departure there followed the horrible, murderous, eternally black night of June 30, 1934, during which so many innocent people were shot by the SS.[3] At the same time, being a great optimist, he still hoped that the storm, which had flared up against him, would soon quiet, that National Socialism would never be able to hold out in Germany, and that he would then be able to return home. But things happened differently. For many years he was chased from one European country to the next.

From Holland, his first asylum, he asked me in a letter to bring him the bare essentials—his clothing, cassock, soutane, underclothes, breviary, reference library, and so on. So I set about it: I had a passport issued for myself, which I received without any further ado, and I traveled to Holland. There was, in addition, so much to consider and discuss in connection with the continued direction of the business, that I had to travel there not only this

---

3. "Night of Long Knives" was a "campaign of assassinations" initiated by Hitler on the evening of June 30, 1934. By the killings, he sought to quell the growing power of the *Sturmabteilung*, or SA (storm troopers), and to promote the focus on the *nationalist* aspects of National Socialism, or Nazism.

one time, but several more times as well. The good Father Albert Maring, who at that time was already sick with an incurable ailment, often came with me on these consultations. For this he too was arrested, on February 3, 1941, one day before me, in Lübeck, where he had traveled from Münster for a devotional course. He was transported first to Münster and later to the concentration camps Sachsenhausen and Dachau, where, after two years of the deepest suffering and unspeakable horror, he died and was cremated, like so many others.

For us it was a matter of course to bring Father Muckermann his essential clothing and the books that were indispensable for his work. I was sincerely delighted to repay the priest in this way, at least in part, for what he had done for us through years of dedicated, boundless solicitude, for he never tired of devoting himself to the realm of God on earth.

Alone or accompanied, I undertook these trips to Holland, which were often not particularly easy, out of childlike feelings of thankfulness and out of the feeling of belonging that develops naturally from years of jointly accomplished work. How many times was I searched at the border from top to bottom! The customs agents rummaged through all my luggage, leafed through the books page by page, and scrutinized the clothing of Father Muckermann that I had in my suitcase. What must they have imagined at the sight of the priest's black garments in a lady's suitcase? Naturally I was asked, and every time I found a passable excuse. Sometimes, a woman who had been employed solely for this purpose stripped me down to the chemise in order to determine whether I had on my person foreign currency, or other forbidden money or forbidden writings. Once, in Gronau, I had to wait many hours for the next connection because my train was miles away by the time I had submitted myself to the endless searches. Those were certainly harrowing hours.

Yet I never brought anything forbidden over the border, such as foreign currency or any writings; even Father Muckermann told me that he wouldn't have another quiet hour if I tried to bring forbidden material over the border. Therefore I did not need to have a bad conscience in the least bit, nor did Father Maring. If we really had wanted to risk some kind of border offense, what would have happened to us at the border, where the SS stood with the customs men checking passports and searching luggage and clothing?!

These trips of mine to Father Muckermann in Holland were my only offense. Because I brought his clothing, his underclothes, and his reference library over the border to him in 1934–35, I was arrested by the Gestapo in Münster on February 4, 1941.

Chapter 2

The SS and Gestapo in Holland

Father Muckermann fled to Holland in 1934. In May 1940, Holland was occupied by German troops. The first thing that happened there was, of course, a thorough searching of the whole country for emigrants. The SS and Gestapo ransacked every last corner. Many people fell into their ruthless hands and spent years in concentration camps or have not been among the living for a long time now.

During my visits to Father Muckermann in Holland in 1934, I had met a German editor several times who, because he was persecuted by the Gestapo, had left Germany with his wife and five children and had, like several others, sought refuge with Father Muckermann. Father Muckermann did the utmost for this family. He sought support for this strapped and now completely poverty-stricken family among the leading clergy of Holland, and the good Dutch gave amply. The editor himself was welcome help for Father Muckermann with his work in Holland, especially with the journal he was publishing, *The German Way*, which came out in Oldenzaal. We found a sympathetic, kindly friend in Oldenzaal in the person of Pastor Franz Stokman, who expressed his willingness to commit the courageous deed of accepting responsibility for *The German Way*. We were often guests at his hospitable house, and since May 1940 I had always worried about him, until I finally heard that he had escaped the claws of the SS and Gestapo by leading a very destitute existence as a longshoreman. With the help of a priest, he had done this in Utrecht under an assumed name for five years, from 1940 on. *The German Way* was also supported in word and deed by the never-tiring "social apostle of Holland," Monseigneur Dr. Poels in Heerlen, who was also able to escape to safety before the German troops' invasion of Holland.

Before German troops marched into Holland, and before the SS and Gestapo established their regime of terror in this peaceful land, the persecuted German editor fled, as I later learned from his daughter in the concentration camp. His family remained behind, frightened a thousand times over. House searches and arrests of the mother and of both eldest children followed. These children were held in custody, separated from one another, in a prison in Berlin; the mother was released to go home to her smaller children after many interrogations. The two eldest, however, remained victims and hostages of the Gestapo, who repeatedly brought them in for the most tortuous, hours-long interrogations, naturally always separated from one another. The girl was told that she should just admit this or that, that her brother had already confessed it, although this was in fact not the case. Many German emigrants were arrested at that time in Holland, as well as many brave and courageous Dutch people who did not carry the torch for National Socialism. They were all subjected to interrogation after interrogation. They were questioned about Father Muckermann, about people who had visited him with whom he was in contact. The names of Father Maring and myself were named by the Gestapo agents again and again. If, in fact, one of the arrested emigrants named our names, as the Gestapo told us during our arrests, it is impossible to say. And if it did happen, then it happened because of weakness, fear, and need, but not because of faulty conduct or mean-spiritedness. Someone also must have testified that other visitors had been with me at Father Muckermann's, people whose names were unknown to the Gestapo. Thus it was that they later demanded from me again and again the names of the priests and men who had been with me in Holland. But they never came over my lips. Therefore, thank God, they were spared the hell of the KZ, the concentration camp.[1]

---

1. KZ is the abbreviation for *Konzentrationslager* (concentration camp).

Chapter 3

"You are under arrest!"

On the morning of February 4, 1941, at around half past eight, I went to holy mass in the cathedral.[1] As I entered through the vestibule, I saw three men standing under the giant figure of Christopher and conspicuously inspecting me. Apparently they were not in the cathedral to worship. All of their mannerisms were too peculiar. They also weren't the kind of non-Catholics who want to visit a church because they are interested in art. If I am not mistaken, one of them even had his hat still on his head. I thought immediately: those are people from the Gestapo; I knew that type well enough. In the course of the past years I had often come into contact with them through my editorial work. Sometimes they scared us and disrupted and impeded our work, without ever finding whatever it was they were searching us for. I listened to the rest of the holy mass, and by the time I left the church I had already forgotten these men entirely.

When I went back to my apartment afterward (I had picked up the skim milk I was entitled to at the little store across the street and had just closed the door of the building), the doorbell rang. I stood with the milk can in my arm in the entrance hall of the building and opened the door. How horrified I was to see these three men from the cathedral in front of me. I immediately understood everything that was to happen to me.

"Fräulein Herbermann?"

"Yes, please, what do you want?"

"Geheime Staatspolizei!" One of them showed his identification.

"Lead us to your apartment! What we want from you cannot be accomplished in passing on the doorstep."

I led the three terrible figures down into an official, little-used room. But the room did not satisfy them.

"We want to go to your living and working quarters!"

---

1. Münster Cathedral was the seat of Bishop von Galen, one of the most outspoken Catholic clergy against the Third Reich.

It set my teeth on edge. The blood drained from my head; my heart seemed to stand still. I could hardly take another step.

I set down my milk can and had to take them up to my beautiful, large work room. I had hardly opened the door when one of the three rushed to the desk, pulled the desk drawer out, sat down in a low rocking chair, the drawer on his knee, and there, comfortably rocking, read every piece of writing the drawer contained. The second man rummaged through the side compartments of the desk, while the third set about turning everything on its head in the adjoining bedroom.

I asked what the meaning of this was and what exactly they were searching for in my apartment.

"Just wait and see!" was the short reply.

My telephone rang. I went to pick up the receiver. Then the oldest of them approached me brusquely and made things clear to me:

"You may no longer use the telephone! You are under arrest!"

He pulled the plug out of the contact so that it couldn't ring any more.

It took me a while to come to my senses. The horrifying realization was awful: Now you are no longer a free person! From now on you will find yourself in the claws of the sinister Gestapo.

Until noon, and thus for many hours, my apartment was ransacked. Manuscripts, documents, letters, and books flew about in wild confusion and lay in all corners; clothes and laundry cupboards were cleared out, and even the kitchen and adjoining side room were not spared.

On the kitchen table lay a bag with five unrationed eggs I had received as a gift the day before. The Gestapo pressed me to tell them from whom I had gotten these unrationed eggs. I replied that they would never hear it from me. It went the same way with a few packets of soap powder, for which I had honestly saved. Here, too, they wanted to know how I had come to possess this small reserve. It was all so ridiculous and looked manifestly like a dirty trick. I pointed this out to them as well: since they hadn't found anything among my papers that could somehow incriminate me, they obviously desperately wanted to find something in this other way.

Finally I was commanded to pack up some nightclothes and toi-letries. My red slippers were in the bedroom. With a look at these, the head big shot said, grinning, "Take these with you for your delicate little feet!" I ignored the innuendo.

I couldn't make another move alone in my apartment. I had now become a victim of the Gestapo, and coming to terms with that was not easy.

From my apartment they called the headquarters of the Gestapo so that a car could be sent out for my abduction. Without asking me, one of them took a large suitcase from my bedroom and threw into it all letters, manuscripts, documents, etc., my desk had contained. Then I heard the car below honk. I turned around once more in my apartment, every piece of which had been earned with laborious work and which I had only owned for a few years. Then I looked one last time at the pictures of my loved ones, at the portrait of my twin sister, married in America; I caressed with this last gaze the backs of my many rows of books; and then, like a sleepwalker, I let myself be brought down by the three men who had affixed the lock and seal of the Gestapo on every room of my apartment and kept the key. Arriving in the hall below, I asked to be allowed to take leave of my neighbors, the three devoted sisters Schlemann, to whom I was bound by a special affection; this was granted me grudgingly, naturally under surveillance, so that I couldn't say another word to them. The three good old women had already noticed what was wrong. Mutely and with tears in their eyes, they shook my hand. We would only see each other again after my release from the concentration camp. . . .

The car stood before the door, as did the three agents with my large suitcase. I had the first station of my cross behind me.[2]

---

2. Nanda here refers to the Catholic practice of following the twelve stations of the cross, the path Jesus took to crucifixion. Icons representing the events of the twelve stations can often be found on the right and left walls of Catholic churches. Devotions relating to these stations are a particular feature of Good Friday services. Several subsequent references by Nanda to the stations, in a metaphorical sense, are found throughout the memoir.

Chapter 4

The first interrogation

At a frantic pace we headed for the headquarters of the Gestapo on Guten-
berg Street. The first impression that I got of this building had a shattering
effect on me. This gray, sinister box was crawling with officials and clerks,
with defiant women, all of whom turned their eyes on me, while I, entering
the building, felt as if I were dead.

I was led into an office room and stood there with dead eyes. One
of the men, who had probably noticed that I was close to fainting, told
me to sit down. The three men who had arrested me were in the room
with me, then two more came in and, after some time, yet two more new
agents. How long all this lasted I no longer know, for one loses all conception
of time in such hours. The two men who entered last were very elegantly
dressed, poised, courteous, and friendly to one's face, and thus all the more
dangerous. They were quite exceptionally well-seasoned emissaries from the
Berlin secret police's Reich Security Office: this was the agency superior to
all Gestapo headquarters in the Reich. On the previous day, these two had
arrested Father Maring in Lübeck and had transported him to Münster on
the same day.

The interrogation began. Such an interrogation is more cruel than
the worst treatment of animals. Imagine: a defenseless woman against seven
agents of the Gestapo. Right on the very first day I said to myself quite
consciously: You will show them no weakness, name no names, answer
as little as possible, and refuse to give evidence in any given case. An
introductory lecture was held for me: neither silence nor resistance would be
of use to me; the sooner I would confess to everything and betray as many
people as possible, the sooner I would be granted my freedom again. I told
them I had nothing to confess and that I was not aware of any transgression
of any law of the land on my part. Since they had taken my passport away
from me already at the apartment, and since it obviously bore various stamps
from the trips to Holland, I immediately admitted that I had been in Holland

a number of times and pointed out that this fact did not in any way violate the law of the land.

A thousand questions attacked me from all sides: "How did Father Muckermann make it over the border? You were with him?" Everything was stated rather than asked. But they didn't get far with me using such methods. "Where did Father Muckermann live in Holland? Who was there with you? What did you discuss? What clergy were with you there aside from Father Maring? Do you know Dr. Poels and Pastor Stokman? How often did you visit these gentlemen with Father Muckermann? Did you write articles for *The German Way*?" Yes, I had done it, but without signing my name, and the Gestapo never found out about it. I didn't answer any of the questions, and they now began to make threats: "We'll force you to speak . . . We have ways to do it right at our fingertips." I let them ask and threaten, always thinking to myself: What I don't want to tell you, and what could incriminate others in your Gestapo-eyes, you will never hear from me. And in the midst of it I prayed to the Holy Ghost for the courage to be strong.

After a few hours the gentlemen from Berlin withdrew, but the interrogation continued with five agents. The winter sun, which had been shining brightly at midday, had long since gone down. I looked at my watch. It was already after eight, and I still didn't know where I would be spending the night.

Finally the director of the Unit for Political Catholicism (that's what was posted in large letters on his door) said that he would bring me to the police prison and that the interrogation would continue on the following day. Again I was put in a car and, accompanied by my three true paladins, driven to the police prison. I was dead tired, and that was fine with me.

Chapter 5

The police prison

The police prison in Münster lay underground. It was a sinister, dirty dungeon, which stank horribly of unkempt bodies, dirty clothing, and the perspiration of sleep.

We entered the room in which the sergeants of the municipal police sat. After the Gestapo people had whispered with them and taken their leave with "Heil Hitler until tomorrow morning," I was asked in a respectable way to give up my jewelry, rings, and watch, as well as my wallet, and, from my cosmetics bag, the scissors and nail file. After my handbag had been searched, I was handed over to the prison guard, accompanied by the sympathetic looks of the policemen. Out of pure exhaustion I had leaned on a wall and could hardly take another step.

"Come," the old guard said to me in a friendly manner, while he reached for a giant set of keys—oh, this key ring with all the keys to the single cells, how often it scared and tormented me in the following months, and never, never, will I rid my ears of the memory of its sinister clanging! "Come with me!"

I followed him down the long corridor through the stifling half-light of the dungeon. I saw the many heavy cell doors. . . . Oh, God, what heartfelt suffering must be hidden behind them! My attendant stopped before one of the doors and commanded me to step inside.

Then I began to cry for the first time on this fateful day, thick, redeeming tears, which I could no longer hold back. Because of the many tears, I saw nothing in the darkness, which was sparingly lit by a dull lamp; I just stood there and sobbed. Finally I sank down onto a stool, my hands on the table, my head on my hands, and cried and cried . . .

The guard came and asked me, "Have you eaten anything today?" No, only now did it occur to me that I had had absolutely nothing since the evening before. Even so, I couldn't have eaten anything, though I did ask urgently for water. The warden brought me cold water in an old enamel cup with a bona fide ring of grime around it. I was truly disgusted, but I overcame this, and drank the entire cupful in one gulp. How much good that did me! The concerned guard had also brought me a thick piece of bread with a blotch of jam in the middle. But I refused it thankfully. He, however, refused to take it back and said that I needed to keep up my energy, then I would certainly get out again soon: a woman like me did not belong in prison. How thankful I was to him for these words. Then he left me, shaking his head.

All of a sudden, though I had thought I was alone in the cell, a raw female voice asked: "Did you have relations with a Pole, too?" I gave a start. On a cot in the corner lay a totally filthy, fully clothed female. I stared at her shyly and curiously, and unintentionally retreated further into the opposite corner of the cell. "No," I said, for I had to make some kind of an answer, "I didn't have relations with any Pole. Please don't ask me anything, just go back to sleep."

"But give me the piece of bread if you're not going to eat it!" No, I wasn't going to eat it and was glad to give it to her. Now she was content, and she greedily devoured the thick piece of bread and snored the whole night through. How was it possible to sleep in a prison? I, too, later learned to do it, just as I slowly adjusted to the informal address of my fellow prisoners as well.

The warden came back and was happy that I had "eaten" the bread, as he said—and I was happy to let him think so. Then he told me to pick one of the three empty cots to sleep on. They were stacked one cot on top of the other. Now I looked around the cell with critical eyes for the first time and saw that on all the cots the bedsheets were no longer white but gray, indeed that the bedsheets stank of dirt, so that I was almost ill when I pulled back the top blanket. I was supposed to sleep here? Not like this! I asked for clean bedclothes. An embarrassed smile was the good man's reply. No, he didn't have any bedclothes here in the prison, they were only changed a few times a year. I told him that I would rather spend the night squatting on the stool. "You're accustomed to other things," he said sympathetically, and went out mumbling to himself. Yes; although I wasn't spoiled by life, I was certainly used to cleanliness, there he was right.

The feeble light burned for another quarter hour. I now looked around the cell more carefully. How narrow it was! Like a coffin, I thought. . . . Buried alive! The complete furnishings consisted of the four cots, two stools, a very small table, and, under the barred and tarnished windows, a small bench. In one corner stood a brown bucket, which had no lid, for relieving oneself; this bucket was filled with excrement and was only emptied every morning.

Quietly, so as not to disturb my very dainty cell mate, I paced back and forth, back and forth. The horror I felt escalated to the most tormenting fear. Now the light was turned off from the hallway, and the horrid gloom of the dungeon surrounded me completely. It seemed to me like I was sitting in a morgue in the company of dead bodies. I thought about all those who had been in and out of here—creatures cast out, corrupted, led astray, guilty and innocent, wretched men, women, and young people. Was the sick Father Maring also lying in one of these cells? Yes, but at that time I did not yet know it.

Across from my window, through which I certainly could not have looked even if it had been daytime, since it was painted over, stood the Lion's Club building, a society club of Münsterers, and cheery music floated over to me in my abandonment. Every once in a while I heard the gentlemen bowling nine pins. I knew the rooms and some of the people who amused themselves there, and it was very hard for me to bear their sounds during this night.

I was still sitting on the stool, crouched up with an aching back, and the whole night through, a night that never seemed to end, I thought of all the good people I loved and who loved me, of the worries they would be having on my account . . .

Oh, Mother! Mother! How many times during this night did I speak your name half aloud, while my soul screamed it from torment in this horror, in this abandonment. Yet I wanted to remain upright in a strong and steadfast belief in Him up above. I wanted to try to "bear the inevitable with dignity," even if my heart almost threatened to break . . .

This night, too, came to an end.

Chapter 6

"You have power!"

You see, this is the tendency of the times, in which the anvil of a horrible destiny destroys all of our joys, and all of our happiness, as far as they can be destroyed at all. God allows this so that the indestructible reveals itself: the point at which He Himself touches the human being, the ground of creation from which the eons descend, the heavenly secret of the cross. One must take it solidly upon one's shoulders. One must say "yes" to it with the last power of love, floating into death. And so all sorrow will immediately become a Hallelujah, the song of triumph of the sorrowful bride, who knows in every hour of the world that her savior lives.

—FRIEDRICH MUCKERMANN, S.J.

In his story "The Dark Night of St. John of the Cross," Reinhold Schneider has St. John speak to one of the Dreaded during his arrest: "You have power, and it would not be difficult for the powers to conceive of a charge and then proceed at their own discretion. But what would be won by that? Beware, you are in great danger, for you have power!"[1]

Yes, they now had full power over me, and it is bitter to feel all of a sudden completely at the mercy of such power. But woe to those who exercised this power so capriciously: they were really in great danger . . .

It had turned into morning, a new morning without sun, full of uncertainty and darkness. During this night I had entrusted myself fully to Him in whose hands every human destiny lies and now wanted willingly to leave up to Him whatever He had in store for me.

---

1. Reinhold Schneider (1903–58) was a German Catholic historian, novelist, and poet. Though he continued to publish historical works and biographies during the Nazi period, his poetry had to be circulated clandestinely. After World War II, Schneider became famous as a writer of virtue and integrity. He was awarded the German Publishers' Peace Prize in 1956.

After the male inmates had first washed up in a common washroom, something I surmised from the calling and rattling, the many steps and noise in the corridor, we two women were also called for washing and hairdressing. My infamous dirty little pig naturally did not even take off her dress, but gave her face a perfunctory once-over with her hands and was already done as I was just beginning: I had the urgent need to revive myself with clear, cold water after these last twenty-four hours.

After this, the wife of the guard was called to clean the cell and empty the bucket, which she did grudgingly and very slowly. In the washroom, I studied the many, many little sentences and sayings and poems, paragraphs and signs scribbled on the wall there, something that was extremely instructive to me. I would like to repeat here some of these statements, sketched out there by inmates as an expression of their perceptions and dispositions, since they make one think:

> "God does not leave his children . . ."
> "We know that after this great need / brightly will dawn the morning red . . ."
> "Freedom in which I believe, which fills my heart . . ."

The word "revenge" was painted on the wall in big letters, next to it a heart, clumsy and angular, with the name of the beloved inside it and the deadly arrow.

Or: "My parents both died in jail. I, too, will perish there. I can't do differently . . ."

These hundreds of sketches and self-confessions I took in at this early hour spoke for themselves; most of them spoke of guilt and atonement, of love and hate, of hopeless creatures who had succumbed to guilt, many of whom had been completely deprived of love.

Around nine o'clock I was picked up for further interrogation, again by two officials from the Gestapo. We passed through the narrow corridor and the extremely thick iron door of the prison into the office of the municipal police, who handed over my jewelry, wallet, scissors, etc. I strongly sensed the antipathy these regular police had for the Gestapo and their disgusting behavior, and as one of the Gestapo people asked me sneeringly how I had slept in my "new home," I noticed how one of the policemen would have liked to give in to an act of considerable violence in the face of such meanness. I ignored this sarcastic question, but, since the opportunity had presented itself, I did ask to be transferred to the court prison, because the police prison was too dirty for me. I was told that I had already been ordered into solitary confinement, so I would be going there anyway in the course of the day. The guard made a disapproving gesture to me, then tapped me on the shoulder and whispered: "You would have done better to stay with us! Here you at least have some amenities!" He was right, but I don't know if I could have stood such filth for a whole half year. . . . When I heard weeks later that every inmate in the police prison was allowed to receive as many packages as he liked, while not one single one was handed over to me in the court prison, despite the attempts of my friends and relatives (and there were several things I would have been very happy to have, since I really suffered from hunger), then I thought of the well-meaning words of the good old man in the police prison. He was loved and respected by the political prisoners who were entrusted to his custody for long periods of time because he was especially humane to and understanding toward them. I heard also that he had supposedly "done time" for a long period once himself, for political reasons, though he was innocent. It was probably for this reason that he had showed special understanding and benevolence toward me. But brooding about whether it would have been better to waste away in filth or receive food packages was for naught, since I had to go into solitary confinement and the police prison was not equipped with any single cells.

Outside stood another magnificent automobile into which I was told to climb. The car whizzed quickly along the streets of my beloved hometown. The funeral bells were ringing from the Lamberti Church, the church of my christening, the church of my childhood and youth.[2]

I was freezing from the watchful and sleepless night. I folded my hands and sent my morning greeting out into the Holy Kingdom, knowing myself to be completely unified with Him, who bore the cross for us. One of my escorts wanted to start a conversation; I didn't answer and sat there with closed eyes until the car pulled up in front of Gestapo headquarters. After I climbed out of the car and the many eyes of the people who worked in this giant building watched me and sized me up again curiously, even hatefully, I held myself up on a railing until I was told to climb the stairs. They sent jeers and mocking laughter up after me.

I was again led into the room in which they had interrogated me on the previous day. Two people already sat at the tables there, and my two escorts joined them, so there were four altogether to whom I had to justify my actions. Still, my silence was greater than my eloquence. I saw my letters and manuscripts lying on the desks. The director of the Unit for Political Catholicism regarded me with his cold and evil eyes. His mouth could be so atrociously friendly that I mistrusted him from the very beginning. The interrogation began again.

Herr Dehm, the head of the interrogation, supposed that it would

---

2. The Lamberti Church, Nanda's own parish church, was also the place where Bishop von Galen (see note 3 to this chapter) delivered many of his most important anti-Nazi sermons.

gradually have become apparent to me why I had been arrested and that I must certainly have become convinced during this last night that it would be better for me to speak than to remain silent. I answered him, "No, I am not convinced of this at all," to which he promptly replied that they would surely know how to force me to be so.

This second, prolonged interrogation mainly concerned the person of Father Muckermann, upon whom were conferred the nastiest invectives, which I am not capable of repeating. The intrepid bishop of Münster, Clemens August Graf von Galen, and the noble church prior, Professor Dr. Donders, also had to submit to a regular bombardment of oaths and curse words.[3] The Gestapo certainly wanted to finger me as the middleman between the bishop of Münster, whom I was "in close contact with" (which was not at all the case, but pure speculation on the part of these awful men) and Father Muckermann. What cowardice not to interrogate the bishop himself in this matter, for he certainly would have been all too glad to show up for such an interrogation! But they lacked the courage for that. Tormenting a defenseless woman obviously amused them. And then they had the idea that Prof. Donders was the secret secretary of the much-hated (by them) group Catholic Action.[4] They could make neither head nor tail out of the group's silent and beneficial work and were trying to read God knows what into it! Here, too, I was supposed to be the secret "mediator" between Prof. Donders and Father Muckermann. Oh, they thought I was so important—and I had only done the work that everyone who knew me knew about. So I also told them that I had never occupied these honorable positions, but of course they didn't believe me.

Their rage over the remarkable, timely, overcrowded apostolic eleven o'clock sermons of the cathedral preacher Prof. Donders in the cathedral was immense. They objected to something specific in his last

---

3. In their January 1942 report on Bishop von Galen, the Gestapo labeled him "a saboteur of the inner front" because he maintained close contact with the leading rabbis, and he had called the Jewish people the "chosen people of God," and they claimed he was a traitor of his own land because enemy countries were translating his sermons and letters and distributing them and playing them on the radio. Even the Royal Air Force (RAF) dropped them from airplanes (Steward, *Sieg des Glaubens*, 104–5). Professor Donders was born in 1877; he was a Catholic theologian and priest who became a cathedral preacher in the Münster Cathedral in 1911 and a professor in 1919. He also served, beginning in 1906, as the General Secretary of the Central Committee of German Catholic Organizations. He was the author of several books on religious topics.

4. Catholic Action was a Catholic laity group founded by Pope Benedict XV and Pope Pius XI. The purpose of the organization was to create a forum for spirituality in the face of the spiritual degeneration of the times. Pope Pius XI called the organization's purpose to promote participation of lay people in the hierarchical apostolate. Father Muckermann wrote a book about Catholic Action, published in 1929, titled *Katholische Aktion.*

sermons; now I no longer remember what this was exactly. In any case the saying of a famous man had been used by the cathedral preacher as an invocation in one of his sermons. I couldn't suppress a smile when the director, who was so proud of his particular position as head of the Unit for Political Catholicism, asked me what exactly an invocation was. This was characteristic of the education of these people, at whose mercy every spiritually concerned person, every priest and every layman, existed, for better or for worse, and over whom they had authority without trial or justice. I at least gave them to understand very clearly that they could not hold a candle to any of these men. Naturally I had to put up with some very base comments for standing up for these priests.

The gentlemen created an especially good image of themselves by dragging the relationship between Father Muckermann and me through the mud. I never responded to any of these allusions and questions; instead I told them right at the beginning, as those kinds of insinuations came up, that in principle I had no answer for such things. "You can't pretend to us that you took these dangerous journeys upon yourself out of pure idealism to your cause. Women don't do that!" Oh, my dear gentlemen, a woman can do much more!

During later interrogations these above-mentioned matters often came up again. I was also accused of writing articles against National Socialism while in Holland and of bringing pastoral letters and sermons of the German bishops abroad. But I told them that one could accomplish this much more easily by mail, which at that time was still running regularly. . . . Yes, they invented a thousand charges against me, but they had not one single piece of evidence in their hands. Their powerless rage grew from interrogation to interrogation. I remained calm and collected despite the continually renewed threats that they would soon make me speak; finally they decided I was just as "pestilent and lying as all clergy."

After this second interrogation, during which I was able to gain great insight into Nazi psychology, I was transported to the court prison late in the evening, where I was handed over to the head guard.

Chapter 7

In the court prison

While the head guard of the women's division of the court prison was still dealing in whispers with the Gestapo, I leaned back a little against the wall and observed the woman who would now be guarding over me in prison. She had good, shining eyes, which I immediately and thankfully noticed. After the Gestapo had left, I had to follow her up the half-dark stairs. There is something peculiar about this cold half-darkness in each and every prison. It is really there only to increase the lonely horror in which the inmate lives. But I saw from the blooming flowers in the corridor of the second floor of this clean prison that at least a good heart held sway here, and that filled me with some level of comfort. It had now become very lonesome and loveless all around me. I suffered inexpressibly. And when the head guard R. led me to my new lonesome cell #71, after she, too, had taken away my jewelry, watch, handbag, all sharp objects, coat, and hat, all the horror and suffering stood there before me so insurmountably that I could have despaired. I begged for strength and tenacity, for a sign from above, just a very small sign, that at least my God was with me. I thought of Christ's hours on Mount Olive and of his most unsettling of all proclamations: "My God, my God, why hast thou forsaken me?"

Worn down, unconsoled, indescribably sad, I paced back and forth in my cell on this evening, again and again, back and forth. . . . The tears I had held back the whole day now poured forth again plentifully. My last energy went into this. But at certain times weakness can even turn into immense strength. Such moments are profound turning points for human beings. I now stood at such a point. On this evening, in this cell, this fact became very clear to me. I grew more calm.

Now, for the first time, I began to look around in my cell, where for five months I would endure great suffering alone with the Lord God and my guardian angel, but where I would also learn and come to understand a great deal. . . . There was a narrow but clean prison bed covered in blue and white, a pillow filled with straw, a small closet with a brightly polished zinc key, a water glass, a blue towel, then a stool with a back and a very small table. Here, too, the unavoidable bucket stood in the corner, but this one was scrubbed clean, though only with a half-lid on top. The walls were gray—oh, so hopelessly gray—and up above on the front side was a barred window the size of about eighty square centimeters. It was too high: even if I stood on the stool I saw nothing more than the roof of the large court building. But if I pulled myself up on the bars, which I later did frequently, I could see down into the small prison courtyard and beyond the high walls to the back entrance of the court building. In the thick cell door I noticed the peephole, which I had seen already in the police prison, through which the inmate could be observed from the hallway. This cell was approximately four paces long and very narrow.

After I had carefully looked around my accommodations, I crept back into myself, and the great bleakness of my situation began to torment me again. Oh, all the grief one feels cannot be expressed! How hotly and acutely a human heart can rebel. And then the powerlessness and great hopelessness, the speechless staring at the dungeon walls. . . . Buried alive! At times there was no glimmer of hope left in me. The deepest darkness surrounded me during the long, often completely sleepless nights. Oh, how I would have liked to hammer with balled fists against this door, force it open, how I could have screamed, unrestrainedly and wildly, as other prisoners in neighboring cells did at times, throwing true tantrums.

Yes, the nights were long, endlessly long. Even today I can see the window bars creeping slowly over the gray floor in the moonshine. Then I often got up, stood on the stool or pulled myself up on the bars, and observed the endless starry skies and my quiet, beloved hometown, which slept under their protection; I saw the towers of the churches that had grown so close to my heart, where I knew the holiest sacrament, the great love of all Christians. I had so much spare time in these months to dedicate myself completely to those things that bring us closer to heaven. Such a long time completely alone with God, would it not bring me closer to it, make me better?

So we human beings are knocked to the floor, left alone, extinguished. Helplessly I lay in my ripping pain, unable to believe the unbelievable, to grasp the ungraspable. Oh, what do we know about the meaning of these things that are so incomprehensible to us? I stopped asking, where no answer could be revealed to me.

Oh my God, my soul sobbed! You have also given power to the pain and the torment in our hearts. And You alone can help me come to terms with this. I cannot comprehend why You created so much unbridled suffering, so much senseless and insane pain. Help me, that I may come to terms with this! Yes, it often seemed to me as if the limits of the bearable had been reached. I pulled together my very last bit of strength. Then only an outer and inner silence remained—the last loneliness. But I wanted and had to remain hopeful, could not become doubtful. For my situation, there was only one thing to do, to master it with composure . . .

Chapter 8

Fellow prisoners

On the third day of my stay in the court prison, the senior guard, S., came to my cell at nine in the morning and summoned me to go with the other prisoners under her guard to the prison yard. I followed willingly and, because it was still bitterly cold in February, I was handed my coat for this "walk," which lasted fifteen minutes and was repeated daily in the future whenever the weather was reasonably tolerable. Outside deep snow lay on the ground. In the cell I froze day and night and still I was not allowed to put on my warm coat . . .

As I stepped into the corridor I saw the other inmates for the first time as they stepped out of neighboring cells, several at a time; I did not have the capacity to look at them, as I was moved too much by how new it all was. The march down to the prison yard was completed silently. I was held separately from the others and came last, with no one next to, behind, or in front of me. When, weeks later, I dared to ask the senior guard why I was being treated as an outcast twice over, even in prison, she explained to me then that this was done according to an order from the Gestapo. . . . As the last in line I could easily observe how all of the inmates (there were about thirty-five) aimed for the middle of the yard where a round patch of lawn was located, around which a cement path led. Always around and around this round path with a certain distance between each individual: this was how the silent women walked for a quarter of an hour. I had to go back and forth off to the side, all by myself, and all the inmates naturally sized up the new one carefully.

When I experienced this "walk" (as it was called in prison) for the first time, I just stared ahead of me and didn't want to raise my eyes, and the few handkerchiefs I had taken with me at my arrest were already so soaking wet that I didn't know what to dry my tears with. Thus, I also didn't see right away what I later noticed: namely, that on the other side of the prison yard another solitary inmate was walking, who constantly wiped her eyes with a handkerchief and couldn't stop crying. Perhaps her fate was worse than mine? A slim, young woman, but very care-worn. It occurred to me in a flash: could that be Frau Ballhorn? I knew her fate from hearsay. As I had heard a few days before my arrest, she had been picked up with her small child at her house in Holland by the Gestapo and then brought back to Münster to the court prison. The child had been given to the mother of the young woman in Münster. My speculation was correct: it was Frau Ballhorn, and, as she told me later, she also knew right away who I was.

From this day on a mute friendship was established between us. Through the daily, speechless meeting, through the knowledge of one another and through mutual understanding and sharing, we became for each other both strength and comfort. She, too, was in solitary confinement and an inmate of the Gestapo, while all others in this women's prison were detained pending trial or were convicted criminals serving sentences. Frau Ballhorn cried even more than I did. If my eyes were red and sore during the first weeks, hers were for months, and at the end she suffered from a facial rash from the constant crying. The poor woman's husband, who had worked steadfastly as an emigrant in Holland in the Catholic anti-Nazi press, was in a concentration camp, and she suffered from terrible homesickness for her child and was bent over with grief.

The detainees and convicts were an interesting group of people in and of themselves, especially to someone who had never come into contact with people of this type. Already in my first days there I had heard in my cell noises, laughter, and screaming, curse words and loud singing from the neighboring cells, although all of that was strictly forbidden; and I had already tried somehow to imagine what sort of people my neighbors were. When I gradually began to size them up and form an opinion about them, and when I thought about what crime this one or that one could have committed, I was deeply frightened by their sinister, pock-marked faces, by the dead eyes that knew how to stare so impenetrably. Anyone who has looked into such faces cannot forget them—haggard and pale with such uncanny, feverishly glowing eyes. Prostitutes, thieves, murderers came and went, indifferent, dull, unconcerned, apathetic, stayed for a short while, or sometimes a long while. . . . On some days it was like a beehive. Some of them smiled, others stared at me. A small, dark-haired prostitute called to me once: "You shouldn't cry so much, you'll get ugly that way!"

In general it can be said that this bunch of poor souls was made up in large part of individuals unfit for human society, with the exception of a very few who had been shipwrecked, perhaps for the first time in their lives. Most of the faces revealed vice and depravity. And yet, and yet, how things were later in the concentration camp! . . .

I suffered unspeakably through the many months of inactivity. I was not allowed to read anything at all, nor to work. I begged for books, but no one gave them to me in the first months. I had a real fear of losing my mind. I asked the chief warden to bring me potatoes to peel at least. But this was not allowed, and I was no longer allowed to bother either of the good guards about this, though they gladly would have helped me. They were to conform to the merciless guidelines of the Gestapo, and I had to reconcile myself to that. This inactivity is poisonous for every prisoner, whether guilty or innocent. I was happy when, after a few months, the prison chaplain Brinkmann secretly gave me a few books, which I read again and again until he brought me new ones at his next visit. He had been given books for me by loyal friends, and after studying them thoroughly I gave them to the prison library. I read, among other things, Stifter, Guardini, Lippert, works of history, and biographies.[1] What a joy, what a comfort, and what a blessing these books were for me!

---

1. Adalbert Stifter (1805–68) was an Austrian author whose novels and stories are well known for their sensitive treatment of nature and rejection of violence. Romano Guardini (1885–?) was an Italian-born Catholic priest who later became professor of Catholic theology at the University of Breslau and often lectured at the University of Berlin. Guardini played a leading role in the Catholic youth movement; he wrote books on youth and Catholicism, as well as on liturgy and liturgical practice. Peter Lippert (1879–?) was a German Catholic priest and author of numerous theological works on the Jesuits and the Catholic Church in general.

Chapter 9

Sundays in prison

Every Sunday provided me with a ray of hope. All week long I waited longingly for the next one. Then I was allowed to go along to the chapel and hear holy mass, to communicate and be united with Him, who is truly our entire love and sustains us, especially in the most bitter and desolate hours. The small but touching sermons of the prison chaplain Brinkmann gave me the courage to be strong. How comforting it was that Lent fell precisely during my time of sorrow, and that I could sing along with a fervent heart: "Oh head covered in blood and wounds, full of pain, full of scorn." It was particularly during these times that the suffering Savior came infinitely near to me. Through many hours during the day and at night I observed His suffering, and I knew why He had suffered, and also why I had to suffer. So I took solace and faith from the tiny chapel back to the gray, sinister weekdays, and even in those hours when the ghost of dark melancholy wanted to take me in its claws, and when I was often close to despair, these Sunday hours gave me the comfort and strength to carry on.

Almost without exception, my fellow prisoners also attended the Sunday services. It was for them a welcome diversion from the wretched monotony of their gray existence. Unfortunately, they often behaved annoyingly and showed more interest in the male inmates (who were also present in great numbers in the prison chapel) than they did for the religious observance taking place up at the altar, so that the guards had to summon them to order and proper conduct. After the service, the guard on duty went from cell to cell and, since Sunday was the writing day for detainees awaiting trial, asked which of the inmates wanted to have paper and ink. For the sake of my relatives I had asked the Gestapo, whom I otherwise asked for nothing, if I might write to my loved ones. This was granted to me, naturally with instructions that every written line had to go through the hands of the Gestapo and every letter was to be delivered to them open. So I was then allowed to write to our old mother in Soest, who heard of my arrest only eight months later, since none of my siblings could bring themselves to communicate this shattering news to her, as she was very ill. As an exception, I was allowed to write the letters to my mother on neutral paper—all other writing paper had the stamp of the court prison on it. I wrote as I had earlier, as if nothing had happened, so that she wouldn't get the idea that something unusual had happened to me. For a long time my siblings and I were successful at feigning good things, until the whole affair started to strike her as curious. In addition, she was used to my regular visits, and now I didn't come any more. What could that mean? What was going on with her daughter? How must she have wracked her brains? Only after I had already been in a concentration camp for a quarter of a year, where I couldn't write her at all anymore, did she ask my eldest brother to tell her what was going on with me; she could no longer live with this uncertainty. Only then did she hear the facts, so upsetting for a mother.

I often wrote from prison to my eldest brother, who lived in Münster, and to whom I have much to be thankful for.[1] He traveled many roads for me and loyally made reports to all siblings and friends. For his part, he told me everything of the family, the siblings, and acquaintances, which I would find interesting; in short, everything he was allowed to and could tell me. To write everything was impossible owing to censorship. About many things I had to read between the lines; we had to remain silent about other things. I remember well how I wrote to him in a letter that I was very hungry (I thought, namely, that he, who was extremely proper about everything and always followed the rules, would perhaps find ways and means, as had the relatives of other inmates, of getting something to me, above all some butter or jam to spread on my dry bread), but I received this letter back with a comment from the Gestapo underlined in red: "Express objections of this sort again and you will be forbidden from writing!" This meant I had to keep on going hungry. I also often wrote to my oldest and truest friend, now eighty-eight years old, Professor Felix Hase, from whom I received a short letter almost once a week, and who even dared to advance into the "lion's den" and to charge the Gestapo agents with holding me innocently. The sympathetic words of this honest man were touching to me. He was the only one of my friends who dared to write to me in prison as an inmate of the Gestapo.

---

1. Nanda refers here to August Heinrich Ferdinand Herbermann, her half brother. He was born in Borken on October 27, 1892, and was a building inspector in Münster. He married Katarina Josepha Hams on April 26, 1923, and had ten children.

Chapter 10

Horror and injustice

Through long, tormenting interrogations by the Gestapo, the weeks after Easter became a true ordeal for me. If I had found sacred peace in my God and, for a time, a few hours of sleep in the night, now the sleepless nights began again. I got up and often prayed for a long time lying on the floor. The thought of atonement filled me completely. Then I paced the four steps back and forth again, again and again, back and forth. The church bells, so dear and familiar to me, rang. . . . You bells of home, how you could ring into the wounded soul, how you can urge on and call, but also torment. I distinguished by day and by night the bells of the cathedral, of Liebfrauen, of St. Lamberti, Aegidii, and Ludgeri. But I could not become weak; I had to control myself bravely. One cannot allow feelings to get the better of one in such a situation.

Large white sheets of paper and a pencil were given to me in my cell for days on end by order of the Gestapo. I was supposed to confess and betray! But the paper remained blank. I had nothing to confess to these authorities, and betrayal was not for me. I could not refuse to write down my résumé, and that was finally finished one day, too . . .

In order to distract myself, I often recited, in low tones, all the poems I knew by heart—pieces from dramas I had learned by heart in school and later on; I also softly hummed all songs that were dear to me. Then again, the scribbles on the cell walls reminded me of the people who had suffered and starved in this cell before me. There were entire life tragedies sketched in there by fingernail, shocking life confessions of unhappy human beings . . .

One day I learned from the guard that two male inmates from our prison had been condemned to death and would be transported to their execution on a Sunday at midday. They lay chained on their cots, and one of them had made several unsuccessful suicide attempts. Now I saw these two men from my window, on the bars of which I had pulled myself up in order to be able to see out; I saw how they crossed the prison yard chained, step by step (it was a sinister sight!), and then were loaded into a police car. I knew that the bride of one of the inmates was in our women's prison and had often seen her during our "walks," white as wax with eyes red from crying. What must have been going through her soul on this Sunday?

My thoughts were also often occupied by Dr. Grüner, a young and talented priest from Vreden, whom I had known there through my good friend T. and who now languished in a cell above me. Because of some statement in a sermon, he had, like so many other priests, also been arrested.

One Sunday, while leaving the chapel, I was taken by the head guard to the cell above, where Dr. Grüner was housed. In an unobserved moment, I dared to look through the peephole in his cell door. There sat this young priest hammering pieces of leather to make them soft on a so-called tripod. Was this his daily work? But I also saw books lying on his table, and it comforted me to know that he could work and read. My thoughts also rested often on the police prison, where I knew the sick Father Maring was. The religion teacher Chairman Friedrichs, who was highly esteemed in Münster and had been arrested a few weeks after me, was also in this prison. I saw them all before me, collected, calm, self-sacrificing. I also wanted to be this way. I offered my suffering up as a sacrifice for them and prayed for them all the more, the more difficult everything became for me. Like saints who used "the dragon as a bridge over the abyss," they walked across vulgarity, baseness, and devilish evil, tranquil and deeply trusting, toward a different life.[1] Yes, one could learn the deepest submission in prison . . .

I remained very calm in the face of the constantly repeated threats of the Gestapo. They could not scare me this way. Certainly I shuddered to think of the kinds of methods the Gestapo was not afraid to use to force people to talk and to extort confessions . . . and how they were still waiting for me to betray some priest or another, or one of my former colleagues. But I was silent or protected them, for which purpose I often had to resort to a white lie. They seemed to see that no amount of exertion and pressing, the solitary confinement, the inactivity, and even the terrible and irritating torture of the constant, tormenting interrogations would ever sway me from my principles; they had even been told this clearly enough by me right on the very first day. Oh, some of these agents looked like the devil incarnate! I was truly afraid of them. The "Director" himself sometimes gnashed his teeth in rage: "And I'll force you yet!" And he only became more angry at my answer: "Do whatever you can't help. You can't do more than kill me!" For me death would have only been salvation from infinite pain. Is death not mild for those who understand it well? Or he addressed me as "Little

---

1. Note the use of the word "abyss" here, a word Herbermann uses in her title to refer to Ravensbrück.

devil!" to which I responded, "I'm sure it will become clear one day in the future which one of us is the devil."

At the beginning a few of these "gentlemen" approached me with such impudence that I dared to demand decency of them: "Before you speak to me and want to receive an answer, please take that cigar out of your mouth and take your hands out of your pockets. After all, you are still dealing with a lady, as you yourself keep emphasizing, who is only 'being held in protective custody'!" Yes, protective custody! How does someone who is uninitiated imagine that? Tormented by forty interrogations, worn down by half a year of solitary confinement, one could not emotionally mistreat and torture a felon worse!

During the interrogations I sometimes felt like a soldier who lies in a firing position and runs out of ammunition, but who still holds his position. . . . Yet my ammunition could not run out, my courage had to keep growing, strengthening itself in rock-solid faith, my will could not waver or sway. God's grace had to hold me up, and did so wonderfully. Again and again I was allowed to experience God's great fidelity.

Chapter 11

Air raids on Münster!

May came full of blooms and warmth, but it remained cold in our gray home. The little piece of sky that I saw through my cell window became more blue every day, and the sun became stronger and more golden. Since I had had to give up my watch, I learned in these weeks to calculate the exact time according to the position of the sun. I couldn't see a single little flower. To me they were no longer there. In general, I suffered a lot in these years, having to dispense with nature entirely, with its green, its flowers, the forest, and the meadows. Oh, our life was so gray, and so painful, too, that flowers seemed to me almost like the betrayers of some secret of nature. They certainly divulged that somewhere life, hope, light, and love could still be found in the world, even for the longing and wishes of an inmate in the protective custody of the Geheime Staatspolizei.

I felt doubly thankful when the chief guard appeared one day in my cell with a magnificent bouquet of roses so that I might enjoy it for a few moments. . . . How I feasted my eyes on the colors and forms, how I soaked up the fragrance! She would have gladly left me one of the flowers, but even this was not allowed.

In the course of the month of June I was picked up several times for the last interrogations. I breathed a sigh of relief from the bottom of my heart when I was finally notified that this was now the very last interrogation, and it filled me with unspeakable satisfaction when the director of the Unit for Political Catholicism asserted angrily that after all these interrogations they didn't know any more than they had already known on day one; he called me "Jesuit pest!" and promised me that he would see to it that I would end up where I belonged. Stupidly, I did not take this threat seriously, and I didn't suspect that this man would yet "recommend" me for the concentration camp. . . . Yes, in his huge ambition to climb up to the highest "post of honor" with the Gestapo, he could become nothing through me, even if he had faithfully applied all the artful tricks and strategies that stood at the disposal of these men. Therefore I had apparently disappointed his hopes all the more, and thus the boundless rage against me! I, however, was still imagining at that time that soon the clock would strike the hour of my release, since the protocol to be sent to Berlin contained nothing that could have justified my transport to a concentration camp. How I would be disappointed!

I had, however, achieved one small relief in the meanwhile. I was allowed to work a bit in the last weeks of my stay in the Münster court prison without the Gestapo's hearing of it. The bliss of being occupied! My God, it cannot be described how inactivity creates unhappiness! How it almost drove me to insanity! I now sewed one button after the other onto military trousers for the firm Mondt, hour after hour, day after day, week after week. I sewed on thousands of buttons in these weeks! Since these buttons were sewed on with a strong thread that cut through the skin of my fingers so that they bled, I had to sit out for a few days with this insignificant but extremely painful injury until calluses had slowly grown up in place of the wounds. As an exception, Fräulein Mondt was allowed to come into my cell in order to bring the work up to me. This, too, was a ray of light, for she always had an understanding word and sometimes even a small, nourishing surprise for me.

Then came the month of July 1941 with the horrible nightly air raids on our beautiful Münster.[1] How I trembled in fear and horror during these nights, God alone knows. We all had to remain in our cells behind thick, locked doors, upstairs on the third floor. I can still hear the lamentations and the cries of fear of the poor inmates. The bombs struck all around us. Now and then in the midst of it I pulled myself up on my iron bars and saw the city bright as day, burning on every corner, saw and heard whole rows of houses collapse, and always the thought: Any minute you will be hit. As soon as one thought, now it's over, a new wave came, and the horror began all over again. These sinister attacks continued for two full hours. I sat on my stool under the window, ducking and cowering like a shy bird, the hair stuck to my head, my whole body wet from fear and dread. During later attacks, inmates from this prison, as well as from the penitentiary, lost their lives, some of them burned alive. It was inexcusable not to bring the prisoners to a safe cellar!

After these attacks had been repeated three nights in a row, it was decided by the district attorney's office that the detainees pending investigation would be released for the moment; felony cases and convicted prisoners would be transported to other cities. This happened immediately.

---

1. Münster had been targeted for air raids by the RAF since 1939. Because it is located near many industrial cities, Münster was also subjected to "area bombings" at night when the RAF simply dropped bombs over large industrialized areas, hoping to hit important targets that could not be specifically located in the dark. By the end of 1941, the RAF had dropped fifty thousand tons of bombs on Europe. Fifty to 75 percent of Münster was destroyed (Keegan, *Times Atlas of the Second World War,* 53, 138).

Only a few exceptional cases remained in Münster. I was among these. I was now literally at the end of my rope, and I asked the chief guard to inquire at the Gestapo about what was to happen to me and whether I might at least be allowed to spend nights in the cellar. Two more terrible nights followed. The chief district attorney himself came to my cell after the fourth attack and asked me how I had fared during the nights. He felt for me as a human being and would have gladly made modifications, but, unfortunately, it was not within his power, as he assured me. He, too, was enraged by the inhumanity to which I, a defenseless woman, was being subjected. No one should be left alone in a securely locked cell during such attacks. This district attorney must have intervened urgently with the Gestapo for my evacuation. All of a sudden the chief guard appeared before me one evening. "Herbermann, you will be picked up by the Gestapo immediately. Where you are going, we don't know." I found myself in a state of indifference. My hopes of release were dashed. So proceed onward! Proceed to suffer, proceed to pull together all strength, until it is no longer possible. But human beings can truly bear a tremendous amount. And for me this meant, despite all hopelessness, that someday I must emerge from the claws of the Gestapo, someday I would be home again. Such longing, in combination with a solid will, made me strong again in these hours.

Chapter 12

Toward an uncertain future

With mixed feelings I left my silent cell. Yes, if walls could speak! I left the house of horror, took in the peculiarly oppressive quality of this large prison one last time; my eyes wandered up the dungeon walls, I thanked the guards, who could not comprehend why I was being tormented. Often they had said to me, especially in the last days, "Now you will certainly be released!" Oh, to be released! Freedom! Golden freedom!

In the office of the prison I was handed over to three officials of the Gestapo and had to climb into a highly elegant, open car, without anyone telling me where the trip was headed. I was too proud to ask. So I drove again through the familiar streets of my hometown, which was, in the terms of those days, already deeply wounded. Next to me sat one of the agents, and when I was greeted at the main market during our trip in the open car by a lady with whom I was acquainted and silently returned the greeting, he snapped at me: "You are not to greet, you are an inmate! Have you not grasped that yet? If that happens again, then you may experience the shock of your life!" I made no reply.

Now the car drove between the city hall and the city winery down a narrow lane and stopped in front of the police prison, with which I was now well acquainted. I stayed in the car with my left-hand man and heard only the words: "Now we'll load on the priests!" It was then clear to me that the clergy who were being held prisoner there were to come along with me. But to where? To where? To greater horror, to deeper misery and deprivation? And then, on the stone stairway that led down to the prison, Father Maring appeared, the sight of whom alarmed me greatly. He stood before me covered in filth, emaciated, his good-natured child's face grown long. What had these five months done to him! Behind him (I could hardly believe my eyes!) was Father Augustin Benninghaus, S.J., tall and serious, but implacable. So he, too. I hadn't known it. He, too, died in Dachau, a priest after God's own heart, who for years simply held his devotions and never paid attention to politics. He had supposedly, as I found out later, said something during a

93

devotional course for conscripts, a trifle, which an appointed spy betrayed. And there stood a third priest, Instructor Bocks. This last man was told to sit down in back of the car next to me: "The Jesuits must not sit next to Fräulein Herbermann! Any speaking with one another is forbidden!" Those were the instructions we received. The two Jesuits now sat in front of me, I sat between Instructor Bocks and the agent, and the two other Gestapo people were up in the front of the car. It was a great solace to me to have these priests around me and to not have to be alone with Himmler's bandits during this night. Chairman Friedrichs had already been transported to a concentration camp.

We set off again for the headquarters of the Gestapo. Where would we be kept now? I imagined with terror that we would be housed in the cellar of the Gestapo building. As we arrived in front of the building, we were commanded to get out. We went through the long halls of the building and back up the rear stairs again. Despite the fact that we had a guard in front of us and behind us, Father Maring dared to whisper to me: "Be brave! I'm praying for you!" I could only answer: "You can depend on me!" as one of the men had already detected this exchange and threatened us with a slapping. And he smacked the priest in his tired face. . . . Another deep, sad, long glance that expressed a silent agreement, an understanding and knowledge and mutual sharing of the burden. A questioning glance on my part across to Father Benninghaus, since I had no idea why they had locked him up too, and already we had arrived at the door of the room in which I had had to subject myself to so many interrogations.

The three priests were commanded to remain in the hallway. One of the agents stayed with them as a guard, and I had to go into the conference room, where I was offered a chair in the corner behind the door. I was mockingly notified that in order to "safeguard my life" (oh, what did these people care about my life and wasn't this life harder than dying?) I would be taken out of Münster on this very evening. Then the endless paperwork was accomplished which accompanied every transport of prisoners.

Now the priests were called in and notified of the same thing. They received this information just as mutely and readily as I had. "In order to safeguard your life." . . . These men dared to say this, men who had murdered thousands of priests in the concentration camps of Germany, not to mention the many spiritual-emotional murders of priests who, physically and mentally broken, wasted away all too quickly as a result of the tormenting persecution in Germany.

We waited another two full hours for our transport, without yet knowing where we would be taken. All eyes were leveled mockingly, with grins and curiosity, at me, who had stayed alone in the room, and they all sized me up as if they had never seen me before. Had I been changed and transformed by the torment and fear of the last days and nights? Had I not, on the day of my arrest and delivery to the prison, already died a death which one is not capable of describing more closely?

At midnight we finally set out. Down in the yard stood two smaller cars that would transport us further. Father Benninghaus and I were now ordered into one of the cars, and the two other priests had to get into the second car. Two savage fellows climbed into the first car with us, and three climbed into the other car. Silent, dead tired, my soul full of pain, I sat in the back of the car. Now I was, in addition to everything else, supposed to take leave of the city which, of all the cities in the world, was dearest to my heart. Father Benninghaus, in an unobserved moment, made the sign of the cross of benediction over me. I gave myself over willingly to that which was to come and stopped paying attention to the paths we took.

As we arrived in Bochum, we were greeted with heavy artillery fire.[1] There was a full alarm, and the enemy bombers sang their heavy, horrible battle song above us. The car pulled up in front of the prison. Two officials, one from each car, got out, went in, came back after a while and whispered to the others, but loud enough for me to hear: "No room!" They pondered for a long time and then got back in. On we went. But apparently they had taken a wrong turn, for they kept pulling over and asking passersby for the Herne police prison.[2] Hopefully there was a place for us to stay there! I was so tired. I would have gladly fallen asleep never to awake again. My patience was exhausted. Only the grace of God could still help me, still hold me up, for my last strength was failing me. But things were the same for the three priests, who were all over sixty years old. Their pain and suffering grieved me very much. Only to sleep, we wanted only to sleep. Finally the police prison was found in the dark of night.

We climbed out. It was long past midnight. In the distance one could hear bombs falling and heavy artillery fire. There was probably an attack on Dortmund. After the Gestapo had rung the night bell several times, an enraged voice, which seemed to have been disturbed from a deep sleep, finally answered. The door was opened. We four inmates had to wait in the big, long hall with a guard. We were not allowed to put down our luggage. How nasty and common these agents were to the priests of God! Silently I repeated one short, fervent prayer after another.

After the Gestapo had given the robust police sergeant what must have been exacting instructions about our treatment, or rather mistreatment,

---

1. Bochum is a city in northwestern Germany, approximately sixty kilometers southwest of Münster, which was heavily targeted by the RAF during this period. Seventy-five to 100 percent of the city was ultimately destroyed (Keegan, *Times Atlas of the Second World War*, 138).

2. Herne is a town in northwestern Germany, approximately ten kilometers north of Bochum.

in his office and had taken leave of us with the comment, "Good luck! You'll certainly be released soon!" they took off in their cars. But they already knew that both Fathers, and I, too, would be brought to a concentration camp! The police sergeant commanded us in a raw manner to follow him. We went first up a stone stairway, which was many steps high. Upon reaching the third floor, the three clerics had to stop. I threw one last glance at these tormented priestly figures, who stood there like their bound master, and shut my eyes, which burned too much to look anymore. This departure was inexpressibly difficult. I was taken further up, further and further and further, step after step! We must have arrived up under the roof, and, in fact, not one more step led up any higher. I stood before a large door, which was unlocked and opened by the police sergeant with much noise, such that the whole building could have awakened and been scared by it. Then he opened a low, gray door, and I entered a solitary cell! Cold and damp confronted me despite the humidity outside. It was completely dark in the cell.

Yes, I can still remember well how I entered this cell for the first time, in the middle of the night, roaring and resounding with the hail of bombs and artillery fire, and in a summer night so warm, that one mourned the loss of freedom even more strongly than on dim winter days and bleak winter nights.

"Your cell," the police sergeant declared to me, growled something else to himself, turned the light on, threw the door closed behind him, and turned the light in my cell off again immediately from the corridor. "If there's an alarm, you are to get up and get dressed immediately!" he yelled back to me at the last moment. There I now stood, my eyes full of tears. How was I supposed to find my way around this unknown room? In the moment during which the light was burning I had seen nothing of the cell, out of fear that I could expect at any second a few slaps from this insulting police sergeant who seemed horribly brutal to me, so different from the guards in the court prison in Münster. I stood in the dark, heard his raw voice insulting the priests below me, heard the cell doors open and slam shut with a bang, heard how someone was beaten. It could only be one of the priests . . .

"Dear God, enough is enough!" Yes, I yelled it out loud in this horrible night. I was at the end of my tether. Now God would have to go on without me, the Father would have to lead His child, whose strength and will failed her, alone. Meanwhile the all-clear signal had been given.

In the darkness I sought the cot, stepping carefully, feeling along all the walls, from one corner to the next . . . I could not find a cot. Then it finally occurred to me that there were cots that could be clapped up and fastened to the wall. My hands searched and finally found an iron frame. I unfastened the chain. With a giant bang, the heavy frame came crashing to the floor and landed on my right foot, which hurt for days afterward. For

God's sake, if only the police sergeant didn't come back up! I was terribly afraid in the darkness and didn't dare breathe for several minutes, straining my ears to hear whether he was coming up the stairs . . . but everything remained quiet. I found a blanket on the cot and wrapped myself up in it, freezing and shaking. It smelled disgusting.

I had only been lying stretched out there for several minutes when the alarm sounded again. So I got up and got dressed again. Perhaps we prisoners will at least be brought to a cellar here? But no, no one came. Everything remained quiet in the building, although the droning of the enemy machines could be heard for long, frightening minutes. I sat on the sharp, iron edge of the cot and was at pains not to fall asleep. Again I folded my hands: "Dear God, make me strong!" Finally the all-clear signal sounded and soon after that I fell soundly asleep.

Chapter 13

"Please don't beat the priests!"

The next morning I had the time to look around my "new home." The furnishings were paltry. First there was the cot, on both sides of which hung two thick chains. I still believe today that it was a cot to which felons or inmates condemned to death were chained. Mental images of people who had lain here and suffered before me followed me night after night. Besides the cot there were also a stool and a table. Located in one corner was a latrine with flushing water in which, during the time of my prison term in Herne, I always had to wash my laundry and stockings, lying on my knees in front of it. What else could I do? No one here took care of the prisoners' laundry as they had in Münster.

Again and again, despite all hopelessness, whenever the prison bell rang and I heard steps approaching my cell and the sinister rattling of the unforgettable, large ring of keys, I hoped that freedom was greeting me and I was being fetched for release. How one can still hope against all hope! And when the cell door was opened, I thought: how nice it must be when you are allowed to open a door yourself for once, when you can open a window whenever you please.

I heard again and again the loud noises of stamping feet and screaming voices, which penetrated through the walls to me from other corridors. Many foreigners were in this prison. Why they were being locked up I was never able to learn. Later on when I was allowed to move freely in the corridor, I sometimes looked through the peepholes of the men's cells. There they all lay, twenty or thirty men, mostly Italians, next to one another on the cots, or on the ground when there weren't enough cots, talking, gesticulating, or brooding silently. It was a depressing sight. Sometimes I also encountered these men in the long hallway, which I swept and scoured for fourteen days. Their glances sized me up, in part sympathetically, in part curiously, but also hungrily and greedily. Some of them were dirty or downright degenerate. In the great July heat some of them wore their shirts stripped down to their hips. Italian songs full of pain and longing rang out from the cells. I imagined the wide sea and a gondola: "O sole mio. . . ." And from the women's cells, as if in answer, resounded: "Sleep my darling, close your eyes; all that I have on earth is you. . . ." Much deep longing slumbered in these imprisoned creatures. On this floor, high up under the roof, there was seldom a guard, and most of the inmates conducted themselves accordingly.

The first days in this foreign prison were especially depressing for me. I couldn't take it anymore, at least that's what I thought. But it is consistently established anew that human beings are capable of tolerating the unspeakable. Night after night alarms, with never a true night's rest, and complete inactivity during the day. I asked for books and got dime-store novels passed into my cell, trash, which I laid aside enraged. I often heard the inmates being beaten and insulted with common language. I was very worried about the three priests, who were now languishing with me in the same building. At times I heard the name Maring, and I am certain that the poor, sick Father was beaten repeatedly in Herne. This left me no peace, and I often cried.

After approximately eight days, the police sergeant appeared in my cell all of a sudden and asked quietly, which was not his way normally, why I had actually been arrested by the Geheime Staatspolizei. He said that he had never had such a person as me in his prison before. I told him briefly and very reluctantly what he wanted to know, since I harbored a great deal of anger toward him for beating his prisoners. Shaking his head, he listened to my report and said that he couldn't comprehend it. Finally he became very gentle and confessed to me that he had observed me repeatedly through the peephole. I shouldn't cry so much, he said good-naturedly, and asked if he could do me a favor. It was a complete miracle that this man spoke to me so nicely all of a sudden. "Yes," I answered him, "I won't cry so much anymore if you don't beat the priests anymore, they are just as innocent as I am!" Then I told him of Father Maring's life and work—of his research; his patents; his impressive and interesting book on the firmament, *The Cathedral of the Cosmos* (Münster, 1939)[1]; his great love for children; his carpenter's bench at which he worked in silent pleasure, creating so many beautiful wooden toys for children at Christmas; his terrible sickness and partial blindness, which he had acquired in the laboratory during scientific experiments—and I begged him urgently not to beat Father Maring or the other priests and prisoners any longer. The police sergeant became thoughtful and quiet, and

---

1. Nanda refers here to Father Albert Maring's book *Der Weltendom und sein Bauherr. Ein Blick in die Bauhütte des Weltalls. Mit 24 Bildern und 1 Sternkarte* (The cathedral of the cosmos and its builder: A look into the "construction site office" of the universe, with twenty-four pictures and one astronomical chart) (Münster: Regensburgsche Verlagsbuchhandlung, 1939), most likely a treatise on cosmology written from a Christian standpoint.

to his credit, it can be said that from this day on he didn't beat another inmate, at least I no longer heard it in the following weeks.

He now came to me in the cell frequently and gave me bread, and once he even brought a piece of cake from his wife; he left my cell door open during the day so that I could move a bit in the corridor. I asked for books, but he had none other than the cheap novels; I asked for some occupation, still he said he couldn't expect me to clean the prison. But I was so glad to do it. So every day I cleaned the long hallway and the office rooms of the Herne criminal police adjacent to the prison. Life became somewhat more bearable for me.

Once while I was cleaning windows I heard people speaking to each other in the little prison yard below. I leaned out and saw Father Maring and Father Benninghaus in conversation with a layman. So the priests were allowed to stroll a bit. How happy that made me! I coughed so that the gentlemen below would notice me, since I knew that it would also make them happy to see me. But they didn't hear my cough. So I sang softly the Lenau song "Three Gypsies I Once Saw Lying in a Meadow." It was the song that Father Muckermann and Father Maring had loved so much, and which I had sung for them out loud so many dear times in the course of our years working together. The good Father Maring reacted immediately, as did Father Benninghaus. They waved and nodded up to me, again and again. We literally beamed at each other in our squalor from the joy of this short reunion. That was my last encounter on this earth with the two Jesuits, who went to Oranienburg-Sachsenhausen[2] a few days later and were then transported after several months to Dachau, where both died, or, as we more appropriately expressed it in the concentration camp, "had been died."[3]

A merry, twenty-year-old Jew from Dortmund, the small, round Käthe W. (who had supposedly had something to do with a German soldier) helped me with the cleaning. She sang and warbled all day long and clung to me with every fiber of her young, passionate heart. She touchingly shared everything that she had with me; for her mother brought her some nice packages of food in prison. Here we were allowed to receive packages. But

---

2. Oranienburg and Sachsenhausen were two separate concentration camps near each other north of Berlin. Oranienburg was one of the earliest and largest of the concentration camps located within Germany, but it was dissolved in the mid-1930s. Thus the priests to whom Nanda refers here were most likely sent to the Sachsenhausen camp, where approximately 200,000 prisoners were held during 1936–45, at least thirty thousand of whom were killed there (Gutman, *Encyclopedia of the Holocaust,* 321–22, 1091–92).

3. The phrase in German is *gestorben worden sind,* a passive construction of the word *sterben* (to die), which is not normal usage in German (as it is not in English). Most likely this phrase was concentration camp parlance developed by inmates to "pun" on the Nazis' claim that no one was systematically killed in the camps, but that people simply died there.

when the first packages from my relatives, who were so happy to finally be able to get something to me, arrived in Herne, I was already in the concentration camp and they were never distributed to me. This small, bubbly, good-natured Jew was also delivered to the concentration camp Ravensbrück shortly after I was, and was later transferred to Lublin or Auschwitz. In the concentration camp she always spoke only of her mother.

Chapter 14

On a transport

The evening arrived on which I was to learn what stood before me in the near future. It was the end of July. The police sergeant, with whom I was now in good favor, came into my cell quite agitated. For a long while he stood before me silent and embarrassed. I could see that something out of the ordinary was weighing on his soul, but he had to be out with it and start talking. It was no use; nothing I said helped. Finally I said: "Tell me the plain truth! I'm prepared for anything!" and slowly it all came out of him. I was supposed to pack up my few belongings, for early the next morning I would be going on a transport with the final destination of Ravensbrück Concentration Camp for Women at Fürstenburg/Mecklenburg. I couldn't respond; I was mute and motionless as I had been at my arrest and had to pull myself together to the utmost in order not to fall to the ground. So, I would be spared nothing. The most horrible thing the human mind could conceive of, the concentration camp, now awaited me. In God's name then, I suppose it had to be. Who knew whom my suffering might benefit? Again and again, I always surrendered myself to this comforting thought in the most difficult hours. Everything in life has its reason, even if we cannot fathom what this reason is. It is true that if we let ourselves be led through suffering properly, we will always be blessed. We grow in times of great difficulty and need to and must bow down in humility to the unavoidable. Such sorrow is stronger than we are. In such hours of trial the little verse often came into my head that our good, late father liked to cite: "Let God's will be, even if it pains me, and its reason I may not see." And so I reconciled myself with my lot and packed my belongings. Next to me stood the police sergeant, now so gentle and sympathetic, who was not capable of grasping this fact. Yes, this man, who had accomplished his handiwork so crudely and meanly on the surface, whose hand slipped so easily, now cursed what was being done to me and wished the whole Gestapo would go to the devil!

I did not sleep during this night. I was picked up the next morning at six o'clock. In front of the prison the police car designated for transporting inmates was waiting, the "Black Maria" as it was called by the specialists.[1] I climbed in. The single cell in which I was stuck was so small that I, though overly thin, could hardly turn around in it. The car stopped at the Bochum train station. We went with the police sergeant in uniform through a gaping lane of people across the barrier and up to the platform where we had to wait for our train for a very long time. A woman was already standing there with a constable. The policemen spoke with one another. The woman who stood there, who was most likely also supposed to go "on a transport," made a tattered and degenerate impression, as did almost all of the inmates who joined us on this trip.

The train finally pulled in. I was astonished to see that there were prison cars, of which I had known nothing up to this day. We had to get in. A narrow way led lengthwise through the car, to the right and left of which were located small cells, some of which were already overflowing with male and female inmates. What a horrifying image this was! The compartment or cell doors all had small windows, naturally barred, and behind these windows one saw only eyes, deep, probing, dark eyes, grieving, sallow faces, withered from long prison or penitentiary incarceration, with the waxen potato-sprout coloring of convicted and sentenced prisoners. I was housed in a cell in which there was normally room for four inmates, but in which six or seven women with luggage were already located. We practically lay on top of one another. This was all new to me, and therefore it affected me deeply. Everyone now wanted to know where I was from, why I was in custody, and if I, too, was being transferred to a concentration camp. . . . Oh, and the talking and answering struck me as so difficult. Soon I deduced from their carriage and affectation that I had found myself completely among prostitutes.[2] I was quite alone among them. The train went very slowly, stopped often and for long periods. New inmates came aboard. But we couldn't even look out and figure out where we were.

Finally, in the evening, we arrived in Hannover, where we were unloaded.[3] In my estimation there were over a hundred male and female prisoners, among them a young priest, whose hands were bound. We had to wait on the platform for about a half hour, stationed in rows of four, subjected to the curiosity of a gaping crowd, until a huge contingent of police sergeants with trained dogs finally came and we were led away, followed by a thousand

---

1. Called a "grüne Minna" in German, the "Black Maria" is a police vehicle similar to a paddy wagon used for the transport of prisoners.
2. This is Nanda's first encounter with women arrested by the Nazis for "moral degeneration." During her imprisonment in Ravensbrück, she had much more contact with prostitutes.
3. Hannover is a city in north central Germany, approximately 230 kilometers northeast of Herne, where this transport began.

eyes, all of which were staring at our misery. I thanked heaven that none of my loved ones encountered me at this station of the cross. And these dogs, these dogs! I couldn't comprehend it. Was that really necessary?

In front of the station stood a number of trucks into which we climbed. We had to climb up high, and fell down from weakness. But under the curses of the police and in the face of the trained dogs we made it through pure fear. Soon we had arrived at the large prison where everyone had to get out. We women were handed over to an older, female guard, the men to several male guards. I looked over at the young priest once again and could hardly break my gaze from his bound hands.

Now we were all deloused on body, head, and clothing. Thank God I never had lice. Then we got a piece of bread, and I had to go with four prostitutes into a ground-floor cell that had no cot at all. Five of us women lay on two straw sacks. Even though I gathered myself together, it was very difficult and painful for me to have to sleep so narrowly pressed together with the prostitutes for the first time. Out of pure disgust I lay on the very edge; their conversations were unclean and consisted solely of sexual experiences. But how long I lived with them later in the concentration camp in much closer quarters than here, and how deeply I took some of these poorest of the poor into my heart!

After a thin soup on the following morning, we set out again. Like soldiers we stood at attention in the prison yard, waiting for the truck that would bring us back to the train station. Again this crowd of people, which I so hated, again these looks, again the chained men, among them the young cleric. Oh, Father Maring and Father Benninghaus and Chairman Friedrichs had been brought to the concentration camp just like this in chains! (Instructor Bocks had been released all of a sudden from Herne.)

We were loaded in again, just as livestock are loaded, and journeyed on, hour after hour, in the densely filled, small cells of the prisoner wagons on a slow train. And it was an experience to be so closely packed together in heat of over 30 degrees Celsius![4] When we arrived in Berlin in the early hours of the morning, we were all completely exhausted from hunger and thirst. And yet, only after five hours was there a small piece of dry bread and some coffee to drink. This transport, for me eternally unforgettable, was the proper prelude to that which was to come . . .

---

4. Thirty degrees Celsius is the equivalent of 86 degrees Fahrenheit.

Chapter 15

Berlin-Alexanderplatz

A huge contingent of police and dogs received us at the train station in Berlin. Small and large prison vehicles stood ready to transport us away. A portion of the inmates, people who always had to be making noise, was raucous. The others were silent and brooding. So much was going through my mind. We were unloaded into the yard of the large, world-renowned prison "At Alexanderplatz," where hundreds of convicts, inmates in protective custody, and detainees pending trial awaited their further destiny.

We went up many stairs in this giant, sinister building. High up on the fourth or fifth floor we were assigned to cells. I entered a large cell with a number of others. Since it wasn't light out yet and no light was turned on, I saw nothing in the first moments. An indefinable smell surged up against me. Slowly my eyes adjusted to the darkness and I began to distinguish things. I was shocked when I discerned person after person lying here on the floor of this cell. I stepped on people, even though I made every effort not to. Curses rang out against us. They were enraged by the nightly disturbance. There was no place free, and since the prostitutes who had been brought in with me had stronger elbows than I did, they had found a spot more quickly, or had crept in with one of their compatriots who was lucky enough to be sleeping on a cot, while I stood there still at a loss and not knowing where I should sit down. Finally I noticed a free spot by the latrine in the left corner by the window. So I laid down there. The latrine was full of filth and excrement; the flushing mechanism didn't work. I was sick to the point of vomiting, but where else was I supposed to lie? Just sleep, sleep! With my coat as a blanket, without any kind of padding beneath me, I lay there, head on my arms, my lips and tongue dry from thirst . . .

But what was that? Suddenly my whole body itched, and I found not one second of peace in the few hours left in this night. When it had gotten a bit lighter, I examined my body and was horrified to find so many bedbug bites. Yes, it is no exaggeration, I saw and killed hundreds of bedbugs in these four days and nights in Berlin. Never before in my life had I made the acquaintance of these bothersome and tormenting animals, not even in another prison. In the capital of the Reich, in the city of the "illustrious Führer" of all places, in the largest prison in Germany, everything was filthy, bug-ridden, and filled with lice. I was so sad, so unhappy! I cannot describe how I suffered under this pestilence. In this cell, which had about sixteen cots to offer, over a hundred women and girls lay on the bug-ridden floor. There was not even a place for us to sit there. I think there was one single bench there for over a hundred inmates.

During the day I had time enough to examine my new situation. From the almost seventy-year-old honorable craftswoman from Saxony, who had made some harmless, disparaging comment about Hitler and for that had already been in the penitentiary for an entire year, down to the sixteen-year-old prostitute, every age and almost every class was represented. Two silent nuns, praying the rosary, sat in one corner, young and old Jews, hounded and persecuted, sat or lay together in small groups. And on the cots, the prostitutes sprawled. Some of them behaved respectably, but most of them were unbearable for the rest of us. Afflicted with bodily diseases that were unleashed and allowed to flourish in the human underworld, bearing all the marks of a horrible moral plague and ruined body and soul, these outcasts bore their sad lots partly as a burden, but at the same time heartlessly and indifferently. At all times of the day inmates were fetched from this cell. Hardly had the cell been emptied out of a few inmates when it would be immediately overloaded again with new ones. It remained overly full. How I longed for my clean cell in Münster! And the Third Reich's authors and National Socialist propaganda speakers were always bemoaning the conditions in Russian prisons in their books, writings, and lectures! They had absolutely no reason or right to get upset when even the largest prison in the Reich's capital was completely filthy, filled with lice, and bug-ridden! It could never have been worse, even in a Russian prison. The issue of the toilet was especially painful. Each person had to relieve herself in front of all of our eyes, and the seat was coated day and night. One cannot imagine it if one has not experienced it oneself. What I am reporting here will certainly seem to the reader like an exaggeration, but it is fact. The prostitutes acted out the craziest things with one another on their cots. No one could help. One night it was so bad that it came to an abusive fight among the prostitutes resulting from mutual jealousy. The two nuns, a few other courageous inmates, and I decided to ring the night bell; for no respectable person could participate in this any longer, this would be an absurd expectation. The guard came, pulled apart the prostitutes, and led a few of these raving monsters out.

There was precious little to eat in Berlin. In the morning a piece of dry bread, at noon a thin soup without potatoes, and in the evening another piece of bread, or again an indefinable watery little soup. At the sight of my fellow prisoners, the old Russian prison song, which, according to Dostoevsky, was often sung by inmates imprisoned in Siberia, went through my head:

> "Only cabbage with water they give to me,
> But still I eat it as greedily as can be."

The bedbug plague became more unbearable with every passing night. As soon as it got dark, the vermin emerged and plagued us poor creatures. I must be especially susceptible, because one other prisoner and I were, without exaggeration, bitten from the soles of our feet to our scalps and even down to our very fingertips, while the others had significantly fewer bites to show. It is tragic that these bites began to itch anew, even after weeks, whenever it got dark. I sat on the floor scratching, hour after hour, every night. Others sat during the day and mutually deloused one another with a fine-tooth comb. A number of them were completely covered in lice. I was at least spared that in my long confinement. If an outsider could have taken a look at this pathetic cell for only a few minutes, he would have had to assume that he was in an insane asylum, except that insane asylums are clean, for at least they are usually run by Sisters of Mercy.

Despite everything, however, I tried my best to keep my composure, although I was never rid of the burning longing for my life and my loved ones, not even here. Sturdy strings bound me to life, and these strings are hard to loosen. I was also held up and borne by the certainty that there was no shame for me in what I was experiencing and suffering, and that so many innocent people had to bear the same thing unjustifiably. And I knew that they did not let the most horrible and revolting things get the best of them either, and that they always held their confidence up high! How did the sensitive poem of Schönaich-Carolath[1] go again?:

> We shall grasp the palm
> of the ship captain of Nazareth,
> for when the stars go dim,
> bearing light through the seas he goeth.

Yes, for me, too, all the stars had gone dim, but, trustingly, I kept holding on tightly to the hand of the "ship captain of Nazareth." And that alone can fill the soul with comfort and happiness in such hours. Above all,

---

1. Nanda may be referring to one of two German authors here. Christoph Otto, Freiherr von Schönaich-Carolath (1725–1807) was a popular author of patriotic verse epics. A later author, Emil, Prinz von Schönaich-Carolath-Schilden (1852–1908), was a poet and novelist whose work was characterized by a regional flavor.

the deep value and great riches of our Catholic faith seemed to me in this bitterly difficult time like the most costly thing the world had to offer. What occurred between God and my soul could not be taken away from me by the most brutal SS man, or the commonest Gestapo agent, or even Herr Heinrich Himmler himself.[2]

These four days and four nights in Berlin finally passed, even though the hours crept by slowly, all too slowly. I lay scratching on the floor during these nights, sad and deathly ill in my soul, and with burning homesickness in my heart, further subjected to the stench of the open latrine, which was used by over a hundred inmates, day and night. I would never see so much filth again. How was this possible in Germany? I asked myself this over and over again.

---

2. Nanda's family eventually appealed to Himmler for her release. After some time, the request was granted.

Chapter 16

Into the concentration camp . . .

On the evening of August 1, 1941, the guard called out the names of the inmates of our cell who would be transported to the Ravensbrück Concentration Camp for Women near Fürstenberg in Mecklenburg. Among them was my name. We were escaping from one hell only to head toward an even worse one. At three o'clock in the morning we had to stand ready for departure in alphabetically ordered rows of four. Our names were called out again and again for purposes of inspection. Every one whose name was called had to identify herself. There were about one hundred twenty inmates, the oldest over seventy years old; among them were career criminals, prostitutes, nuns, Jews—women of all classes and every age. Around five o'clock we finally left. Again we boarded the prison cars. It was crawling with police and dogs. With a heavy heart, I sent out one last mental greeting from the train station to my two Berliner siblings, who had no idea of my stay there. Then it was back into the prison cars amid the hellos of indiscriminate prisoners and the curses of the police and the barking of the dogs. I saw that many of the cells were filled with male prisoners who were being brought to the concentration camp Oranienburg-Sachsenhausen.

After a few hours' journey we arrived at the new cross station, Bahnhof Fürstenberg. Unutterable grief filled my soul. There stood the SS, there stood the female overseers with the trained dogs who would torture us so often in the future. A horror overcame me, body and soul. We were literally thrown into the trucks that stood ready for us. Some of us, the little old people and the weak ones, could not make it in so fast. "Old piece of s——t . . . get up there now or you'll get a lashing!" Our first greeting was of this nature. All my limbs shaking, I climbed onto the truck, and already one of the SS people was grabbing a club and pressing it into the backs of my kneecaps so that I fell to my knees. None of the inmates said a word. Amid so much horror even the most destitute and downtrodden lost their ability to speak. Oh Mother, Mother, how I thanked God that you could not see what was done to your child!

Far down from the beautifully located air-cure spa Fürstenberg,[1] of which we obviously saw nothing since our trucks were covered, the concentration camp for women lay hidden away behind giant walls encircled by electrically charged barbed wire (this was indicated by the pictures of black skulls posted ahead of it). I can still remember well how I first set foot in the concentration camp where I would now live for a long time, suffering and bearing deep pain I never could have imagined before this. It was about nine o'clock in the morning. The gigantic entrance gate was crawling with SS and overseers in uniform.

We had to organize ourselves in rows of four in front of the office of the chief overseer: luggage was not to be unloaded and there was strict surveillance with dogs in front, behind, and next to us.[2] So we stood, hour after hour, until the late afternoon, without even receiving something to drink in this blazing August heat. Toward evening they finally began to let four prisoners at a time into the office, where, in a large room, an overseer wrote down personal information and the reason for consignment to the concentration camp. When I gave the answer that I had been arrested for being Father Muckermann's secretary for many years, I received my first beating, and it was so severe that blood poured from my nose. Then we were led into a small room where, amid the jeers of the guards, we had to take off and give up everything we were wearing or carrying. When it was my turn, a little old granny also came up, who was so nervous that she was not capable of unbuttoning her clothes. I wanted to assist her, but then I was given yet another beating. Robbed of our clothes, which were thrown into a corner, we stood there stark naked. SS paced back and forth between us. For hours we stood there in our nakedness. For me it was the most difficult thing. Some

---

1. Fürstenberg, the closest town to the Ravensbrück camp, is scenically located in an area surrounded by lakes, including the Schwedt See, which was quite close to the actual camp. In the 1930s, Fürstenberg was a popular vacation spot for Berliners, favored for its close location (about ninety kilometers from the city) and for its fresh air and scenic naturescapes.
2. The camp hierarchy of Ravensbrück personnel was as follows:

> Lagerkommandant=camp commandant
> Schutzhaftlagerführer=camp director of "Protective Custody" Camp
> Verwaltungsführer=administrative director
> Arbeitsdienstführer=director of work service
> Gestapobeamte der Politischen Abteilung Gestapo=officials of the political division
> Lagerärzte=camp doctors
> SS-Schwestern=SS nurses
> Oberaufseherin=chief overseer
> Aufseherinnen=overseers
> SS-Wachmannschaften=SS guards (Zorner, *Frauen-KZ Ravensbrück*, 29)

Though the top echelons of power were occupied by men, Ravensbrück had the largest number of female SS guards and overseers of any camp—550–600 (Feig, *Hitler's Death Camps*, 138).

cried out loud. I remained mute. Then we were led into yet another room, where the new arrivals were deloused, one after the other, by two Jehovah's Witnesses who were also inmates.[3] Wherever a single louse or a bug was found, the poor creatures' heads were fully shaved. And so many had caught lice with long incarcerations in unsanitary prisons! My head was clean. Of the prisoners who were delivered to the camp on this day, at least fifty women were shaved bald. Some began to scream like wild animals, others accepted it resignedly like sacrificial lambs. After the delousing we were brought into a bath area with many showers. The first had to wait until the very last were undressed and deloused. Then we went under the hot downpour, which did us good. My body was so cut up from the Berlin bedbugs that I had to allow myself to be affronted with many jeers from the SS and female overseers even on the first day, for the red spots just wouldn't disappear. Yet the jeers didn't affect me. After this shower bath everyone received a blue towel and was then "clothed" as a proper prisoner. Underwear and clothing were for the most part uniform. Everyone received a shirt, which was more gray than white, a skirt, and, as long as the supply lasted, knickers. These gray knickers were so long that they stuck out ten, and sometimes even twenty, centimeters below the skirts. And we had no thread, no needle, to make the knickers shorter. Only later did we learn how to "organize" such things. Finally, everyone also received an apron. Mine had at least twelve patches in various different colors. But what did it matter to us? Now we were all equal: nuns, Jews, prostitutes, criminals, "enemies of the state," old and young. These shorn women's heads were horrid to look at. In all that time, I was never able to get used to these shorn women, although I had to get used to very many other things. They looked like gnomes. Was this hell?

---

3. Jehovah's Witnesses were imprisoned because they refused to serve the war effort, to take an oath of allegiance to the Third Reich, to make the "Heil Hitler" salute, or to serve in the army. For an especially detailed description of the Witnesses, called *Bibelforscherinnen* (Bible students) in German, who were imprisoned in Ravensbrück, see Buber-Neumann, *Under Two Dictators*, 219–56. The Jehovah's Witnesses were a group apart in the camp, known for their extremely orderly and clean barracks and their refusal to try to escape, which led the Nazis to entrust them with positions of responsibility. They could gain release by simply signing a document to the effect that they would no longer be active in their faith; very few ever sought release in this way.

Chapter 17

Shocking impressions

If the word love could cry,
It would have long since cried itself to death,
If the word love could bleed,
It would have long since bled to death,
If the word love could die,
It would have long since died.

—Prof. Dr. A. Donders

We "admittees," as the newly arrived inmates were called in the concentration camp, were now brought by the overseers to the so-called admittance block. Now I could observe to a certain extent, as far as was emotionally possible on that first day after so many shocks, the conditions and organization of the camp.

Long block houses, in which the prisoners ate and slept, stretched out along both sides of the wide Camp Street.[1] The inmates were divided into various groups: there were blocks for political prisoners of all nations, for Jehovah's Witnesses, for Poles, for criminals, for Jews, for Gypsies, and for asocials (among them the prostitutes), and later for Russians, Ukrainians, etc. In the foreground of the large yard stood a giant block house, the kitchen, then other various domestic buildings with cellars, pantries, etc. In front and to the left of the large yard was one single, friendly-looking, white building: the casino for the SS and overseers. Opposite that, on the other side of the yard, was the house of horrors—one could see from its external appearance what it held within: the detention- or cell building, with which I later was forced to make bitter acquaintance.

---

1. For Camp Street, please refer to the map of Ravensbrück in the photo section.

We admittees were first brought to the admittance block, where we fell onto stools in complete exhaustion.[2] Here, too, it was overly full; there was too little space absolutely everywhere. In the day-rooms, in which people sat, there were sixteen to eighteen inmates sitting at tables meant for about ten people. People fought for the stools, just as they did for the cots. People here were screaming, making noise, laughing, cursing, mocking, singing, dozing, and crying. The block had two hundred and seventy cots, three stacked atop each other. Since I had held back in order to escape the noise a bit, I got a cot on the third level, where I almost hit the ceiling with my nose. In the meantime there was something to eat. I couldn't touch anything on this evening, but greedy eyes were already waiting for my portion, which I gladly gave over to them. I sat at a table together with at least ten prostitutes and other prisoners, almost all of whom had been shorn of their hair. They behaved like pigs. My God, in what kind of bizarre society had I ended up! As I lay on my cot at night, what conversations I heard there, what expressions! The craziest experiences from bordellos were related aloud and recited, lewd songs were sung, and I lay alone in the midst of this, godforsaken, scratching myself throughout the night with a feverish head. So it went for weeks until the itching finally stopped.

Thousands of thoughts went through my tortured brain. Would things keep on in this way? Could one even keep on living here at all? Would I never be alone again? Never again be able to deal with my God composed and undisturbed? Never again, when liberating sleep didn't want to come, would I be able to converse for hours with my loved ones far away, as I had so often done in prison? Tortuous was the certainty of never again being allowed to be alone by oneself, with one's own thoughts and one's own homesickness! During the days I had to perform hard labor outside, together with the other inmates under the strict guard of the SS, overseers, and dogs! Thus during the day, too, never again alone!

It was certainly a peculiar society in which I had ended up and with which I had to remain bound for so long in the face of death and destruction. And it wasn't only peculiar, but also dangerous, full of envy, grudges, lies, and baseness. Certainly there were exceptions, but not very many. How exemplary and obliging the nuns were, how modest the staunch craftswoman from Saxony, whom I had met in Berlin, how reserved and full of sorrow the aggrieved and persecuted Jews. We found ourselves together in free moments and comforted ourselves in our commonly borne sorrow. The majority, however, was depraved. Mutual betrayal and wrongful accusations

---

2. All new inmates were required to stay in the admittance block, sometimes referred to as the block for new arrivals, or the quarantine block, for a period of approximately four weeks, after which they would be transferred to a different block on a more permanent basis.

by the inmates against one another made life into a hell, a hell within a hell. There wasn't a trace of womanliness or shame left to be found among these individuals. The commonest expressions, like "brainless cow," "old piece of s——t," and even worse were part of the daily routine. I was a thorn in their side from the very beginning since I was reserved and just different from them, and often during the first weeks these inmates had fun tormenting me, teasing me, and mocking me. I couldn't participate and held back, but this didn't suit them. My table mates, to whom I often gave my piece of bread or potatoes, stood by me, however, and defended me in whatever way they could. But this only happened so that they could get something from me again at the next paltry meal. Yes, they would have sold their souls for a piece of bread or a few potatoes. . . . Poor people, they had already become animals, and would soon be placed far below animals, as the following remarks will prove.

Chapter 18

The first four weeks in the concentration camp

Heavy is the labor, heavy are the chains,
Year after year under the hot blaze of the sun.

In the first days there were all kinds of formalities for the "admittees" to attend to. First the inmates had to go to the "records department," where photos (full face and profile) were made of every newly delivered prisoner, which were added to her file, so that in the case of a possible escape (which was not rare) the woman in question could be apprehended again more quickly. We had to stand there waiting hour after hour until we were finally shown in. Everything occurred under strict guard.

On the next day we were taken to the political division, where the newcomer, already completely tormented, was asked all manner of possible and impossible questions. Here we received our prisoner numbers.[1] I got number 6582. The next day we were taken en masse to the tailor, where we received a little piece of white fabric on which the number was printed in black, together with the triangle. Woe to her whose number or triangle detached itself from her dress while she was working! This could even be a cause for detention and other hard punishments. There were triangles in all colors here. The political prisoners got a red triangle; the Jehovah's Witnesses a purple one; the prostitutes and asocials a black one; the career criminals a

---

1. Prisoners' numbers began in Ravensbrück at #1416, as 1,415 people had been prisoners in Lichtenberg, over 800 of whom were transferred to Ravensbrück in May 1939. Numbers were given out in sequence and are thus some indication of the time of a prisoner's arrival. For example, Margarete Buber-Neumann, who entered the camp in August 1940, was #4208; Nanda, arriving a year later, was #6582.

green one; the convicts also wore, atop the green triangles, a thickly imprinted black Z; Jews got a yellow triangle; inmates who had been delivered to the camp because of *Rassenschande* wore a yellow one with an upside-down black one atop it.[2] The triangle and number had to be fastened to the upper left arm. The red triangle and the number 6582 now shone resplendently from my arm. We were also supposed to identify ourselves to the commandant and the chief overseer, as well as to the overseers and SS by naming this number. The identification went like this: Inmate Herbermann, #6582.

Before every guard we had to stand at attention. How nasty and horrible the encounters with the guard personnel often were! They embittered the poor inmates all the more through their unfounded, arbitrary, and senselessly brutal treatment, and the hate of many inmates grew boundlessly. Fists were balled in hot rage. As in every prison, knives and sharp objects of any kind were strictly forbidden in the concentration camp. And yet everything was there in the blocks, it was just "organized"; those who had many previous convictions (of which there were very many in this concentration camp) had a special talent for doing this. I would never have wanted to do it; the penalties resulting from the frequently occurring searches and pocket controls for such objects were too heavy. Many let themselves be dissuaded by nothing. If their knives had been taken away and they had a severe punishment behind them, the next day they would already be arranging for new ones. But I don't want to foretell anything without first reporting of the first days and weeks in the camp.

Every morning at half past four the sinister camp siren sounded, in a tone similar to our all-clear signals after air-raid alarms. We sprang up quickly from our cots and everyone streamed noisily into the washroom. For two hundred seventy inmates there was a washroom in every block with about fifteen or twenty sinks. Everything was always backed up. Everyone wanted to be the first in line. The quarreling and bickering began this early in the morning. This was doubly depressing. I renewed my unhappiness with this company each and every morning. Then those who still had hair at all combed it quickly and smoothly backward. Parts, curls, and so on were not allowed. After that we got dressed hastily and the "bed" was made. I tormented myself up on the third level, almost hanging in the air—I could only hold myself up from one side since my cot was directly next to the window. This was a new vexation every new morning! Woe befall us if the

---

2. *Rassenschande* (race defiling) was the crime of sleeping with a non-Aryan. The Nuremberg Laws (1935)—the so-called Law for the Protection of German Blood and the Reich Citizenship Law—prohibited such sexual contact. Offenders were often made to march through the street with a sign around their neck reading "Ich bin ein Rassenschänder." Such persons were subject to arrest and imprisonment.

edges of the sack of straw or wood shavings were not straight! They had to be dead-straight, as if measured with a ruler. I never quite figured out the art of doing this. The controllers came daily to closely examine and inspect the cots together with the edges of the straw sacks. How I trembled in the face of this control! The others could generally do it much better than I could. Making the cot almost drove me insane in the beginning. Not that I was afraid of food deprivation (I had already taken that upon myself), but the punishment of standing for hours in the rain and wind and bad weather after the exhausting and grueling heavy labor of the day was a great torment.[3] And my bare feet were already painful enough. Finally a good soul was found who helped me. For this she received my piece of bread. Yes, in the first weeks I gave up my piece of bread almost every day for this reason. We could not be found out, for there was a punishment for doing this, too. And since the inmates were very jealous among themselves, I could only slip the piece of bread to the person in question very secretively. I was too shy and was taken advantage of by all sides.

By turns, ten to twelve inmates had to pick up the black coffee in heavy pails in the morning, which was then distributed by the block elder and her two barracks elders. Block and barracks elders were preferred inmates and wore a green band around their left arm. But their tasks and responsibilities were dangerous and difficult. To guard over hundreds of inmates as block elder, to be responsible to the SS for everything that took place in the block, to have to know about everything, absolutely everything: this was no small task, and many had to innocently take on bitter punishments and, often enough, confinement in the dark.

---

3. Buber-Neumann describes the three levels of punishment at Ravensbrück: "punishment standing without food"; "solitary confinement in a dark cell"; and "twenty-five lashes" (*Under Two Dictators*, 193). This account generally corresponds to the three levels of punishment outlined in the camp's "Code of Criminal Procedure." Level 1, *Ordnungsstrafen* (order punishments), included the following types of punishment: warning with threat of punishment; punishment work during "free time" under the supervision of an overseer; forbidding a prisoner to write or receive personal letters; withholding a prisoner's lunch or dinner but requiring her to maintain a full workload; assignment to the punishment block; or assignment to a cell with a hard bed after a day's work. Level 2, *Arreststrafen* (arrest punishments), included the following types of punishment: "medium" arrest (level 1), up to three days, in a lighted cell with a wooden cot, with only bread and water; "tightened" arrest (level 2), up to forty-two days, in a dark cell with a wooden cot, with bread and water and "full meals" only every fourth day; and "strict" arrest (level 3), up to three days, in a dark cell with no possibility of sitting or lying down, with only bread and water. "Strict" arrest could be used on its own or for a day at a time as an "upgrade" of "tightened" arrest. Finally, Level 3 punishments, *Körperliche Züchtigung* (physical punishments), consisted of beatings on the behind and the upper thighs. Between five and twenty-five lashes were possible, and the camp director determined the number of blows in each case. (The "Code of Criminal Procedure" is reproduced in Litschke and Schlaefer, *Der Zellenbau Ravensbrück*, 4.)

The prisoners had to obey the barracks elders and, above all, the block elder. The block elder did have all kinds of rights but even more difficult duties. It was much better to disappear among the masses in a concentration camp than to occupy a position of responsibility; I had to learn that myself as block elder later on.

After we had hastily gulped down our coffee and bolted the rest of the piece of bread we had received the day before (if there was any left), the siren sounded again, and we went out to the first roll-call count. In front of each of the approximately twenty-five blocks (by the time of my release about ten new ones had been added), the inmates stood in rows of ten, one behind the other. The roll call was usually taken by the chief overseer or one of her deputies and lasted almost an hour. And if the overseer had miscounted, everyone had to fall out and fall in again, over and over again, until the number had been clarified in some way. When the roll call wasn't correct, the commandant often showed up and everyone began to tremble. Whenever he happened to feel like it, this or that inmate had to strip naked before him and before all of us on Camp Street. He was the most horrible human monster that I have ever experienced. It was not rare for kicks and beatings to be distributed during the roll call. At the crack of dawn we stood there at attention, freezing even at the height of summer, with bare feet. From April 1 to October 1 all inmates went barefoot. This was a catastrophe, and above all troublesome for the heavy roadwork outside. The feet of most of the prisoners bled, had open wounds, and were thickly swollen. I have never again seen the kinds of foot diseases that I saw in the concentration camp. I felt immensely sorry for the very old and sick inmates. How many silent tears flowed during the morning roll-call count. We were never rested, but always nervous and always agitated, and the homesickness, horror, and uncertainty burned in our souls. During these early roll calls I begged heaven every morning for courage and strength to face the newly dawning day. One had greater need for these gifts from the Holy Ghost in this hell than anywhere else in the world.

The first four weeks in the concentration camp are more clear in my memory than all the following months taken together. They were so shattering. I thought I knew from hearsay much of what went on in concentration camps. I had also read a book in Holland in 1934 that sketched out the conditions and proceedings in a concentration camp.[4] But the images I could and had created for myself from this account were mere shadows

---

4. How much was known about concentration camps this early outside Germany? Some evidence can be gleaned from Germaine Tillion, who mentions a book she read, prior to 1942, titled *Under the Nazi Whip*. "I knew that concentration camps existed; in particular (and quite by chance), I had read a book on the subject. . . . This rather restrained book, along with other accounts by German refugees, gave me some idea of life in these camps—an

compared to what took place before my eyes in the camp and what we inmates discovered only little by little. I simply could not come to terms with the thought, with the fact, that something so horrible could be carried out against people by other people, and especially by German people. I felt as if I should always be apologizing to the foreigners and telling them: What goes on here is not German, most German people know nothing of this! These concentration camps are wholly a monstrous creation of the criminal dictators of the Third Reich and certainly not of the German people.

After the first roll-call count, the work call or work formation took place, and then (just as in Siberia) the hardest forced labor was demanded of the inmates. One crew shouldered spades and went digging, another had to build roads, and still others had to carry rocks, transport coal, dig up earth, paint, build, and grade. A huge work crew went to the large barracks of the Siemens factories everyday, in which armament work had to be done.[5] These barracks were ten to twelve minutes away from the concentration camp, and the inmates worked there to the point of exhaustion. The last bit of strength was pulled out of their weakened bodies. We who performed this hard labor envied those who were able to work in the workshops of the camp (sewing, tailoring, weaving, shoemaking, etc.), although here too the most difficult demands were placed on each individual. Of course, in order to be assigned to these operations one had to be able to produce in the specified area; for this I was too inexperienced. To get into one of these operations at all as an "admittee" was impossible. So I set about the difficult, unfamiliar, hard

---

idea which, I'm afraid, only scratched the surface" (*Ravensbrück,* 4). She mentions that its author was a German actor, but gives no further information on the book and it is not listed in the bibliography in the French edition of her memoir.

5. Inmates in Ravensbrück were assigned either to *Innenkommandos,* work forces inside the camp who performed tasks such as cooking, washing, nursing, or cleaning, or to *Außenkommandos,* work forces who left the camp in the morning and traveled by foot, truck, or train to factories or other sites where they performed hard labor, often in the service of industry. In Ravensbrück, inmates were put to work in several areas. Many inmates worked in the service of companies owned and operated by the SS, doing agricultural work, raising Angora rabbits, producing textiles, weaving, knitting, and sewing, among other things. A second group of inmates worked for private industry, performing agricultural and trade work. A third group of inmates was put to work in a branch of the Berlin-based electronics company Siemens (to which Nanda is referring here) that was built at Ravensbrück. These inmates were to produce armaments for the war effort. Because the work at Siemens (and other armaments firms) was very delicate, women were the preferred laborers. Many young girls were also employed there. While working, the inmates continued to be guarded by the SS and were supposed to fulfill a specific quota of production each day. If the quota was not met, the women would be persecuted with extra punishments. Because of the complex and delicate nature of the work and the pressure to meet quotas, as well as the extra walk to the Siemens plant each day that Nanda notes, work in the *Außenkommandos* was often even more demanding and draining than work inside the camp.

outside labor. During the first weeks I had to carry potatoes on my back and unload rocks all day long. We were not allowed to put down the heavy sacks to rest a bit. Merciless overseers drove us like a herd of livestock, their trained dogs on their leashes and their pistols in their holsters. The consequence of this overly hard labor was that many prisoners fell over and could go on no longer. I, too, sunk to the ground several times a day at the beginning. When one loads more and more onto a conveyor, the horse will eventually stop and won't pull anymore. My body was too weakened by the six-month dungeon confinement, and I was hardly used to the outdoor air anymore. Out of pure misery my eyes always welled up with tears. I couldn't hold them back. But these tears were like a red flag for the overseers. With kicks and punches, setting the dangerous dogs at me, they helped me up again. There were overseers who encouraged us to take our lives on the electrically charged barbed wire; they emphasized the fact that then they would have one less "eater." Kicking and punching, as well as setting the dogs on us poor victims, were everyday occurrences. No, even if I had the good will to adapt myself to anything, to endure a lot, and to be master of my destiny, I could not reconcile myself with this. It was so un-German, inhumane, and disgraceful; it was subhumanity, torment conceived of by monsters, the most horrible torture. My bare feet bled and hurt. Again and again I looked sadly at the very old inmates (some of whom were over sixty or even over seventy) who had to bear the same things, and said to myself: If they can and must bear it, then you must stand it, too.

For weeks then I had to push rocks in wheelbarrows. To keep these shaky, hackneyed, and overfilled carts in balance was almost impossible. Since I was especially clumsy at the job, I sometimes tipped the whole mess over. Then I had to take beatings and kicks and whole bombardments of insults from the guards. Oh, the poor "old pig" sure felt sorry for herself! Yes, fear, horror, beatings, and biting dogs were our most loyal companions at work. Once one of these trained beasts took hold of me as well. And what beasts these beasts of people had made out of good-natured animals! I screamed in fear. But, thank God, only my apron, dress, and knickers were torn. Never in my life had I been afraid of animals, but here it was justified, and all the inmates trembled in fear of these large-breed dogs and German shepherds, whose sinister whining and barking provided us with the most horrifying camp music early every morning during the roll-call count. But I also learned here that humans can be even worse beasts of prey.

I did what I could. Hour after hour we toiled in the hot sun without even being allowed to take a drink. Often we could no longer bear this thirst. How thankful we would have been if a good soul had given us a tiny sip of water. But no one was allowed. I still remember one hot September day. We were tottering from faintness, our tongues had become as heavy as lead, and our lips were completely dried out. Some were crying. I poked an old Gypsy, since I could tell from looking at her that she couldn't stand it any longer, and said to her: "Don't cry! Just two more hours!" She answered: "But you're crying, too! Don't think I'm crying for myself. My children!" A few more short minutes and she was lying unconscious next to me. The overseer who was on duty poked her with her boots: "Old piece of s——t, come on, get to work!" But the poor "brainless cow" didn't hear a word. I breathed deeply and would have liked to lie down next to this old, good-hearted Gypsy, never to wake up again. A half hour later the Gypsy vomited, and kept on without stopping, turning round and round in circles. I got very dizzy from this, and a few minutes later it was my turn, and then four or five others'. I was seized by such shocks that I sank to my knees and, with my fingers clawing at the rock pile, kept on spitting. No one said another word. We only kept hearing as if in a half-sleep the voice of the overseer: "Old sows, rotten pigs!" I squatted on the ground until the last bile came up. Then I only felt a certain nausea and went on working shakily like the others.

At noon we went back to the block for an hour. In rank and file (often we were ordered to sing) we had to march "home" from work, and the rows and quarreling and insults began again in the block. What a burden it is to have to live forcibly in such company! Such a mass of people and thugs, penned up together as they were here, is no place for someone who doesn't belong with them, who simply can't participate. And you could cut the air with a knife in these blocks even during the day (not to mention at night) since many of the prisoners just let themselves go, unrestrained in any way.

We ate our sparse meal, many as greedily as animals, casting furtive glances to the right and left to see if they couldn't ferret out something more here or there. If I turned my head to the right, it could happen that a neighbor to my left filched half of the few potatoes on my plate and had already made them disappear. As quickly as a magician! Yes, these neighbors of mine were slippery customers. I was powerless in their presence. Of course, I did learn in the course of time, as lengthy as it was, to assert myself in their midst.

After eating, there was another work call again, a large march along Camp Street, five at a time in rank and file, and heavy labor until evening. Stepping away from work for a few minutes was only allowed on very rare occasions. This was an embarrassment. The prisoners who couldn't wait any longer let everything go below them. And many were sick and suffered from diarrhea as a consequence of the bad food and from abdominal troubles of all kinds because their clothes were soaked through for days on end. I was boiling with rage! What sicknesses would develop from this and last for life!

I suffered so much in the first week that I completely lost the ability to speak. Each person is endowed with a natural level of tolerance, and I had reached this level. The work call after eating lasted for half an hour. It was pathetic. Despite all energetic attempts at pulling ourselves together and clenching our teeth, our last strength still dissipated, and I can still remember well how I fell unconscious to the ground on two consecutive evenings during the first weeks, something that had never happened to me in my life. During these spells of unconsciousness we were not, for example, carried back to the barracks, but rather thrown on the ground outside in front of the blocks, with no one to take care of us. Not even an inmate was allowed to do that. Some inmates got cramps, had tantrums or dizziness, ripped out whole clumps of hair, and lay there screaming and groaning, without any help.

Anyone who was still human in this hell simply couldn't look at it or listen to it.

The prisoner already knows for himself that he is an outcast from human society, but who wants to force him to forget that he, too, is human and that, even in the most abject situation, he has the right to be treated humanely? This treatment, or rather mistreatment, was below all human dignity. And what a miracle a bit of goodness and love could have wrought among the poorest of the poor!

In *Memoirs from the House of the Dead*, in which Dostoevsky reports of his banishment to Siberia, he writes aptly: "Since the inmate is in fact human, so one must treat him in a humane fashion. Oh God, truly humane treatment can even make someone, for whom the image of God has long since faded and grown dark, human again! With these unhappy creatures in particular one must act in the most humane way. That is their joy, their saving grace. I met (in Siberia) such noble-minded commanders who thought in this way."[6] (I didn't meet any in the German concentration camp besides perhaps a few respectable SS people and overseers.) And Dostoevsky further reports that he observed the effects that such treatment by a good superior had on these debased people: "A few friendly words and the prisoners felt

---

6. Dostoevsky's book is a fictionalized account of his experiences in a prison labor camp in Tobolsk, where he was jailed from 1850 to 1854 for his radical political activities (which consisted primarily of participating in a Socialist discussion group and reading some forbidden writings). Nanda seems to have modeled her manuscript on Dostoevsky's book to some extent, as this description of Dostoevsky's memoir suggests: "Goryanchikov's [the narrator's] account begins in an almost anthropological manner, with a distanced narrator describing a remote and remarkable society. Almost immediately, the cruelty and the uselessness of the prison system emerge in discussions of punishments and of the unrepentance of the prisoners. The hostility between the peasantry and the gentry, and their shared sympathy with escapees and released captives lead naturally back to the beginning, with its graphic depiction of the harm this prison system does. . . . But the great power of the book lies not in such teachings but in the harrowing lives the inmates live as they eat, sleep, bathe, pray, go to the hospital, drink themselves into insensibility, work for themselves, or on labor details, or recount their deeds outside the camp" (Terras, *Handbook of Russian Literature*, 105).

like they had been reborn." Let it be known here that I read Dostoevsky's reports about his many years of banishment to Siberia with doubled interest after my release from the concentration camp, and I have to admit that the German concentration camp was in many respects significantly worse, and its commanders and hangmen much more inventive in the area of torment, torture, and vulgarity, than ever was the case in Siberia according to Dostoevsky's report.

Completely exhausted, we returned from work to the camp in the evening, often consuming our meager piece of bread amid sobs. After the evening roll-call count, the inmates could stroll along Camp Street for another half hour and chat with each other, if they were in the mood for it. In the first weeks, however, I preferred to climb up onto my cot . . .

Chapter 19

As "barracks elder" with the prostitutes . . .

It's not easy, tending wild flowers,
for of these there's oh so many an ilk,
and each one produces its own bloom,
one of them raw, another silk . . .

Early on life's bitter sorrows
caused your hot mouths to be sealed shut,
you had to bear incarceration,
and by fate you were chafed and cut

Homesickness, horror and privation,
hard labor from early to late,
nights long and dark and filled with sorrow,
until death comes to annihilate.

From the above-mentioned admittance block, I was transferred to Block V, which housed political prisoners of all nationalities. It was a more bearable, more well-mannered environment than that in the admittance block. This block was also fully occupied, but each inmate still had her place, her own stool, her own cot. There were women and girls from all classes, social strata, and political parties. Party solidarity made itself felt here as well, and soon I had figured out who was on the right, who on the left, who belonged here or there. Although it was strictly forbidden, some couldn't resist making their views outwardly apparent; it was only too understandable. They had brought their ideals with them into this hell, they suffered for them, and it was quite humanly understandable that they would champion their opinions here. Later I liked to listen to them, for there were clever people among them. In general, there were many educated women represented here in Block V:

social workers, nuns, teachers, officers' wives, Austrian social democrats, noblewomen, an old mother superior over seventy years old, writers, several witty and very lively French women,[1] representatives of all different parties, bourgeois women: everything, absolutely everything could be found here. There also were fortune tellers and even little farm maids who had had relations with a Pole or another citizen of an enemy nation. The latter usually had a prison or penitentiary term behind them and came to the concentration camp for an as yet uncertain amount of time. These mostly simple and good-natured girls were shorn of their hair by order of the Gestapo when they were delivered to the camp, and sometimes several times in a row in intervals of a few weeks or months; in addition they were given ten to twenty-five lashes with a cane, often repeated up to four times.[2] I will come back again to these blows, the meanest and most vulgar of mistreatments ordered by Himmler and carried out by the camp commandant and his accomplices and, unfortunately, by his female assistants as well.

One evening after the roll-call count, the entire Block V had to line up for Chief Overseer Langefeld who found it especially amusing to make the inmates wait for hours in front of her office after a day of hard labor.[3]

---

1. Tillion estimates that 8,000–10,000 French women were imprisoned in Ravensbrück; of these, she estimates that 25 percent were what she terms "common criminals": thieves, informers, and prostitutes who had infected German soldiers; the rest she describes as political deportees, women who were involved with the resistance or were related to someone in the resistance (*Ravensbrück*, 34–35).

2. This form of punishment at Ravensbrück was specifically permitted after Himmler's visit to the camp in 1940. A special wooden structure called "the beating block" held the prisoner in place for the punishment, and the prisoner was often made to count the lashes aloud.

3. Johanna Langefeld was chief overseer in Ravensbrück from 1941 to 1943 (with the exception of a six-month period during which she served at Auschwitz). Buber-Neumann records that Langefeld began her career as an overseer, and later a chief overseer, in the first concentration camp for women, Lichtenburg, in 1936 (*Under Two Dictators*, 263). According to Irmgard Heike, Langefeld was an unemployed single mother who asked for work as a prison warden so that she "could do good among the poorest of the poor" ("' . . . da es sich ja lediglich um die Bewachung der Häftlinge handelt . . .': Lagerverwaltung und Bewachungspersonal," 233). Langefeld's career trajectory then took her into concentration camp administration. Buber-Neumann, like Nanda, saw both a good and an evil side in Langefeld. Buber-Neumann notes that Langefeld was transferred to Auschwitz in early 1942 along with the first transport of 1,000 prisoners from Ravensbrück to Auschwitz (247). But Langefeld was horrified by Auschwitz and requested her transfer back to Ravensbrück after six months there. Buber-Neumann observes that Langefeld was particularly protective of Jehovah's Witnesses and had a soft side for many of the "politicals," two of whom she saved in Auschwitz (265). Buber-Neumann worked in Langefeld's office upon Langefeld's return from Auschwitz (262), as did Nanda (see chapter 33), though the two never mention each other. Eventually, as Buber-Neumann notes, "Frau Langefeld [was] arrested and brought before an S.S. court charged with a variety of offenses, including that of having shown sympathy towards the Poles. She was discharged for lack of evidence, but removed from the service" (281).

However, I never did see her beat an inmate. She could even sometimes muster up an understanding heart for certain people. But she was cold and indifferent from so many years of work in the concentration camp. She stood by at all canings that were meted out. I think this was an order from above. When she finally appeared on the evening in question she let her eyes, which nothing could elude, wander critically over the almost three hundred inmates of our block and sought me out. She asked me about my profession, age, and so on, and then ordered: "You will go to Block II as barracks elder."[4] I was given a terrible fright, for Block II was the prostitutes' block, the most infamous in the whole camp. For this reason I dared to beg her not to send me to this block; I made the objection that I was no match for the prostitutes. She, however, replied: "You will go there whether you want to or not!"

I received a green band around my left arm, packed up my belongings, and, deeply unhappy about this new assignment, walked that very same hour over to Block II, as I had been ordered to do. I would have rather remained at my outdoor labor. But for us outcasts there was no "rather," an order was an order and that's that. It was time again to subject myself to the unavoidable.

What did my assignment as barracks elder now consist of? In every block there was, as I mentioned before, a block elder, and, since the block was divided into two halves, A and B, each half had a barracks elder. The barracks elder lived in direct and constant connection with the inmates, who were under her command. The block elder, whom we had to obey, presided over the barracks elders. I had the great luck of hitting upon a very dear block elder in Block II, Sascha Dziuba, an ethnic German who had been the secretary at a Polish consulate, a magnificent, upstanding, and respectable human being, who became my true comrade. Unfortunately we were only together for a few months. She was released one year before I was; I was her successor as block elder. For a short time we two bore our difficult fate together. We block and barracks elders had to give an account of everything that took place in the block to the block director, in our case Overseer Gode. Let it be mentioned for the sake of truth and her own defense that Overseer Gode was one of the most respectable and humane overseers in the entire camp, a praiseworthy exception. She was truly loved and honored by the inmates, and she had compassion, which cannot be said of most of the other overseers. When she asked me in the course of a conversation why I had been arrested at all, and I described my case in brief for her, she confessed to me that she never would have become an overseer in a concentration camp if she had known beforehand what goes on here. She

---

4. Accounts of Block II are also found in the memoirs of Wanda Poltawska and Margarete Buber-Neumann (see pages 253–60).

never beat the inmates; rather, she tried to understand everything they did and to help them.

Alas, if the commandant and the administration of the camp had learned of her goodness toward us inmates, she would have been heavily punished! How enraged she was by the canings dealt out to the inmates of our block in particular almost every week!

As barracks elder, I had to take care that the day- and sleeping-rooms were kept painstakingly clean. A few prisoners who had "indoor duty," and were thus liberated from outdoor labor for a short time, stood at the disposal of the barracks elder to help with this work. These were only half-workers, often with high fevers; it was not rare for them to be so miserable that they could hardly hold themselves up on their legs. One had to lend an efficient hand oneself so that everything would pass muster before the strict eyes of the commandant, the chief overseer, and the guard personnel. Tables and stools were scoured snow-white with sand every Friday, windows and doors scrubbed and the cupboards washed down inside and out. In the same way, great cleanliness was the rule in the dormitory, with its 135 cots on the B-side of the block, and the maintenance of this cleanliness was entrusted to me. I had to check every bed and, if sick people lay on the cots, take care of them, as far as that was possible in a block without medicines or bandages. I was especially glad to do this, and the prostitutes readily submitted themselves to it. We set store by the utmost cleanliness in the toilets. But one could wipe up every hour there; again and again they were soiled with filth and excrement so that one almost got sick whenever one walked in there. In the day- and sleeping-rooms, too, cleanliness could not hold on for long amid the elements of this block. It was often repugnant, for there were inmates who found great joy in making it dirty again, right at noon after the dormitory had just been cleaned at great pains and without the aid of any cleansing agents; some even used the dormitory as a toilet. Many times I caught inmates who took their food dishes into their cots at night and relieved themselves of their greater and smaller needs in them. Everyone will understand that I had to step in forcefully, even if only for the sake of the other, clean inmates.

Overseer Gode knew that the block and barracks elders of her block did more than was their duty in this regard, and therefore she left our assignments up to us quite independently. She herself had to go out with outdoor commandos during the day and was only present for a short time in the morning and evening, very seldom longer.

Chapter 20

Alone no more!

The communal life in Block II was extremely difficult and became more and more unbearable over time as a result of extreme overcrowding. There were no more cots for many of the inmates. They lay several to a bed; many had to sleep on the floor. The inmates of Block II were mostly prostitutes, young and old, ranging in age from seventeen to seventy. It is hard to understand what it means to hold in check and take care of these often fully corrupted people. I had to serve out the coffee to them in the morning and the food at noon and in the evening. My arms often became crippled from doing this. In addition to this there was the unhappiness, the hate, the envy, the grudges, the reciprocal accusations, and insults of the nastiest sort. Unfortunately it often came to betrayal among these women of quite inferior natures. If someone had, out of hunger, stolen only two raw potatoes, then someone else went and told on her fellow inmate. Then there was an announcement and, following that, a punishment report, and then, at the proclamation of punishment, the bitterest punishments, often canings and detention, were imposed. And these people, gentle ones and rough ones (a remorseful one could hardly be found among them), defiant and morally depraved, had to live among one another and with one another, eat at one table, often sit in pairs on one stool, sleep next to one another on a cot. Vulgar brawls occurred repeatedly, which we block and barracks elders had to settle. This was not easy. They scratched and bit and lashed out, these poor, loveless, excessive, unruly human beings.

And they knew how to steal! It was a near daily occurrence that dry pieces of bread were stolen from a number of inmates out of the cupboard. This mostly happened while the others were sleeping. Sometimes I caught someone at it in the middle of the night. I had already suspected one of them on several occasions, but I always lacked proof. I exhorted her just to confess, but she assured me, crying, that she had never stolen. Oh, but I knew, Bertha, that you already had six weeks of detention and twenty-five lashings behind you for theft from comrades.[1] How well-meaning I was with you, giving you a piece of my bread so many times, often secretly smuggling a few of my potatoes to you at noon—and yet, you couldn't do differently! When I caught you stealing you ran away from me and threw the whole piece of bread, the meager day's ration, which was worth its weight in gold for us, into the toilet. And when, in the same night, I searched your straw sack, where you all liked so well to hide your stolen rarities, there I found eight to ten pieces of stolen bread. Some of them had already become moldy from age and dampness. And the poorest people, from whom you had stolen them, were starving at hard labor. You had to atone bitterly for this! You knew that theft from comrades could not be excused in the camp even by block and barracks elders. No one had more than anyone else, and everyone was starving. What has become of you, a person without stability, without a will, without faith, without God?!

And where can you be today, Gisela, you who made life so sour for me as barracks elder and later as block elder, that I often could have despaired?! Gisela was a prostitute of at least fifty years age and had, as she often told me proudly, already celebrated her twenty-fifth anniversary as a prostitute. She was a slippery customer, lying and cheating until she made a ruckus. You, too, Gisela, knocked away the hand that reached out to you helpfully. You grew up in bordellos. Do you still remember how you stood before me and told me: "I've been a prostitute for twenty-five years and am proud of it"? And in the same breath you challenged me: "Do the same as I do!" No, I couldn't do the same as you do. My heart ached during your explanation, and inexpressible sympathy for you and your comrades filled my soul. And yet we always got along with one another. Hadn't you, poor thing, been in the concentration camp for ten years already? How could you become a better person, come to repent, in this environment? No, a concentration camp in the Third Reich, under the terrorism and bestiality of Himmler and his cronies, could not make a person of your type better, but only even worse!

And Auguste, you little witch of almost seventy years age, how mutinous you were, you were always the bone of contention in the block, despite the fact that we block and barracks elders made many allowances for you, since you were so old and gray! If only four to five potatoes could be distributed to each inmate because there were simply no more left, then you created mutiny and claimed that the smallest and most rotten had been

---

1. Herbermann's use of direct address here is a bit odd and an unusual peroration for a camp memoir. It is almost as if she seeks ongoing dialogue and contact with former inmates. It is unlikely she expected them to respond to such passages in the book itself, as she tells us (see her note at the end of the memoir) that she has changed many of the names.

picked out for you. And if I brought you the dishes of the others, to show you proof that no one else had more than you, then you fumed even more and became boundless in your rage. Oh, I know well, all of you, all of us, starved. For this reason you also couldn't be taken completely seriously, for a starving person can, if he exercises no self-control, turn into an animal in his greed. But to retain any stability with you all was overly difficult, even impossible.

But Anni, the beautiful, blonde prostitute from Hamburg, she could pull herself together; in this she was an example for all of you—that one can be respectable if one exercises self-control. What has become of Anni, who was released a few months before me? I often conversed with her, she told me about much of her life and pursuits. She had the firm intention of becoming a different person, performed her hard labor silently, was quiet, and never quarreled. Yes, she was one of the few whom one was glad to have around. I had given her the address of my relatives in Soest in case she was released and directed her to have recourse there, where someone would certainly be able to put her up somewhere and would help her to start a new life. And she did write, as I learned from my relatives after my release, again from Hamburg. But her address was not given so that a further exchange of letters was impossible. Does she earn her money as a respectable person now?

You too, Else, I cannot forget. You belonged in an insane asylum and not in a concentration camp, in which one could, nonetheless, certainly go insane quite easily. Whenever an airplane droned above us, you suddenly stopped, got very excited, waved with both hands, and screamed crazily: "He's sitting in there, my Heinrich, my Heinrich!" Everyone made fun of you, especially the SS and the overseers, but you were only to be pitied.

And my poor Anneliese, you who often clung to me in your misery and defenselessness, like a child to its mother's skirts, whenever someone wanted to do something to you. And they often pounced on you, your fellow prisoners! Death already stood in your hungry, greedy, large eyes when I first met you. Your body, which I often scrubbed down for you, since you were so unclean and always wore wet underclothes smeared with excrement, was as gaunt as a skeleton, the abdomen fat and hard. How greedily you plunged on the potato peels and ate them with two hands like an animal. Often you stretched out your gaunt hand, smiling and begging: "Do give me your peels!" No, I didn't want to give you the peels, you just got sicker from them. I preferred to give you a potato from my ration. But afterward you took the peels anyway, out of the wood barrel that stood in one corner of the block for garbage. How many times did I take you away from the compost heap, you and many others, who dug like animals for whatever cabbage stems, leaves, peels, and stinking remains lay there. I exhorted you all not to do that anymore. You knew what hard punishment awaited you if you were caught!

And I pointed out to you what serious and unpleasant sicknesses could result from this and had already so often resulted from it. How many inmates died from typhoid! You always promised to change for the better, but were back there again on the same day, whenever a guard wasn't standing there. You died in the detention building after twenty-five lashes, you unhappy soul!

And I think of you, Thea, you who were sick through and through, you who haunted about at night in the block and scared the sleeping women. You no longer knew what you did. One night as I lay sleeping on my cot, you beat me with both fists so that I started up scared. You stood there, draped with blankets, like a gray phantom. I wanted to take hold of you, but you began to rage and jumped out of the window, with me and several other inmates behind you, until we finally caught you. It was an icy winter night and the full moon, with its countless good stars, stood shining in the sky. I called you by name again and again. You didn't listen, threw yourself on the ground, went completely insane and called repeatedly out loud: "I, too, am crucified, just like Jesus Christ!" Yes, you poor thing, you too were crucified. We wanted to take you back to the block using all our force, since we knew that the night guard would come and take you away to the house of horror and death. But you shoved and lashed out with your hands and feet and would not let yourself be picked up and carried by the three of us. Then the night guard came, the SS came with the dogs, and I had to accompany you into the cell building, where a straitjacket was put on you before my eyes. You never made it out of the death house alive either.

I have yet to tell of you, beautiful, little Frieda! Many a night I sat on your cot while you convulsed from your severe attacks. I am still happy today about the fact that you always said to me: "You are my mother! I never had a mother besides you!" Yes, Frieda, you told me of your whole fate in life. Through tragic life circumstances you had landed in a bordello all too early, and begged me to help you so that you would be ready for a later life. I did what I could. You knew it. Wasn't it nice, when we prayed the Lord's Prayer together deep in the night? And you begged: "Say the prayer again!" You in particular could have begun a different life someday in freedom, you had a good foundation for that. But you disappointed me and volunteered yourself for the bordello in the Mauthausen Concentration Camp for Men, where the delivery of ten female inmates had been requested. I applied all my powers of persuasion with you, reminded you of your resolved good intentions, of your poor condition. Yes, I warned you that you would never survive it, and I was right. You never came back from Mauthausen.

To elucidate what I have been describing here I have to report that approximately every three months, eight to ten inmates, primarily from my block, were requisitioned for the bordello of the Mauthausen Concentration Camp for Men, as well as for other camps for men. The prostitutes were chosen by the commandant, the inspector, and the chief overseer, and could also volunteer themselves of their own free will. It is a horrible fact that people who had been imprisoned for their depravity, and for "endangering human society," were now commanded by the state, which held them for this precise reason, to be depraved again. After the stipulated time, these inmates came back and new ones were chosen. What I heard from these inmates who returned from Mauthausen and other KZ's was gruesome. I will leave it up to others to report of this in more detail. The prostitutes who were sent to Mauthausen or other camps received somewhat better food, didn't have to perform any other work, had beds rather than cots, and received money, which was paid out to them by the camp administration in the case of their release. All of these superficial, material advantages exercised great powers of attraction over them. Of the five marks each male inmate had to pay in this bordello, the prostitute received fifty pennies; the other four marks and fifty pennies were pocketed by the state.

I want to mention one more of my wards, Hermine, a young, fresh, healthy girl from somewhere in the Rhineland, who was hard to tame because of her hot temper and her defiance, which was often taken to an extreme, and who caused me a lot of headaches. One afternoon she fled with five other inmates from outdoor labor. It was a frequent occurrence that inmates took to their heels; I couldn't blame them. But most were caught again very quickly by the SS and the Gestapo, and then it was terror with no end, from detention to canings to the punishment block. This punishment block was an extra block for those inmates who were guilty of some special misconduct. Often enough this "special" misconduct consisted of insignificant trifles. But this punishment block was a concentration camp within the concentration camp, with constant food deprivation, the hardest labor, and an overabundance of daily mistreatments. So Hermine had fled with five other inmates. They had taken the triangles and inmate numbers off of their clothes, stolen cardigan sweaters somewhere, and so these people, hungry for freedom, had dared to take flight. While her five companions were caught again very quickly, even the most wily SS and Gestapo could not find a trace of Hermine. I don't know anymore exactly how long she was gone; I believe almost a year had passed when all of a sudden it was said in the camp: "Hermine is back! She's up there with the new admittees." Since I had to take care of something in the office of the chief overseer anyway, and was curious myself as to whether this "camp rumor," of which there were many, was true, I set off immediately to convince myself of its accuracy. In truth, there she stood, elegant and fresh, smiling and provocative in the manner of prostitutes, and whispered to me as I walked by: "Nanda, it was worth it!" Further commentary about this would be superfluous. As I learned later, she had supposedly lived with a man in Berlin and from there had gone back to her home, where she was discovered by the criminal police. And now she came back as a "backslider," as those who were delivered to a concentration camp for the second time were called. The most horrible punishments awaited her. If I'm not wrong, she received, and survived, twenty-five lashes four times, as well as long weeks of detention and punishment block. She was that tough. But, according to her own pronouncement, the year of freedom was "worth it."

Chapter 21

Block elder over four hundred prostitutes . . .

We are not as children, who naively play,
by this cold age our hot mouths have been shut . . .
Against our love we have been chafed and cut
and are discarded before we gratify . . .

The current block elder in Block II was generally called "brothel mother" by the prostitutes. And so I had the "great honor," after a few months' work as barracks elder, of being promoted by the administration of the camp to mother of the prostitutes. I don't know what I would have given to have avoided this post. I was not the robust person who unquestionably belonged in such a post. I took everything too seriously, too conscientiously, and I suffered from the threats and vulgarities and betrayals of the inmates among one another. How often I was advised to find myself a thicker skin, but, despite every effort, I did not succeed in this. What can one do if one is simply made a certain way?

When Sascha, our previous block elder, was gone, I stayed behind, alone among almost four hundred prostitutes and asocials, spiritually and intellectually lonesome. Since Sascha, with whom I had on occasion been able to pursue a bit of intellectual exchange late at night, was no longer there, I longed doubly as much to be able to read a good book once again. Having to do entirely without any reading material is not easy for someone who for many long years has had almost solely to do with books. The inmates of Block II did not feel this way. But for an inmate with intellectual interests, this torment existed in addition to the mental and physical torments. Admittedly, however, the average inmate had no inkling of this. Only someone who has experienced the same thing can really completely understand what it means to have to renounce every intellectual occupation, all intellectual needs, in such a hell.

It had become winter, the bitter cold winter of the year 1941–42. Our barracks was iced over, inside and out. If everything had not been so completely horrible, one could have found this block house, completely covered in snow and ice, surrounded by snow meters high, to be quite enchanting. Oh yes, if only. . . . A deep sadness and despair settled in my soul during this winter. I was not permitted to think. The grim cold did its bit as well. To starve and to freeze was our parole. I had long since lost the ability to cry. At some point even the tears stop. Poor, sorrowful life!

My prostitutes could not be tamed. I was hoarse from screaming. It was a torment to have to set up three to four hundred inmates of this kind in rank and file for roll call at the crack of dawn, in complete darkness, and twice a day to boot. I lived from the most extreme expenditure of strength, from an energy which said to me again and again: You must endure! I still wanted to go home again some day, to my hometown—as long as I didn't "croak" in the camp! I defended myself against every sickness, and it remains inconceivable to me, to this day, what unbelievable things even a weak person is in the condition to bear. A strong, untamed faith held me up. The words of Paul often went through my head: "I have the power of Him, who gives me strength!" How visible God's grace was with me, how it held me up again and again; for this I can never thank heaven enough. I knew that everyone at home was praying and offering up sacrifices for me, and the consciousness of this bore me up. I was and remained safe in God's love and in the loyalty and prayers of my relatives and friends, and knew them all to be deeply connected to me in my great suffering.

So I lived on with my prostitutes, watching over them and working for them, being good to them as much as I was able. There were great differences among them, though they adhered to the same depravity almost without exception. A small number of inmates in this block had been delivered to the concentration camp as asocials because of a refusal to work. In manner, disposition, and conduct they were all quite different again. There is one kind who finds her fate hard to bear, who slowly extinguishes like the light of a candle. And the other kind, who is always loud, who takes everything on the light side, who somehow feels at home even in this Sodom and Gomorrah. Oftentimes they had been previously convicted, thirty, forty, fifty, even up to a hundred times and more, had spent their whole lives in prisons, work camps, and penitentiaries, and their youth under welfare. Their fates had made them hard and relentless and very egotistical. They revolved only around themselves. But whenever I heard their life stories, which many of them entrusted to me, then I would have liked to confess to these poor, depraved creatures: You can't be any different! If I had been raised in this way, in such an environment and without the blessings and protection of a good parental home like them, then I, too, might have turned out like them. When they had their "moral times," when they were shaken with pain over their botched lives, then they often threw their arms around my neck and kissed me. I accepted this and repressed my disgust; for I knew that many of them had been afflicted with the most horrible and catching diseases, and that some still were. As one of them lay dying in my arms, she confessed to me: "If only someone would have been as good to me before as you have been, then I would have become a different person. I will never forget you for understanding me! Now it's too late!" I folded my hands with hers for prayer and spoke to her of God and his great love and compassion. When she died a few days later, I was firmly convinced that she had found a lenient judge up above. She would have been happy and ready to open her heart to a priest. But no priest was ever allowed to come to us in the camp. Without any spiritual help they all literally had to perish, often with the aid of the famous "death injections," as we called them.[1]

If one priest would ever have been permitted to set foot in this concentration camp for women and exercise his office, only for one single day, thousands of women from all barracks would have rushed out to him and would have raised up their downcast souls in honest confession and attained salvation. Thus the great and compassionate God had to do it in his own way, and I am convinced that he did it. Yet many people told me that they had lost their faith completely. Oh, how much obstinate disbelief lived inside them! Many of my wards were completely morally ruined in this environment. They performed the most depraved acts with each other, since sexuality was the only thing left for them.[2] They could no longer be helped by goodness and patience. They were totally ruined; physically, too, they were unkempt and dirty. This caused bad air and a stench that was especially unbearable

---

1. Injections of phenol were given to murder inmates in Ravensbrück (Gutman, *Encyclopedia of the Holocaust,* 1227).

2. Christa Schulz cites this passage of Nanda's book as a thinly veiled, prejudicial reference to lesbianism among the prostitutes in Block II ("Weibliche Häftlinge aus Ravensbrück," 141). Schulz also cites a reference to a statement by Tetzlaff, a leader of the Hitler Youth organization, that two-thirds of lesbian women were prostitutes, driven to lesbianism by their disgust at sleeping with men. As Schulz points out, this common societal prejudice was one reason behind the stigmatization of both lesbians and prostitutes in the camps. Because this stigmatization was so widespread, it is very difficult to get a clear and honest picture of relationships between women in Ravensbrück, particularly because there are no extant accounts of the camp written by prostitutes or lesbians, and other women's accounts may be untrustworthy because informed by such prejudices. Like Nanda, Wanda Poltawska refers to lesbianism in prejudicial tones, mentioning it explicitly by name. She writes of an entire Block XI, separate from the prostitutes' block, which apparently housed lesbians:

at night. In addition there were the curses and cackling, the disgustingly unrespectable jokes, which were told out loud, and the shameless laughter that followed. . . . I was extremely put off by all of this. I forbade them of being offensive in this way in the dormitory, where all speaking was banned. But as soon as the feared night watch was over, it began anew. A few listened to me, but the majority did not; on the contrary, they used to the utmost the fact that I hardly made report of this, which would have resulted in hard punishments for disobedience confronting the block elder. Yes, they were often ungrateful and nasty to me, my prostitutes, for whom I made so many allowances, with whom I tried to exercise so much understanding. Then I wished I were back in my outside labor, in order to finally find a little internal and external peace again, which I was never allowed in this hell within a hell of Block II. More than once I was tempted to ask the chief overseer for this, but Overseer Gode, the director of our block, held me back from doing so every time.

They were hard to handle, but they weren't all bad because of this. Many who were worse were certainly running around free outside the concentration camp.

A few of them were, however, true monsters, and I was always afraid of them. Morally they were completely ruined, and in addition they

---

Block II. I go cold at the mere thought of it . . . those women . . . the block where we first understood the full hideousness of that odd word "elel"—LL—the initials of lesbian love.

Within a few days that band of women had completely terrorized us. They stole everything we had: only half our camp rations ever reached us and soon those last souvenirs of freedom—our toothbrushes and combs, together with a few treasures we had brought with us from prison—vanished irretrievably. We couldn't wash, because they wouldn't let us into the wash-room. We couldn't go to the sleeping quarters during the day, because the woman in charge wouldn't let us. She was always "re-making" our beds, stealing anything she could find and spitting on the sheets. It was horrible to have to lie on those sheets after she'd spat all over them.

I managed to shield Krysia from seeing some of what took place while that word, "elel," acquired a hideous, inhuman reality. Whatever will become of us? I asked myself. A couple of years from now, will we be like that too?

I don't really know if Krysia understood why I stopped giving her a goodnight kiss. Maybe she even resented my not doing so. But the incredible goings-on in that block destroyed my faith in the innocence of even the simplest human gesture. I gave up believing in affection or purity.

Often at night it took me ages to get to sleep. At first I couldn't credit what was happening, and watched wide-eyed, torn between curiosity and despair.

The last shreds of humanity were slowly disappearing.

Lesbian love . . . love . . . love . . . (*And I Am Afraid of My Dreams*, 57–58)

Denise Dufournier also mentions lesbianism among French women in Ravensbrück in passing: "I think *Block 27* was the worst, after the Gypsies' *Block*. In *Block 27* they'd put the Jewish women and children, and for good measure they'd put the French criminals and asocials in there, too—prostitutes and so on. There was a certain amount of lesbianism. The 'males' were called 'Jules', and they would carve a cross into the foreheads of their 'steadies'—we called it a *croix des vaches*" (Quoted in Gill, *The Journey Back from Hell*, 327).

were sly and deceitful and therefore dangerous. And we slept together, side by side. Oh, it was difficult beyond all bounds.

This must be a task of the new state and also the Church in the future, to give these children who are outcasts from human society a chance to refine and better themselves in an environment not ruled by whips and rubber truncheons, but rather by goodness, understanding, and patience. Under the terrorism of the SS and Gestapo, under that constant mistreatment, these people could by their natures only get worse. So it was not uncommon that their despair drove them to suicide. In the mornings, some of them hung charred from the electrically charged barbed wire surrounding the high walls. Yes, they were literally driven into the arms of this suicide. Whoever has understandingly and lovingly listened to the fates of these poor things, has lived together with them and studied them, knows what is missing here. The chaplaincy too must take hold here more actively than ever before. But it won't be easy to find the right personalities for this, even among priests. Augustinian and Paulist natures, priests with the patience and forbearance of saviors, would have the calling for this, and women, too: not the old maid or devout churchgoer types, but women who are close to life, schooled in sorrow, and seasoned in battle, with large, strong hearts. "Hard as a diamond, tender as a mother," as Lacordaire so aptly puts it.[3] In this book I would like to appeal to the Church and the state that something drastic be done in this area very soon!

There are inmates, convicts, who remain dangerous to the general public after a sentence determined by the court and served out—often these prisoners, as I already mentioned before, had been convicted up to thirty or fifty times. Such individuals cannot be released back into the freedom of human society without further ado. But it goes against all justice and all humanity, as was all too often the case in the National Socialist state, to simply transfer inmates who have served their prison or penitentiary terms over to a concentration camp, which was a hundred times worse than any prison or penitentiary, as everyone can witness who was acquainted with both. We were all homesick for our prisons, for our penitentiaries, where we were at least treated as human beings by the respectable administration and were not subjected to the caprice and bestiality of the most vulgar and perverse creatures. In so-called protective custody the inmate must be treated humanely at first and not with kicks, beatings, whips, and rubber truncheons. Woe befall anyone who guilelessly and capriciously tormented such inmates as had been dealt enough blows by fate already, something that happened hour after hour in the concentration camp! Only then would all their rage

---

3. Henri Dominique Lacordaire (1802–61) was a French priest, theologian, and writer who was particularly successful as a preacher at Notre Dame in Paris.

truly break forth, particularly among those who had been serious about improvement and, heaven knows, had pulled themselves together like heroes to fight bravely against the "lusts of their own flesh." Through mistreatment it's suddenly all over again, and the last flicker of good will is extinguished, never to flare back up again. Then such tormented and mistreated people let all moral inhibitions drop and become even worse than ever before.

Oh, those who have once been marked (whether justly or unjustly) must bear their taints for a lifetime, for they are profoundly afraid deep in their hearts, and they feel it, they can tell that we fear them, even loathe them. And when they are mistreated so awfully and capriciously? They never forgive that, and the cleft splits apart, wider and wider, deeper and deeper. They knew well that those who beat and whipped them gained pleasure from their pain. They could never get over that. And for this reason they remained full of mistrust. The pain sharpened all of their senses to the extreme. They became like wild animals, who unconsciously plunged into the abyss.

Chapter 22

Eight days of confinement in the dark— raging underworld

Oh, my times, so inexorably torn,
so void of stars, in life and thought so careworn,
like you, to me no one, no one will appear.
The sphinx has never held her head so high,
yet to your right and left you look awry,
ere the mad abyss you cry in pain and fear.

—HERMANN KLEMM

I had already had to accompany quite a few of the great number of people entrusted to my care to the detention building. This was always a journey of sacrifice, for we inmates all knew that the building of detention cells was the most horrifying thing the human brain could ever devise. How I was always so glad and ready to believe in even the most depraved and outcast of human beings! But since I have become acquainted with this building I know that there is no animal on earth that can be more horrible, more vulgar, more cruel, more unbridled than this beast, the human being.

In this building of cells the canings were dealt out personally by the commandant and the guards, men and women. But the majority of the overseers (and even the SS) did not volunteer themselves for such vulgarities. This particular commandant, however, the SS-Obersturmbahnführer (senior storm trooper) Kögel, was the most vulgar of inhumane monsters that one can possibly imagine.[1] Equal to him in this rank was the Overseer

---

1. Max Kögel was commandant of Ravensbrück from 1939 until October 1942, at which point he was replaced by Commandant Fritz Suhren. Kögel, who went on to serve as commandant at Majdanek and Flossenburg, was eventually arrested by the U.S. Army and was found dead in his cell in 1946 (Feig, *Hitler's Death Camps*, 457).

140

(later Chief Overseer) Mandel, a satanic female who naturally got along particularly well with the commandant.[2] The beautiful, young Overseer Erich, who was later transferred as chief overseer to the Jewish camp in Lublin, also belonged in this category, as did Overseers Hasse and Binz and a few others whose names escape me.[3] It was characteristic that only the overseers who were most brutal were quickly promoted.

Early one morning we had just finished making the block spic and span clean, and I was sitting making my daily entries regarding the inmates for the block director, when the corpulent, greedy, and brutal figure of Commandant Kögel appeared in our barracks. We few inmates who found ourselves in the barracks at this time began to tremble, for his appearance never brought good tidings. As block elder I had to step up to him, stand at attention, and report: "Block elder Herbermann reports for Block II, occupied by 397 inmates." His eyes looked at me as if he wanted to eat me up. He stepped up to the oven, saw that a small fire was burning in it, and said only: "You're coming with me!" I followed him. One of those moments had arrived again in which all the blood in me congealed and I became as pale as the white paper on which I am writing. The camp commandant set me in front of the office of Chief Overseer Mandel and went in, sizing me up again from top to bottom. Swinging his whip back and forth, he called out his order to a passing overseer: "Into detention with her!" I dared to ask why I was being put into detention? "Shut your trap you old pig!" was his answer. He cracked his whip and left.

After a long, fearful wait, I was called into the office of Chief Overseer Mandel, who was quite equal to the commandant in vulgarity and meanness.

"You were heating your block!" I told her that my block director, Overseer Gode, had expressly allowed me to do it, since I could not perform

---

2. Buber-Neumann refers to her as "Mandl." This overseer became chief overseer when Langefeld was transferred to Auschwitz. Buber-Neumann agrees that Mandel was a "sadistic beast" and points out that things became much worse in the camp after Mandel replaced Langefeld (*Under Two Dictators*, 247). After six months, Mandel was transferred to Auschwitz when Langefeld succeeded in securing her transfer back to Ravensbrück. In Auschwitz, Mandel became famous as a particularly brutal overseer.

3. Dorothea Binz was known as one of the most ruthless and sadistic overseers anywhere. Memoirists of Ravensbrück inevitably discuss her horrifying acts of violence against inmates. Binz, who was from a town near Ravensbrück, apparently volunteered to work in the camp, which was very uncommon. Though she hoped to work in the camp's kitchen after having completed an apprenticeship in kitchen prep work, she agreed to become an overseer when she learned that no kitchen work was available. Binz began work at Ravensbrück in August 1939 and remained a camp overseer through 1945 (Heike, "'. . . da es sich ja lediglich um die Bewachung der Häftlinge handelt,'" 233). She was sentenced to death by hanging at the Ravensbrück trial in Hamburg in 1947 (Feig, *Hitler's Death Camps*, 139).

the daily required written work with stiff, ice-cold fingers, and that, according to the prescriptions of the camp regulations I didn't have to ask anyone else except for the block director in this case. In addition, the "yard squadron," which consisted of eight to ten inmates who had to keep Camp Street clean, brought me poplars and a few leftover bits of wood so that we needy, freezing inmates, completely soaked through from the early roll call, could warm ourselves up, if only for half an hour. I dared to bring up all of this. She, however, allowed for none of it, and announced to me: "The commandant has ordered you to be taken into detention immediately!" These words were accompanied by two cracking smacks.

Now the most abject time of my life began. The suffering I was being subjected to and forced to bear, innocently, in my own native land, had become indescribable, so that often I could only think: This is no longer my own native land! The seed of vitality inside me was truly pulverized in this mill of life.

An overseer had to lead me away to the house of horror, to the death house. I was received by Overseer Binz amid many kicks. Two raging dogs, one of them a large breed, jumped at me. One shiver of fear after another ran through me. I was led into a dark cell and the cell door was immediately thrown shut behind me. There I stood in a pitch-dark room, into which no ray of light could penetrate. I could grasp nothing more and was completely at the end of my rope. To think of anything was impossible for me. I suffered a fate worse than death in this hour.

It was the birthday of our dear, good mother in 1942.[4] I will never forget this day when, in the early morning, I had sacrificed to God all the suffering I would endure over the course of the day for the sake of my distant mother. How good it is, Mother, that you did not see me in this misery! Your mother's heart would have been broken. How hard God's tests for me were! It was as if He were no longer there for me. And again and again I submitted myself to His will, despite everything, convinced that everything I was made to bear had to have a greater sense for Him. But now, trying to reconcile myself for an uncertain amount of time with this confinement in the dark, it seemed impossible to me. And yet I had to take on my situation as something immutable and try to master it. Those who are close to God cannot be broken by any fate in life. The stars of faith still continued to shine for me in this sinister darkness.

In complete darkness, I groped for a stool screwed into the floor. I sat down, folded my hands in the darkness, and implored fervently, "You can illuminate the darkness, only You alone." My eyes, which slowly got used

---

4. Nanda's mother, Maria Anna Helene Hülsmann, was born in Glansdorf, Germany, on May 14, 1877.

to the darkness, could discern that this cell was much smaller than the one in the Münster prison. Groping, I paced back and forth, back and forth for hours, sometimes leaning in one corner, sometimes in another. How glad I would have been to die! This was the last straw. I was guilty of nothing, had truly tired myself out worrying about my fellow prisoners from morning to late in the evening, often into the night. Yes, I was sapped of all energy and could not grasp that I was now being subjected to this injustice in addition to everything else.

I heard the groaning and moaning of the poorest creatures who languished in the darkness of solitary confinement next to me, above me, and below me, in cell after cell. Several had lost their minds. No wonder! They stormed and raged and beat wildly against the cell doors, sang crazy songs in their derangement; still others sang old church songs in despairing, bestial voices, completely distorted, until an overseer came and pulled them up, beat them horribly, and sometimes even locked the dogs in the cells with these poor victims, so that the trained beasts could throw themselves on their prey. There were inmates among us out of whom the dogs had bitten huge pieces of flesh; one had lost half her ear, another a piece of her nose, a third pieces of her hand, and so on. Still others were found in their cells having bled to death or frozen into ice, for it was always bitterly cold in this house of death. There I sat with my bare feet in the dark, freezing to the depths of my soul. I no longer believed I would ever make it out of there alive. What people suffered here goes beyond all human powers of imagination, and only God alone knows what we inmates had to bear up to and endure, physically and mentally, in this building.

And always the fearful, tormenting question: Will I, too, be strapped to the rack and caned like so many others? Will I, too, be beaten on the kidneys, so that I later die from bleeding of the kidneys? The first night began in this most horrible of all dungeons. I lay on wood. Everything hurt; I got up again and sat on the floor. Through the silence of the night, the screams of horror of the martyred inmates rang out eerily. Often I heard the despairing call: "Hunger, hunger!" Such savage noises emanated from the people here that I felt like I was sitting in a cage with wild and fatally injured animals. The hours crept by. And yet I looked forward to night, because at least then one of the devilish overseers would not appear in the cell and deal out beatings and kicks arbitrarily. In these days and nights, God was closer to me than ever before. In my soul a light was burning that no one could extinguish.

On the second day of my confinement in the dark I heard male voices in the morning, among them the sinister and fear-inducing voice of the commandant. Then I knew that canings would be distributed again today. And indeed, six or eight inmates were summoned, their names and numbers resounding in the cells! Frightened, I pricked up my ears and heard them being taken from their cells. My heart stood still. Would I, too, be taken away? I perceived the groaning and crying, the slapping of the rubber truncheon, and closed my ears. It was not to be borne. And there was the sinister darkness all around me. But I was not summoned. The chalice passed me by. When the canings were dealt out, as the beaten inmates told me, one of the most disgusting doctors of all, the SS station doctor (who also beat people himself) stood by, feeling the pulse of the poor victim all the while. If overseers were dealing out the blows, this SS doctor sometimes took the whip out of their hands and continued the beating himself in order to show them that they had to beat much more solidly.

Several prisoners (I had some of them in Barracks II) bore these floggings and mistreatments valiantly, often even silently, without issuing forth a sound of complaint. I still remember how one of my prostitutes, who had received twenty-five lashings, told me that the commandant, excited and angry, cried out at the twenty-fifth blow, "Start screaming, you pig!" But she remained mute. It seemed to especially amuse and satisfy this beast to hear the beaten inmates whimpering and screaming. But many refused to do him this favor. It was monstrous that the prisoner was often made to count the blows out loud herself. Woe befall her, however, if she miscounted. Then it started over from the beginning: one, two, three . . . twenty-five.

I saw many of these bodies, covered in blood, beaten to a pulp, burst open. How painful that must be! How it must burn! These areas where one could still clearly see the strokes of the rubber truncheon were thickly swollen. I sometimes cooled these areas and rubbed them with salve or cream to help soothe the unbearable pains of these poor creatures a bit. I begged or "organized" cream or salve in exchange for bread from new admittees, who still brought such rarities into the camp. Otherwise such remedies did not exist.

How could German men and women be a party to beating prisoners, often innocent prisoners, in this way, strapping them to a rack and then letting twenty-five blows rain down on their poor bodies? How could anyone degrade people so basely? And how basely those people who dealt these blows were degrading themselves! They were as bloodthirsty as tigers. No, these were no longer human beings!

And the poor, beaten, skinned, tormented women and girls could not even lie on their cots at night because of the pain. It was horrible when the beatings were repeated four times in a row, at an interval of eight days, which happened frequently. Everything was still raw and bloody from the last blows, and already new lashings were raining down on it. These women bore immeasurable physical pain. And their mental pain?

The leadership of a state that orders such things and lets them be carried out must be thoroughly exterminated. How could such a thing happen in civilized Germany at all? It was Satan who was at work here. How ashamed I was before the foreigners that German people were party to horrors of this kind! When one notes in addition that even the smallest camp thefts and the most petty offenses carried a sentence of beating (if, for example, an inmate stole a few raw potatoes or a dry piece of bread because of hunger that could no longer be tamed, or even if she couldn't work as a result of exhaustion, which was simply labeled as a refusal to work), then one is really left speechless.

Several other punishments were administered in this detention building as well. It must have been truly horrible when they set a prisoner under a dripping water faucet, where drip after drip trickled down on her poor head, hour after hour, until she broke down and fell unconscious and lost her mind forever. Then the death injection was simply administered and the poor soul finally came to peace. My fellow prisoners reported this fact to me.

Or when they used ice cold water to drench people who, in the midst of the coldest winter, were already almost frozen to death anyway, and then left them in the icy cells in their soaked clothing without letting them dry off or get warm. The clothing stood stiffly on their bodies, as when one tries to dry wet laundry outside in the winter and it never truly dries out. In the detention building there was one piece of dry bread and one cup of black coffee to eat everyday. I believe that for most prisoners in this building, even the hungriest, all feelings of hunger were numbed by suffering and torment. At least this is what happened to me. In the first three days I didn't touch my piece of bread.

For eight days and nights I lived in this death house, I lived in this dark cell without light or sun, only with a little coffee and bread, and I really came back out alive, even escaping the canings. When I finally stepped back out onto Camp Street and saw the light of the sun, everything danced before my eyes, and I staggered and tottered so much that inmates who were passing by had to hold me up and support me. My prostitutes hugged me and were crazy with happiness. One of them had saved me a few potatoes, another a little piece of bread, still another had "organized" me a clean pair of knickers and a shirt in the laundry room to give me a small pleasure. I loved them all very much for this.

In the evening a few comrades from the political blocks appeared on the sly to offer me a few kind words and rejoice with me that I had escaped the death house alive.

When our block director, Overseer Gode, came the next morning and caught sight of me, bright tears stood in her eyes. Mine, too. "That you had to endure that, Herbermann," she said. "I had no appetite during these eight days. Twice I visited the commandant and the chief overseer to get you

145

out, since you did nothing wrong!" How thankful I was to this overseer for so much comforting goodness!

I had, however, become more experienced, more seasoned. These eight days of confinement in the dark added to the completion of my stay in the concentration camp by helping me to make the right judgment about this institution of hell. I humbly bowed down under God's will and repeated anew a childlike "Yes, Father."

Chapter 23

We inmates are people, too

I lived on among my prostitutes, but life now seemed to me like a new gift. It had been so desolate and bitter in the dark imprisonment of the last week that staying in Block II seemed to me like a salvation. And they made the effort, my poor, miserable sisters, not to vex me or bother me. I was very touched to observe how some of them troubled themselves. Yes, they too had hearts in their breasts, even if they were broken in most cases. Yet for the majority of this capricious bunch every resolution made was gone with the wind all too soon. They knew well that if they got along with each other, they made me very happy. They also knew all too well that I never would beat them, as many a block elder in the KZ unfortunately had done. While my blood certainly did boil at times out of rage and anger, never once did I lift my hand for a beating.

Soon the discord, quarreling, envy, grudges, wrongful accusations, and betrayal began all over again among them. All of these vices were part of the day's business for them. In particular, two individuals existed in my block against whom I was completely powerless. My predecessor, the highly respectable, brave Sascha Dziuba, had already tried to have these two inmates moved to another block if possible. I did the same. But it was refused me as well. I was told that I should lash out against them and see to it that it was taken care of. But no, my basic axiom was and remained not to beat any inmate. I entreated God every morning anew that I might not forget myself in my often justified, boundless rage, and that I might keep my temper.

These two very difficult inmates in my block had both been "brothel mothers," or madams, as they called themselves, by profession; both were already over fifty years old and both were depraved and morally ruined. They were only out for themselves, for their own advantage, and related out loud, for the benefit of the entire block, the most awful bordello experiences down to the smallest detail. The screaming and applause of the other inmates on these occasions was just monstrous. And there were still some among them who were not yet rotten to the core, for whom these two errant women were pure poison. Yet what could be done? I forbade them from having these conversations, but no sooner had I turned my back when they began to pour out their filth over the other inmates in the barracks all over again. In this regard Block II was a real pool of depravity, and we block and barracks elders were completely powerless to do anything about it.

They treated me like a foreigner who did not belong among them. These two obstructionists had already been in the concentration camp for ten years in 1943. I did try to understand them. And I knew well that people of their type cannot become any better in such a hell. Their basic axiom was: As inmate and prisoner I no longer belong to human society and therefore I have the right to conduct myself accordingly. And they took this to extremes. They were a pronounced example of where people can end up and what they can sink down to when they have no more inhibitions or principles.

When I could no longer stand it in the block and my work was accomplished, I fled to the main Camp Street in the evening, where I breathed real air for the first time. This did me good after the stench in the barracks, and I wandered back and forth, watching the setting sun, which could be so especially beautiful and diverse here. And the sunrises! In the east, the heavens are colored with the most unbelievable hues. I have never seen anything like it again. Yes, "the heavens boast of the Eternal Glory." I often sang this song, and said to myself: Great, almighty God will continue to bring me aid.

We were all allowed to stroll for a short time on Camp Street in the evening, and the inmates went around with furrowed brows, sunken into themselves, tormented and deathly sad. Hopelessly they bowed down under the harsh yoke the horrible powers-that-be had hung over them. Their external bearing already betrayed their misery. Others were proud, sauntered around with heads held high, bearing their fates defiantly; others laughed and made jokes. These were mostly my prostitutes and the career criminals. One heard the chatter of the Gypsies who were as good-natured as children.[1] The youngest Gypsy child was no more than twelve years old, and I had taken

---

1. Gypsies were among the first to be imprisoned in Ravensbrück when a transport of 440 Roma, some of them children, was brought to the camp from the Burgenland area of Austria in June 1939. Roma had been persecuted throughout Europe for many years and were explicitly targeted, along with the Jews, by the Nazi Nuremberg racial laws in 1935. Housed in a separate block, Roma were the primary victims of forced sterilizations in the camp and were often subject to "medical experiments" in Ravensbrück as well. Historians estimate that at least 200,000 Roma perished over the course of the Holocaust, but many argue that this figure is too low. It is clear that between 16,000 and 18,000 Roma were killed in the concentration camps on German territory (particularly Buchenwald, Dachau, and Ravensbrück) alone (Gutman, *Encyclopedia of the Holocaust*, 634–38). We have used the single term "Roma" here, rather than the more common terminology "Roma and Sinti," following the example of Isabel Fonseca in *Bury Me Standing*, 228.

her especially into my heart. As soon as she caught sight of me, she ran to me, looked at me trustingly and in a childlike way with her glittering Gypsy eyes, which were deep as an abyss, took my hand and didn't leave me until I had to send her back to the Gypsy block.

When the night watch, which went from block to block, was over, then we sang a few folk songs together, although it was forbidden, or we sang our prison songs, which were so sad and melancholy:

> "Heavy is the labor and heavy are the chains,
> Year after year under the hot blaze of the sun . . ."

or

> "We know that after this dark night,
> The morning will dawn, red and bright . . ."

Tears streamed down many faces. These songs were full of Russian melancholy. Often they also sang:

> "Every day isn't Sunday,
> Every day there isn't wine;
> But every single day,
> You must treat me nice and fine.
> And when one day I die,
> You must think of me yet,
> Before you fall asleep at night,
> But you mustn't cry or fret . . ."

We often sang this song, a few of us or many of us, and sometimes everyone even hummed along; our hearts ached while we sang it and it often happened that the melancholy of it choked us with tears and our heads fell heavily forward.

My prostitutes could sing with particular ardor:

> "Silent as night, deep as the sea,
> So your love should be . . ."

I liked to strike up our pretty, old folk songs:

> "At the fountain by the gate,
> There stands a linden tree,
> I dreamed in its shade
> Many a sweet dream . . ."

or

> "In the prettiest meadow field there stands my quiet home,
> Many an hour I set out in the vale there to roam . . .
> Oh, my quiet vale, I greet you a thousand times . . ."

Yes, a thousand times a thousand times we greeted it, our faraway homeland, in the newer song, too: "Homeland, your stars . . ." All the pain, all the longing and homesickness burned hotly then in our tormented breasts, and I thought of the song Dostoevsky cites in the above-mentioned book:

> "I will never again be near,
> To my beloved homeland;
> Innocently I'm sentenced here,
> And lifelong I am banned.
> The owl calls from on the loft,
> It rings through field and loam.
> My mind is bleak, my heart is soft,
> I'll never be back home."

At Christmastime a true passion for singing came over the inmates.[2] In the evening a voice would begin from some corner and others would join in:

> "Quietly falls the snow,
> Silently rests the lake,

---

2. Descriptions of Christmas in Ravensbrück can be found in at least two other Ravensbrück memoirs. Gemma Gluck, in *My Story* recalls Christmas Eve, 1944. Some of the women at the "international" table she had established had managed to "organize" candy and tiny sandwiches made of bread and marmalade. They presented her with various gifts, including a highly prized pillow and a small album constructed of smuggled paper and covered with fabric; the various inmates signed the album and many included inscriptions and poems (46–49).

   In her book *And I Am Afraid of My Dreams,* Wanda Poltawska describes the singing of national carols and the effort to avoid tears. "What were our loved ones doing that night? Were there really people, somewhere in the world, who were gathering peacefully round a green fir tree in love and celebration?" (50). Like Nanda, she describes "little toys . . . roughly carved out of toothbrush handles: miniature elephants with their trunks held high as a sign of joy; tiny boats; hearts" (50). These were decorating a tiny tree in the block.

   Both women also expressed the same sentiment about the Nazi Christmas tree on the *Lagerstrasse* (Camp Street): Nanda says it stood there "as if to mock us" and Wanda says: "Perhaps to taunt us, the Germans had put up a tree in the camp street: a tree with fairy lights, which we walked past each day, weary with our duties" (51). Nanda notes that the tree was "completely undecorated"; perhaps by 1942 such "luxuries" were no longer possible.

All Christmas-like shines the moon,
Rejoice, the Christ Child's coming soon.

Soon Christmas Eve arrives,
Choir of angels awakes,
Listen, how lovely is the tune,
Rejoice, the Christ Child's coming soon.

In our hearts it is warm,
Silent are grief and harm,
The sorrows of life pass on,
Rejoice, the Christ Child's coming soon . . ."

In the nights before the holidays, in the hours of two to three o'clock when there was no guard to be seen or heard far and wide, we sang our "Te Deum" according to prior arrangement.[3]

"Great God we praise You,
Lord, we glory in Your strength,
the earth bows down before you
and admires Your works.
As You have been throughout all time,
So You will remain in eternity . . ."

Yes, we also dared to sing this avowal to the tripartite God in this, our cruel life, in the darkest of night. Not only the first verse, but also the second and third, which I had to teach them. There were some beautiful voices among us, and so this "Te Deum" in the concentration camp, in the most debased situation, nevertheless became a moving avowal of faith to the creator of all life. Many a choir director would have been happy with our accomplishment. Here we sang with a fervor generally unknown in life. We outcasts, whether small and weak or big and strong, sang intensely and courageously and without trembling into this grayness, some of us even exulting like the birds on a spring Easter morning. God in heaven must have taken pleasure in it. There was something so vigorous, so deeply faithful, so solid and calm in this singing, and I never would have believed beforehand that such a people so oppressed, tortured, and spiritually tormented would have been capable of such an accomplishment.

---

3. "Te Deum laudamus" is a hymn dating back at least to 500 A.D., sung as part of mass, the divine office, and in thanksgiving to God for a special blessing (*Catholic Encyclopedia,* 14:469–70).

And the beloved Christmas holiday came, which I experienced for the second time in the concentration camp, separated from all my loved ones. For every single one of us this day was grievously difficult and sad beyond all measure; for even the most depraved and wretched prostitute had at least one soul somewhere in the world to whom she felt drawn.

It was very touching to see how the inmates tried to bring joy to one another through small but strictly forbidden presents, since they themselves had nothing. But one became inventive in this great need, even if it was just a little song or a tiny poem (how many I had to compose for this purpose!), or even a piece of bread one had spread with saved mashed potatoes and garnished with "organized" jam or margarine. The whole thing was then embellished with fir greens and endowed with festive propriety by means of a hand-drawn religious picture that related to the holiday. The Poles and our Gypsies were especially talented at small artistic works of this kind. Some people also saved their pathetic little pieces of war soap, which we still got very erratically, so that they could give one as a gift on the holiday. I would certainly have never given it away, since soap was so indispensable here. One often had none for weeks on end. Yet one had to set a special value on personal cleanliness in this "pigpen," otherwise one would go to seed completely.

Charming little animals were also carved from the stems of tooth-brushes of all possible colors; there were standing and sitting dogs, cats playing, galloping horses and heavy elephants. These were all filed with pebbles and detailed down to the finest point. Little crucifixes were also produced from toothbrushes and were perfected very artistically. I smuggled various examples of these small carved objects out with me at my release from the concentration camp and they have been marveled at consistently, even by artists.[4]

We were not allowed to have Christmas trees in the barracks. A giant tree, completely undecorated, stood at the top of Camp Street during Christmastime, as if to mock us. I always passed it with lowered eyes. Nevertheless, on Christmas Eve, large bouquets of fir branches and greens stood in the blocks, despite a strict prohibition, just as if they had grown out of the floor. We really didn't know where they came from, who had magically produced them in the barracks, or where they had been hidden for so long. And lights were on them, real wax candles! Where could those possibly have come from? Yes, these too were "organized" wares, brought

---

4. Photographs of three such small objects can be found in Litschke and Schlaefer, *Der Zellenbau Ravensbrück,* one of the official camp brochures for Ravensbrück published in the GDR. These photos show a small doll, outfitted in a camp uniform of striped dress and kerchief; a handkerchief upon which has been embroidered a woman's face behind bars; and a small mat, embroidered with the date 1943.

from the spinnery, weavery, and sewing room, bits of wax that had been secretly diverted and skillfully made into candles.

As block elder, I had told my prostitutes that I didn't want and wouldn't accept any presents. First, it was forbidden; second, after such holidays betrayal among us, which led to the hardest punishments, was always very high; third, the prisoners always competed with each other to make presents for the block elder so that they could come out a little better with her. I had painfully observed all of this in other blocks and for this reason wanted to avoid any of it. In addition, I couldn't be responsible for the prisoners' making themselves punishable for my sake. A few, however, could not leave it be. It was probably those whose hearts were most devoted to me. They all knew: motivated by self-interest, I was not accepting any presents. No one could expect more special treatment from me because of presents. They all were and would remain equal in my eyes. They also knew that everyone who conducted herself respectably was treated respectably by me. Nevertheless the especially staunch and unflinching snuck up to me secretly, surreptitiously pressed something in my hand or laid it on my cot: "Please, please, take it!" How could I say no? Love knows no prohibitions. So it goes here as well. I received a pretty roll book from one of them, made from cardboard and decorated with colorful bands, which I desperately needed for my daily roll calls. The material for this had also been secretly "organized." Alas, alas, if the commandant or SS guards learned of that!

The Poles, who were completely by themselves in their barracks, held their mass on Christmas day, singing in Latin. Homemade mangers were built. And whenever there was no SS guard present for an hour at noon or in the evening, this moving religious ceremony was celebrated with dignity. A few prisoners had to hold watch behind the door of the barracks. If an SS guard was sighted, then everything was completely cleared away in two minutes, and even the wiliest SS man or the shrewdest SS overseer could not discover a trace of what had just been taking place there. Once I was able to take part in one of these uplifting and moving ceremonies through a personal invitation by the Polish block elder.[5] I felt as if I were in a church,

---

5. Here Nanda is most likely referring to the block elder of the "Polish Block," whom Christa Wagner identifies only as "Danuta" (*Geboren am See der Tränen*, 156). Danuta was a Polish partisan who was arrested for resistance work in spring 1940. Wagner describes the Christmas celebration that Danuta organized for Christmas Eve 1941: "Several green fir tree branches, a few candle ends, a gift table with picture books, odd little books put together from postcards; in addition socks, wool caps, scarves, gloves, all hand-knit or crocheted from unraveled old wool sweaters. Women, girls, above all children at the table. Danuta had initiated the plan to surprise the children in the camp with a Christmas celebration with candlelight and little presents" (156). According to Wagner, Danuta invited Nanda Herbermann to this celebration, where Herbermann met for the first time several women with whom she

and I sang and prayed together with these noble Poles, filled with ardor and devotion. God must have pitied us! He was exalted—even and precisely in the concentration camp.

---

would later develop friendships. Among these were Hannelore Fabian, an eighteen-year-old stenotypist, arrested in summer 1941 after her boss's daughter caught her kissing a French prisoner of war, and Ruth Grynspan, member of a Jewish resistance group in Berlin, who was arrested in 1937 after her group joined forces with a Communist youth group (see 156–57).

Nanda Herbermann (*left*) and her twin sister, Anna Helene or "Leni," 1928.
Courtesy of Joan Hundhausen.

Brothers Clemens Josef Herbermann (b. 1908), known as "Joos" (*left*), and Johannes Wilhelm Leander Herbermann (b. 1900), who emigrated to the United States. Courtesy of Joan Hundhausen.

Brother Joos, SS (Schutzstaffel), 1944. Joos was captured and spent part of the war in POW camps in Huntsville, Texas, and Marysville, California. Courtesy of Joan Hundhausen.

Nanda Herbermann, date uncertain. Nanda sent this photo to her twin sister, Leni, in America in 1950. Courtesy of Joan Hundhausen.

Nanda Herbermann, early 1960s. Courtesy of Bernie Herbermann.

Nanda Herbermann and siblings, November 7, 1964. *From left* (seated), Agnes Herbermann Eller (b. 1917), Sister Lamberta (Anna) Herbermann (b. 1894), Nanda; (standing), Annalies Drees, married to Clemens, Clemens Herbermann (b. 1910), Joos Herbermann (b. 1908). Courtesy of Bernie Herbermann.

Portrait of Bishop Clemens August Graf von Galen, 1933. Galen (1878–1946) was appointed archbishop of Nanda Herbermann's hometown, Münster, in 1933. Copyright unknown; rights: SV-Bilderdienst. Bild 183/R 32494. Permission granted by Bundesarchiv, Koblenz, Germany.

The courtyard of the Alexanderplatz prison, April 1933. Nanda Herbermann was imprisoned here in the summer of 1941, en route to Ravensbrück. National Archives, courtesy of USHMM Photo Archives.

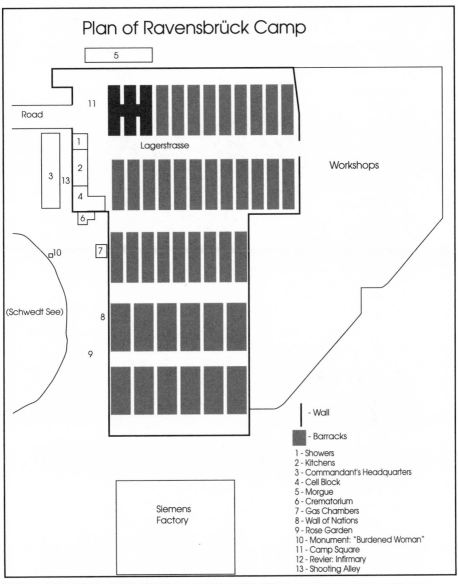

Plan of Ravensbrück Camp

5

11

Road

Lagerstrasse

Workshops

1

2

3   13

4

6

7

10

(Schwedt See)

8

9

- Wall

- Barracks

1 - Showers
2 - Kitchens
3 - Commandant's Headquarters
4 - Cell Block
5 - Morgue
6 - Crematorium
7 - Gas Chambers
8 - Wall of Nations
9 - Rose Garden
10 - Monument: "Burdened Woman"
11 - Camp Square
12 - Revier: Infirmary
13 - Shooting Alley

Siemens
Factory

Map of Ravensbrück Concentration Camp for Women, drawn by Jamison Conley.

Ravensbrück Concentration Camp for Women. Arrival of a new transport of women, ca. 1940. Dokumentationsarchiv des Oesterreichischen Widerstandes, courtesy of USHMM Photo Archives.

View of the barracks at Ravensbrück, 1940–41. Lydia Chagoll, courtesy of USHMM Photo Archives.

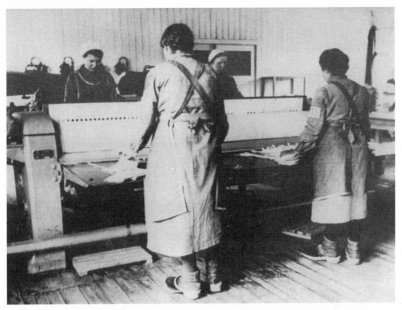

Forced labor of women prisoners in the camp laundry, 1940–42. Mahn- und
Gedenkstätte Ravensbrück, courtesy of USHMM Photo Archives.

Female prisoners at forced labor in Ravensbrück, 1940–42. These women are pushing large carts filled with construction materials along a track. Mahn- und Gedenkstätte Ravensbrück, courtesy of USHMM Photo Archives.

Ravensbrück inmates at forced labor, 1939–45. Lydia Chagoll, courtesy of USHMM Photo Archives.

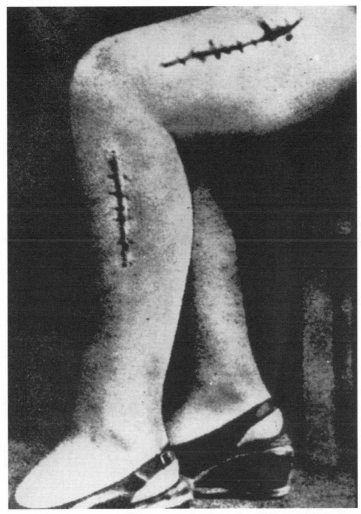

Photograph of the leg of a survivor from Ravensbrück who was subjected to medical experiments at the camp in 1942. The disfiguring scars resulted from incisions that were intentionally infected with germs, dirt, and glass to simulate war wounds; these wounds were then treated with experimental sulfur drugs. This photo was taken after the war and used as evidence at the Nuremberg trials against Nazi doctors, which were held between October 1946 and July 1947. Copyright unknown; rights: SV-Bilderdienst, Munich, Germany.

Reichsführer-SS Heinrich Himmler inspects the Ravensbrück Concentration Camp for Women, 1941. In chapter 29, Nanda Herbermann describes one of at least four visits Himmler made to Ravensbrück. Mahn- und Gedenkstätte Ravensbrück, courtesy of USHMM Photo Archives.

Women prisoners in Ravensbrück Concentration Camp. Probably a liberation photograph, 1945. Dokumentationsarchiv des Oesterreichischen Widerstandes, courtesy of USHMM Photo Archives.

Chapter 24

The sick among us

In my comments thus far, I have already reported some things about the sick among us. The ailing in my block demanded very special care and nursing as well as time to recover. Since the block was overcrowded (270 cots and at times over 400 inmates) many lay in threes on two cots; others had to sleep on the dirty floor. I tried to organize whatever straw sacks I could get hold of. We scrambled to get these; for the other blocks were also overcrowded, and hundreds of admittees were added every month. The sick people in our block also slept on the floor, at least most of them; for it was dangerous, with the constant cramps and attacks, for them to sleep on the second or third level, and above all it was difficult to transport them down from the top cots. This required tremendous strength, which we block and barracks elders did not possess. So they lay on the floor, lashing out around themselves, raving, ripping whole bunches of hair out of their heads, passing out; still others suffered heart pains, fell unconscious or experienced nervous fits during which the wood floor beneath them would quake. Poor, poor creatures! They belonged in the tender care of good Sisters of Mercy, and instead they had to waste away here in misery. Almost every night I made cold compresses; for this we used our blue towels, for we had absolutely no materials, let alone medicines.

I think with sadness of the old goblin with her pock-marked face, who, according to her tales, had just managed to survive in her meager life by begging and peddling. She peddled here in the concentration camp as well. It must have been her great passion. The pockets of her dress and apron were always filled with twine, pebbles, potato peels, needles, bits of leather, tatters, etc.; in short, everything that lay around on Camp Street or in the corner of the barracks found its way into her pockets. Almost daily I emptied these for her; for if the SS guards found it during work, she was beaten and shaken up and pulled by the hair. I wanted to spare her such torment and torture, this poor, seventy-year-old vagabond. Now I brought this old woman to the sick bay in my arms on a dark winter night, in which a storm swept around the barracks and it snowed and rained, for I could no longer help myself.[1] She was deathly ill, ranting and raving with fever. The other inmates complained and grumbled that they couldn't sleep. So I sought help in the sick bay. But we two were kicked and labeled "sow pigs" by the doctor whom we met in the hallway, only because I had asked for help for a doomed woman who needed help so badly. This "doctor" ripped the balled up little piece of humanity from my arms, threw her on the floor, grabbed her by the hair and pulled her through the corridor, until he finally showed her to the door with his boots, and I, too, flew out like a football. Both of us lay in a puddle, filthy and wet from top to bottom. I jumped up again quickly and soothed the poor little grandma, who was now completely out of her senses and no longer understood my well-meaning words. Then I took in my arms the little sack of perhaps eighty pounds, which I was just able to carry with my weight of ninety pounds, and brought her back to the barracks, where I returned completely out of breath. I sat next to the old woman on the floor for a long time during this night. She spoke, confused and frightened. I kept talking to her, but she no longer understood me. I silently prayed for the dying woman and begged God to finally grant her salvation. Even if she had erred in her ways on this earth, I knew that even through years of error, people are never entirely outside the graces of God. I asked for mercy on her poor, ill-treated soul; I am certain that she had it better in death than she ever had it on earth. The next morning she lay stretched out on her straw sack, with inexpressible and unimaginable lines of suffering on her small, white face. Now she had finally gone home, she who had never had a home on earth. For some day, all those poor people who have erred or been cast out must also go home.

Despite the danger of being kicked or boxed on the ears in the sick bay by doctors, overseers, and the brown nurses (though not all of them were nasty), I often went to the sick bay late at night to beg for help and medicines for particularly serious cases. Sometimes I succeeded. Then I was very happy, despite all the insults and mistreatments I had to submit to as a destroyer of nightly peace there: but we were used to that.

Once a week each block had a sick-bay hour. I had to appear in the sick bay as block elder with the sick inmates from my barracks, naturally in rank and file. A few of them were helped, others were not. Many who were in need of help were thrown out brutally. As a result of going barefoot from April 1 to October 1 there were many horrible and disgusting foot

---

1. The sick bay, or *Revier*, as it was called by inmates, was, for the most part, a dreaded institution in Ravensbrück, one that inmates sought to avoid at all costs. Sick prisoners were more likely to be treated with brutality than medication. It was located near the main gate; see the map in the photo section. This is also the site of the infamous medical experiments performed on inmates.

diseases. Many were covered by the ugliest rashes over their entire bodies. I had never seen so much misery before. Blood poisoning, from which the prisoners usually died, was not uncommon.

The seriously ill were admitted to the sick bay completely arbitrarily. Some of them received their "death injections" there. I can still see the tall, ugly, brown head nurse and the way she held these shots hidden under her apron! And how these poor victims struggled! They knew what was happening. Oh, they could have been helped and saved by conscientious treatment and appropriate medicines.

It was a true blessing for many that inmates were employed as nurses in the sick bay. It speaks well of the German nurse, and of German women in general, that only a very few signed on here voluntarily as nursing personnel; for even a person with an ironclad constitution could not have participated voluntarily in what went on here. Since not enough employees could be obtained, inmates had to step in here as well. They were glad to do it, for they knew that there they would be able to show many of their suffering and dying comrades-in-sorrow a last act of kindness, silently and secretly. Much that was good and noble was done by inmates for other inmates in this place.

I saw some of the poor victims lying dead in their boxes, naked, completely naked. I was able to shut the staring, sad eyes of one young Polish woman as I was passing by without being noticed. Most of the dead people disappeared without being seen by any inmate, with the exception of the prisoners who were occupied in the sick bay. We often saw the black death car come, which picked up the corpses from the sick bay and transported them to the crematorium: Lord, give them eternal peace after so much torment.

What vile doctors had to decide about the life and death of thousands of prisoners, and how they tormented these poor people and how they reveled in this torment—it cannot be described. These were true slave drivers, who have innumerably many innocents, Germans as well as foreigners, on their consciences. Involuntarily I often had to think of the noble doctors with whom I was familiar and friendly from my days of freedom. I thought of the always helpful and good-natured Dr. Vonnegut in Münster, in whose station in the Raphael Clinic in Münster I had lain so many times, surrounded and cared for by never-tiring Sisters of Mercy, and I thought of the noble head doctor of that clinic, Professor Dr. Ramstedt. And here? Fatally injured creatures with souls bleeding to death and with completely sick bodies were mistreated rather than treated, were beaten rather than comforted.

There were days of terror for the entire camp when we were told: Today a doctor's commission is coming again from Hohen-Lychen. There was a large sanatorium there. A number of inmates were chosen according to their personal files, mostly Poles, for the employment of their often beautiful, healthy bodies for medical tests such as skin transplants and experiments on the strength of bones. These victims were used as "guinea pigs" and made into cripples for the rest of their lives. It was a terrible shame, and the poor prisoners cried out in their deadly peril like hunted animals; they resisted, even fled through the barracks window when their names were called out— but still, none of this helped. I saw some of these women and girls after such violent operations. They had thirty to forty centimeter-long deep scars on their thighs, calves, and shins. They were pale and emaciated, and usually destined to die. And they knew it. Murder, murder, murder! It screamed inside me, and my heart burned with the rage and pain of this sight. Newly born children of young mothers, who had been taken into custody during their pregnancy, were killed, or the fetuses were aborted before birth. In the sick bay I myself heard such a small being crying, who was murdered fifteen minutes later. I knew German and foreign inmates who confessed to me after their delivery to the concentration camp that they were pregnant and hoped that they would be released in time. But they were not released, nor did they bear a child. Shame, nothing but shame, which released these murderers over the once so esteemed and now so unhappy German fatherland, which was under the power of criminals! Oh, it horrified me! And I knew the day would come when innocent German people would themselves have to atone bitterly for the crimes and atrocities of these terrible offenders.

Chapter 25

Clothing and laundry problems

Underwear was a catastrophe. As I already mentioned at the beginning, many inmates did not even have knickers because there were none in stock. We often wore undershirts and other underthings for weeks on end without being able to change them even once. The more inmates that were delivered, the harder it was to wash laundry. It was strictly forbidden to wash a piece of laundry, and yet it did happen secretly among those who did not want to go to ruin in filth. However, it could only be done in the summer; for then the laundry dried overnight. In the winter, however, this was out of the question. Woe were we if a piece of laundry, which someone had hung up to dry somewhere in a hidden corner, was found! We had to wear our striped inmates' garments month after month without their ever being cleaned. They were often covered in filth and slime from the outside labor, smelling like sweat and unwashed bodies. In the summer our garments were plain blue, thin, and usually faded. Often enough we stood there at the crack of dawn in the morning at the roll-call count in this insufficient clothing, with our teeth chattering.

In the summer, from April to October, there was no footwear of any kind, neither stockings nor shoes. I already mentioned how the inmates suffered from this and how many sicknesses arose from it. The stockings we received in winter often had no ascertainable color anymore. But we were happy to have at least something warm on our feet. At times there was even a good, respectable pair of stockings among them. My prostitutes fought and beat each other up over the best pair. There were also, however, reasonable and content women among them who had already gotten over their dear vanity and preferred warmth to beauty.

The distribution of the so rarely disbursed clean undergarments was a difficult and thankless task for me as block elder. After I had divided the laundry as much as I was able into three sizes, large, medium, and small, I passed them out to each row in whatever order they lay in. But my unruly prostitutes simply threw those items that did not suit them back again, and some even lobbed them at my head. Then the curses began. These curses were infectious, and though I so wanted to be just to everyone, I could not, much as I would have liked. Sometimes I had to call an overseer to help me with the distribution of the laundry in order to be able to accomplish my task amid all this wildness.

It often happened that clean underthings, which we had had to leave tied in a bundle overnight at the foot of the cot for inspection by the SS guards, were stolen. In their place there lay on the next morning dirty, completely filthy undergarments. What was there to do but to put on, with great repulsion and disgust, this underwear of another, for there was often a clothing and underwear inspection with pursuant punishment if no undershirt or knickers could be found on one's body. Yes, my hair often stood on end over so much meanness and baseness of the prisoners to one another.

It went similarly with the distribution of stockings in the winter. To pick up undergarments and stockings and aprons for four hundred people from the laundry room, and then afterward to deliver the dirty laundry back to the washing room in exactly the same quantity in bundles of twenty or thirty, was no small task. It caused me much irritation. But the distribution of stockings of the most various colors—black, gray, brown, cotton, and wool—was most particularly agitating. I tried to grant particular wishes. But I couldn't give everyone what they wanted, because there just weren't enough to go around, and so there were beatings and curses, even fits of rage and long faces and accusations against the block elder. I will gladly admit that some inmates had it badly. Some of the stockings were so short that they didn't even reach to the knee. And there were no garters to be had. Stolen strings had to help out here. Some had one long and one short stocking; others one cotton and one woolen one. Although I myself do not like to wear woolen stockings, since they easily cause itching, I took a woolen pair anyway for the sake of the others, in order to make one more heart happy again in this way.

The question of shoes was even more catastrophic than the matter of stockings. Shoes, leather shoes, only existed in exceptional cases. Over the winter we wore wooden clogs, open at the back, with some kind of substitute war material over the gap in front. This bad material ripped open again and again, and one shuffled along as well as one could. It was a torment to walk in this bad footwear, especially during the required marches, where we had to march back and forth singing in rank and file. Such a tragic image! My clogs and those of many others, which were much too large and wide, often fell off during these marches, and then we heard again: "Old piece of s——t, pay attention! Back! And march by again!" Or there were kicks and beatings. Our feet were often worn out by these ill-fitting shoes, the gaps in front sore and covered with blisters.

And then the kerchiefs! No inmate was allowed to appear on Camp Street or at work without a kerchief on her head, even in the summer. Our scalps could never air out; we always wore this troublesome scarf, even during hard labor outside. Among many inmates an all-too-early, heavy hair loss could be seen, which was caused by this. We looked like scarecrows in these kerchiefs, one exactly like the other, the only difference being that some kept themselves cleaner than others.

A clean handkerchief was very rare: if things went well perhaps once every six to eight weeks. They were simple gray linen handkerchiefs, which already looked like filthy cleaning rags after several days' use, sometimes even at distribution. The majority of inmates conducted themselves accordingly. They spit out and blew their noses wherever they were standing or sitting. If one of my trusted table mates took out her handkerchief during the meal, I often couldn't eat any more. I'd rather not discuss it any further.

Chapter 26

Camp punishments

The individual and camp punishments were extremely diverse, and often innocent people had to suffer along with guilty ones.[1] Whenever some camp theft had been committed and the inmate in question did not come forward, the commandant would order food deprivation or standing punishment. Hour after hour we had to stand at attention until we would fall unconscious—for hours during the day and for hours at night. When I let my eyes wander over my poor, tired comrades-in-suffering during this standing punishment, when I looked at their slackened faces, their terrible misery, this mass wretchedness of thousands, then all this no longer seemed like reality to me. Each individual prisoner was guilty of absolutely nothing.

If, for example, a towel or other piece of laundry was found in the sewage works, there was food deprivation for everyone, that is, no midday meal. And that is really something when one is performing the heaviest and most backbreaking labor. Anyone can imagine what the mood was like on such days, how the vices of the inmates of my block in particular surfaced in the crassest ways.

Many victims came into the detention or cell building, into the so-called death house, every week, sometimes for three days, for eight days or more; and there were even detention sentences of six to eight weeks and beyond. Some victims never surfaced again.

The most horrible of all punishments was, as has been mentioned already, the punishment of beating, the whipping of poor prisoners. I still think often of Irma, an inmate in Block II, a singular, fearless, good-natured, but also dangerous girl. She told me very composedly that she had been under the whip since childhood. Her mother had been a prostitute, her father a pimp. She had been driven out into the streets by these "parents" at the age of fourteen, in order to earn money. Woe to her if she came home without any money! And at first that happened to Irma quite frequently, for she was

---

1. Please refer to chapter 18, note 4, for a description of the punishment system in Ravensbrück.

still small and inexperienced at the time. Then the canings came raining down on her child's body, which was still developing. She told me that her body and back had actually never been free of traces of whip marks. She was beaten constantly, until "I let myself be whipped by lewd and perverse men later on in the bordello. . . . Everyone whom it pleased beat me, and now I am being whipped here in the concentration camp for the fourth time already, and I have gotten used to it." Irma was one of those who never let out a sound of pain while the whippings were being dealt out, and who also hardly spoke about it afterward. She also did not particularly suffer as a result of it anymore. It was just a part of her poor life. She herself stated that she could no longer count the number of canings she had received in her young life. This poor little mite was one of those who often had attacks. I took her under my wing, took pains to prove to her that there was indeed some goodness left in this world, even for her. Deep sadness comes over me still when I think of this poor Irma, who was certainly beaten to death, who most likely lingers among the living no more. She was visibly fading off in that direction: even then one could tell from looking at her that she had tuberculosis.

When I think back to one particular day in the camp, hot rage wells up in me even now and my fists ball up in anger. It was in the summer. The entire block of Jehovah's Witnesses was supposed to build air-raid shelters for the commandant and for the SS settlement stretched out in front of the concentration camp. This work had been especially delegated to the Jehovah's Witnesses by the nasty Commandant Kögel because he knew that any work for the cause of war is strictly forbidden by their statutes. He wanted to force them to do it. But, together, they all staunchly refused to carry out this order. The commandant, exasperated to the extreme, ordered ten lashings for every Jehovah's Witness. They all had to fall in to receive this punishment. I can still see this procession of mostly old, dear little grannies. As a unit, it can be said to their honor, they were the most respected, most peaceful, most helpful, and most patient inmates in the entire camp. Now they were being driven like a herd of cattle to the slaughtering block, in this case to the rack, to which they were tied in succession. Each prisoner was tied to the rack with leather straps for the administration of the punishment, and then it began in succession. But they prayed, silently and resignedly. They conducted themselves heroically and took these ten lashings for their "beliefs" steadfastly in stride. When they stepped out of the detention building again, they tried to retain their bearing as much as they could. Many of them crept along, bent and bowed over in pain, with their violated, old bodies. There were several women of sixty and over among them. I thought of my mother. And they were almost all mothers, whose sons were for the most part fighting on the front. But what did the bestial commandant together with his vulgar SS hangmen care about that? What did Herr Heinrich Himmler care about that? Some of the old grannies did not survive this beating.

I had a conversation with a few of them some days later. I asked them if they still had bad pains. They smiled silently, but the fire of rage was glinting in their eyes over this disgrace brought on them and their "sisters" (as the Jehovah's Witnesses call each other). I personally held the Jehovah's Witnesses in high esteem, though otherwise I certainly could not have declared myself to be in agreement with their views, for they truly understood how to love and to suffer.

In the barracks of the Jehovah's Witnesses there was never quarreling and squabbling, no theft, and no betrayal, as there was in so many other blocks, above all in Block II. They were always good and modest and friendly to everyone.

I must mention here as well that on this day, since the commandant and his accomplices had already beaten until their arms could beat no more and had tasted too richly of the satisfaction of their unbounded power over the bodies and souls of their victims, the commandant appeared in Block VI, that of the career criminals, with the inspector (that beast!) and asked the prisoners who were housed there which of them would like to volunteer to beat the Jehovah's Witnesses further. He promised them better food for a few weeks and the advantage of not having to work for a while. Two young, strong, female fellow prisoners actually volunteered to commit this disgraceful deed. I would never have thought that possible, even among the most depraved inmates. But this fact proves as well the kind of people we had to live among.

The entire camp was already completely enraged by the orders of the commandant. However, when these two pathetic creatures now volunteered for the beatings, all of the inmates became frantic with indignation and swore revenge on the two career criminals. After the administration of the canings, they could no longer let themselves be seen on Camp Street or in their own block: they were spit on and beaten up, and the prostitutes and career criminals fell on them and beat them so thoroughly that they sought refuge with the chief overseer. The result was that these two had to go to the detention building for some time, where they were treated especially well and got plenty of light and food. My prostitutes, who had participated in the retribution, however, got confinement in the dark and canings, and then had to spend a year in the punishment block. Never again did I see the inmates of our barracks in such an extreme state of agitation as on this fateful day.

Chapter 27

The lice plague

Despite my best efforts and those of the two barracks elders, our block was still filled with lice all too frequently, just as were many of the other blocks. What caused this? The laundry problem was despicable, and the cleanliness of a great number of the inmates left much to be desired. There were even a few, as I mentioned earlier, who took their dishes with them into their cots at night in order to relieve their smaller and larger needs into them purely for the sake of convenience. Although I vigorously forbade that, and often undertook an inspection late at night when everyone lay sleeping (on orders from the block director), nonetheless it happened again and again. These people were all too resourceful and shrewd. I don't know where they could hide the dishes during these thorough inspections. In addition, we had four to six bed wetters in our barracks at times: their sacks never got dry, and this caused the worst air and only gave the vermin more opportunity to reproduce.

One can imagine that inmates, who for the sake of convenience relieved themselves on their cots, also did not keep their bodies or their clothing clean. Some evenings I scrubbed the dirtiest among them from top to bottom with a brush. If there was no soap there, it had to be done with sand. Since there was no warm water in the barracks, one had to undertake these washings with cold water. These little pigs just had to put up with it. It was their responsibility to keep clean, and there was always plenty of water there. It cost me enough of an effort to have to wash these often scab-covered, stinking bodies of inmates who were, to make things worse, often significantly older than me. They were not children any more, and yet I had to take it upon myself, for everything fell back on me. And I did it with rage, though certainly restrained; for my strength and nerves eventually failed me some days as well.

One Sunday morning I was ordered to delouse the heads of the over four hundred inmates of my barracks and check every one of them for hair lice. Sunday after Sunday I had hardly had a quiet hour of time to myself, and this work really rubbed me the wrong way, especially on holy Sunday, when I so liked to be alone for an hour in the evening, or together with like-minded people from other blocks. And I of all people, who had such a pronounced repulsion and disgust at vermin and uncleanliness, had to do it! But it had to be done according to order, and I had to make a report of my successes to the chief overseer in the evening.

From morning until late into the evening, I stood behind the stool, fine-tooth comb in hand, taking up one head after another, one body after another, and searching them for these disgusting animals. Everything had to be registered exactly, so that no inmate could elude this lice control. Some of them were just crawling with it. My barracks elders helped me loyally, although one of them was usually all too glad to leave any special or unpleasant work up to others. Whenever I found hair lice, I had to send the inmate in question to the sick bay for treatment and shaving; those who had head lice were shorn bald by inmates who were employed solely for this purpose. I could protect no one from this.

In the evening there was a lot of wailing and cursing. I felt deep sympathy for the women who were robbed of their often beautiful hair in this way. Many of them no longer even possessed a comb with which to care for their hair. I had long since broken my comb up and given away the other half. Combs were easily stolen, and one could no longer buy them in the camp in 1942. Some people owned little combs with literally only three or four teeth left. How, then, could they keep their heads clean, without ever being able to really wash their hair properly? And if they got them clean, others infected them anew with the vermin. I personally never had a louse during my incarceration.

Chapter 28

Reverie

How I liked to stay sitting at the window of our barracks in the evening, when everyone already lay in their cots, and to dream of my blessed, past freedom, to give myself up completely to the memory of my loved ones. Such evening hours were certainly very rare, for the duties of the day often detained me until well into the night.

The view of the starry skies on cold winter nights, which awakened so much longing and homesickness in me, was indescribably beautiful.

The past stood up before me in large, bright images. Details came into my recollection that I never would have remembered during normal life. But the whole difficulty and tragedy of my situation lay heavily on me. And the future? What will it bring? How does one ever get out of this hell? And does one ever get out? This uncertainty is a horrible torment. Every penitentiary inmate knows: after two, four, six, ten years I will be released and then I'll be a free person again. I didn't know it. Only after my release did the Münster Geheime Staatspolizei inform me that my warrant had read: "Until one year after the end of the war." Homesickness . . . it is worse than the most horrible sickness, more painful than all other privation and neediness. Would I ever see my home again, my mother, my seven brothers, my good sisters, my loyal friends? Since mail came only rarely, and even then had often been lying around the camp for weeks already by the time it was distributed to us, I was constantly worried about my relatives. Five brothers were in the armed services, the other loved ones at home in constant danger from bombing.[1] How I brooded! And yet, the more without prospect the situation, the greater the hope. This was the hope of the hopeless.

---

1. Nanda's mention of her five brothers who served in the army refers to (the italicized name is the name by which the brother was known): 1) *August* Heinrich Ferdinand (b. 1892), a building inspector in Münster, who was drafted into the army in 1939, and was a POW from 1945 to 1947; 2) Franz Josef *Clemens* (b. 1910), an editor in Westphalia and the father of four, who was drafted into the army and was a POW in Russia until 1950; 3) Clemens *Josef* (b. 1908), owner and executive director of a cinema in Reutlingen, who was captured by

Amid this reverie and brooding I heard the prisoners groaning in their sleep, often from deep down in their chests; the restless ones among them could be heard tossing and turning on their creaking cots, still others could be heard coughing loudly and unpleasantly. The chatty and communicative ones were still whispering to each other late into the night. They probably couldn't find the peace, the sleep which was so beneficial, either. Some of them told others of their lives and deeds in the world, of their loved ones at home, and those who could never, ever leave it be, whispered to each other the dirtiest of jokes. All too often a suppressed, vulgar laugh reached my ear. And there in another corner, a poor, beaten inmate cries out in pain: the sore areas burn, and lying down is a torment. Another has a rattle in her throat and gasps for breath: a bad attack of the heart. I make one cold compress after another. There are no soothing medicines whatsoever. I stay until the attack has passed and then lie down sadly, very sadly, on my hard bed for five or six hours, hours that are interrupted often enough by some incident or by the SS guards. And in the morning it is once again my charge to be the first one up! I no longer knew real peace and privacy, which would have been so beneficial.

I was always seized with rage when the guards appeared late on cold winter nights to search the dead-tired inmates on their cots to see if they had kept some piece of underclothing on in the cold under their thin blankets. Then the inmates were dragged from their cots and beaten, the underclothes were ripped from their bodies. One lay there freezing throughout the night and could find no sleep from being so cold. But in our wretched desperation we put everything on the line and put our underclothes back on after the first night watch. To starve and to have to freeze in addition is inexpressibly bitter.

During some bright summer nights I also sat pensively at the window and dreamed while looking up into the broad, endless, starry skies. . . . Oh, home, the stars that shine upon you. . . . Then it became still inside me, completely still. The many thousands of lights shone comfortingly. And the loyal stars held their star sermons for me in their own way. They preached to me of God's greatness, His goodness and compassion. But they also preached seriously and deeply of the pathetic pettiness of human beings. I often thought that all human madness would have to go to wretched pieces under this silent, starry sky. What are human beings in the face of these universes? One becomes very humble and very mute here. But out of this

Americans; "Joos," as he was known, who was held in POW camps in Huntsville, Texas, and Marysville, California; 4) *Heinz*, or Heinrich Josef (b. 1902), a salesman in Berlin, who was a Russian POW and escaped by promising to be a spy; and 5) Heinrich Bernhard *Ferdinand* (b. 1912) who was declared missing in France in 1944; he was drafted into the Navy and served on a U-boat; some family members believe he was killed by fellow German soldiers because of Nanda, an apparent "traitor" to the Nazi cause.

pettiness one's soul grows larger in the calming consciousness that before the greatness of God even the poorest, most debased and outcast person is worth more than all universes. And so I nestled trustingly into God's fatherly arms and knew that even in the concentration camp I wasn't completely deserted. In my soul it became light and bright again, for the best light for a fatally injured and suffering soul comes not from this earth but only from the eternal heavenly heights of the great Lord. Yes, the starry skies were my sad life's favorite sanctuary.

Despite all the pain over my lost freedom, despite my realization of the tragedy of being buried alive, of not being allowed to live or breathe as a free being any longer in God's free world, I became calm and collected again when I was awakened by such thoughts during nights like these. I still had to fight with many difficulties and torments of the soul in order to come to terms with my hard fate again and again. I could not accustom myself to it, as could many of the inmates of Block II, and yet I still had to bear my destiny, bear the irrevocable with composure; I had to, for the love of God, for the love of people. I said to myself very deliberately that it was better for me to go through this than Father Muckermann; for if he had fallen into the claws of the Gestapo and SS, he never would have escaped them again. What had one of these Gestapo bandits said to me during an interrogation in Münster?: "We will rip the guts out of Muckermann's body when we get our hands on him!" Instead he could work in distant places for the benefit of a better, more moral, more honorable Germany, which we would then be able to call our home and fatherland again.

I certainly had the will to bear it, but my strength did fail me at times. The constant unrest around me, the eternal torment in my soul, my completely shaken nerves, and my weak physical constitution all played a part in this failure. The constant need to pull myself together, to exert my last energy, to have to order around the others, the horrible screaming during the roll-call count three times daily, where the four hundred inmates simply did not want to fall into line—all of this required the utmost expenditure of energy. And the environment in Block II! People without any self-control, without any culture, disorderly, unruly, gloomy, sullen, quarrelsome, defiant, disobedient, filled with hate. They had only contempt, even for those who meant well. Nothing is more terrible than having to live in such an environment, which was completely foreign to me. I was not one of them and they let me feel it. So of necessity I fell into a dangerous isolation among them.

There were few quiet and peaceful people in this barracks. They may have been silent and still, but they were also mistrustful and stolid: they had been tested too much and often deadened by life. Silently they carried a last glimmer of hope in their souls.

The completely despairing, those who believed in nothing anymore and hoped for nothing more, were totally inconsolable. The condition of their souls must have been shocking. People cannot live without hope, especially not in such a situation, and it was these poorest of the poor, who had already lost confidence in God, people, faith, home, fatherland, and themselves, who sometimes even became insane or suicidal. And if I had not had my strong, intractable faith, this most valuable of all merciful gifts, I, too, would have ended this way.

Happy was the inmate who drew the conclusion from all this insanity and horror that there must still be a world of faith, if life here was to retain any kind of sense at all! Happy was she in whose soul those stars still shone, which had stood over the happiness and dreams of her childhood. Wherever these stars still shone, there the tortured heart despaired and brooded no longer, for there this heart believed.

Chapter 29

Heinrich Himmler's "visit"

How does that sound: a visit?[1] Yes, such a thing existed, even in the concentration camp—and what a visit it was! The Reichsführer of the SS and the chief of the German police in person. This man, for whom we all felt only the deepest contempt, came with his staff and entourage and "visited" the concentration camp, which was controlled by him and completely subject to his commands.

A few days beforehand the visit was announced in the camp. Then there was a race back and forth; everything had to be cleaned down to the last iota. All barracks, the offices, the kitchen, the detention building, all the workshops were turned on their heads as if a king were coming, when it was, in fact, the devil incarnate who was coming! How I was disgusted by such a great expenditure for this one person in the midst of the worst of all wars, this person who had ruthlessly taken from us the gifts of human dignity and freedom, granted by our creator and by nature, and had debased us into animals! The majority of the inmates felt as I did, but there were a few lucky optimists among them who thought that Himmler would perhaps generously release them during his visit. We had heard in the camp that Himmler had, in a magnanimous gesture—what melodrama!—arbitrarily released some prisoners on several occasions during his visits in the years before the war. And some of my poor prostitutes believed that this luck would bloom for them, too. They even cleaned themselves up in their own way in order to please "him."

I still remember precisely that for the first time during my stay in the concentration camp, Himmler's visit, which was always connected to a tour of the camp, was scheduled for a morning. It was an awful rainy day, as we often experienced them, and huge puddles formed on Camp Street,

---

1. Himmler made at least four visits to the camp during its existence. After his visit in January 1940, corporal punishment was instituted by his order for the first time in the camp (Buber-Neumann, *Under Two Dictators*, 208).

which had been cleaned painstakingly and with great effort the previous day. In the streaming rain we inmates stood at attention on Camp Street, soaked through to the skin, hour after hour, waiting for the All Powerful. But no Himmler came. We kept on standing past noon, stood like soldiers in rank and file, literally stood until our legs poked through our bodies. What did we care about this man? But this did not matter: he was interested in us, his serfs. And it must have been an indescribable feeling for him, in his urge to dominate, to be able to rule over these thousands upon thousands of women and proceed at his own discretion.

Finally, however, everyone said: He's here! It is strange how prisoners always know everything. He had probably not even set foot in the concentration camp yet and already everyone knew: He's coming! Necks craned, and still it lasted hours before the reception formalities with the commandant, the political director, inspector, chief overseer, and the SS reporting had been completed, and we prisoners "had the honor" of being allowed to see Himmler face to face. Despite all my aversions, I looked at this face very thoroughly. Letting his eyes glide over the thousands upon thousands, he walked, followed by his staff and surrounded by the commandant and the rest of the camp administration, down the long rows of inmates set out in rows of ten. That was all. No one was released. The hopeful were disappointed again. Afterward he visited this or that block, and there were idiots among the inmates who actually felt flattered by this. I personally breathed a deep sigh of relief when it was all over. Himmler's "visit" was repeated three times during my stay in the concentration camp.

Chapter 30

Small performances

Anything that could somehow create a diversion for the inmates, or even amuse them a bit, and do them a bit of good by carrying them away from the consciousness of being an outcast for a short time was naturally forbidden, as always by threat of punishment. And yet, despite the SS guards, there were a few relaxing hours of diversion here and there. By and large the hours used for this purpose were those during which the SS and the overseers were having their parties and there were only a few guards in the camp. However, this was certainly not very often the case.

Among the inmates of Block II there were several with artistic talent. A few were inclined toward theater acting, others toward music, dancing, and movement. Naturally, I gladly turned a blind eye when I noticed that something was afoot again. Let them amuse themselves. Then afterward they would be more tolerable, more balanced, and happier for a few days.

One must imagine our life: the outcast existence, the lack of freedom, constantly having to live under the gun, the oppressive uncertainty that burdened every single one of us. Oh, how many years would they have to bear it here yet and how sad would they be? The situation was desolate for every single one of us, so without variety, so gray upon gray, like the darkest rainy day. And now, for an hour, a little bit of cheer and diversion! My prostitutes had the ability to completely release themselves from their prisoner existence at such times, and so to enjoy these hours fully. That was impossible for me. But I gladly took part in their joy externally and also participated in the various performances by reciting ballads or poems or scenes from classical dramas. They liked it best when I played Gretchen from *Faust* for them.[1]

---

1. The classic German tragedy, *Faust. Der Tragödie erster Teil*, was published by Johann Wolfgang von Goethe in 1808. The play, whose mythic story lies at the core of German cultural tradition, concerns Faust, a scientist, who, driven by his thirst for knowledge, makes a pact with the devil, Mephistopheles. When Faust meets Gretchen, a morally upright German girl, he attempts to resist her charms, but spurred on by the devil, he cannot resist

I had to do that again and again. It was also not difficult for me to imitate Hitler in his movements and gestures. That drew an applause every single time, which I had to forbid, since I was worried that the guard could hear the noise and then . . . unimaginable! We would have all been brought to detention.

The youngest of my block were great at dance performances. They danced singly or together with remarkable grace; they mimed love scenes with one another that could have certainly been shown on any stage, at least in terms of movement and expression. The accompanying costumes were absolutely fantastic. Yes, inmates manage many things a free person would not suspect. They were rich with inventions, and when they had their good hours, they were like children and their common cheerfulness was pleasant and refreshing.

Yodels were also sung. There was a great woman from Munich in our block who was equipped with an unbelievable voice and sang one yodel after another out loud, standing high atop a stool.

The SS and overseers were imitated and ridiculed, and since I have always possessed a particular inclination for such things, I also aped our inspector, who obliged me to do so through his animalistic, curious, apelike appearance. Yes, when I walked by this man, often I secretly made a face that corresponded to his appearance.

Other prisoners dressed up like men. Our knickers had to function as pants. They were able to accomplish this with few means and with such aptitude that no one could recognize them.

Sometimes the whole block was in motion, young and old, even grumblers and sourpusses danced along; they danced and danced until they fell giddily into each other's arms. For accompanying music, a comb was taken, tissue paper was laid over it, and then the rhythm and the various melodies were blown on it. And, happy to have had an hour of diversion and merrymaking again, they laid themselves, refreshed but still excited by all the romping and frolicking, down in their wretched beds.

The reader must not think that such hours in the concentration camp occurred frequently. No, they were extremely seldom and always a great risk. If someone had betrayed it, the whole block could have been taken into the detention building, especially the block and barracks elders who had silently watched the goings-on, or even participated. In the eyes of the

---

seducing her and encouraging her to give her mother a sleeping potion, which eventually proves fatal. Faust leaves her and Gretchen discovers that she is pregnant. When Faust returns, he discovers Gretchen in prison, sentenced to death for the crime of infanticide. Faust hopes to rescue her by using the devil's powers, but Gretchen, maintaining her moral stance even in the most tragic of situations, refuses his help. See the introduction for further information on Herbermann's prewar work in the theater.

commandant and the administration of the camp, every hour of happiness among the inmates was a crime.

When everything had become quiet again after such hours, I crept once again through the two dormitories A and B and observed the languishing, disillusioned, pale faces and was so happy that these outcasts from human society had once again experienced a bit of joy.

On one such evening, after I was already lying on my cot, I heard bitter sobbing. It was coming from the third level. I climbed up and asked the sobbing Toni what was upsetting her so much. Toni was nineteen years of age. "O Nanda, Nanda!" she cried sadly. I knew of her sorrow, the unpleasant situation of her family, and stroked her feverishly hot brow and comforted her as much as I could. She was happy that someone was being good to her and soon fell asleep, still crying softly. The next morning she crept up to me secretly with a small mirror she wanted to give me; she knew that mine had been stolen from me on the previous day, together with all my toiletries, from the cupboard. A mirror was a great rarity in the concentration camp, and naturally coveted by us women because it was almost indispensable. But I didn't accept it, for I knew how difficult it would be for her to miss it. And I told her that she was still younger and prettier than I and so she needed it more. I could still manage to fix my plain hairdo without a mirror and had absolutely no desire to look at myself in the mirror very often. She accepted my refusal properly, and was visibly glad to be able to keep the little mirror.

Chapter 31

Mail censorship

We all awaited Saturday with great excitement and impatience. This was the only day of the week on which the mail for the prisoners was distributed. The block elder picked up the letters, which had been laid out for each block in the roll-call room of the overseers, which was next to the office of the chief overseer. It is certainly understandable that I quickly leafed through the letters and packages meant for Block II every time, to see if something was there for me. And if there was a letter for me, then my heart beat wildly with joy; if, however, nothing was there, as happened so often—for we were only allowed to receive one short letter of fifteen lines every four weeks—then my disappointment was great.

When I received my first letter in the concentration camp from our poor, sick mother, which was so full of worry and goodness, such as only a mother can write, I cried bitterly, out of profound melancholy, for a long time. Now the good woman knew everything, and probably bore my fate even harder than I did. Once I received from dear friends a postcard with the Münster Cathedral on it. In the background was dear old Münster, my hometown. Although we were obliged to rip up our mail, I never parted with this postcard until my release. Yes, I can confess without shame that I slept with this card every night and looked at it for a long, long time every evening. "I greet you from far, far away, dear home, I greet you!" My eldest brother wrote to me regularly, reporting all the news from our large family. Unfortunately, I never received some of his letters. For months on end, I went through a period of wild emotions, when I was especially worried about everything dear to me, without receiving one single line. The letters were often cut up, whole parts were scratched out with a knife, other sentences crossed out with a thick red or blue pen mark. My mother, who always commended God's protection on us children in all of her letters, had written in her first letter the sentence: "God bless you, my child!" This simple wish of a deeply religious mother for her poor, tormented child in banishment had been thickly crossed out by the mail censorship office with a red pen, and next to this, in large letters, was the word "Rubbish!" That they would dare to debase so profoundly the most heartfelt feelings of a mother who had raised twelve children, of whom five sons were now stationed at all different fronts! But similar comments could be found in almost all letters in which the name of God was simply mentioned.

The prisoners often had only a completely empty envelope handed over to them. The letter had simply been taken out. Oh, it was shameful, and there was much crying on these Saturdays after the distribution of the so ardently desired mail! Others received perhaps two complete lines; everything else had been cut off. This also happened to me. Oh, first the joy of having a letter, and then this disillusion. It would make you cry!

And these letters often held very sad news. Many an inmate lay bent over the table crying: one's mother had died; the husband or brother of another had fallen in action; a child at home was deathly ill; a brother was missing or wounded. These evil tidings were quite diverse. Since we had some Gypsies in Block II, almost all of whom could not read or write, they came to me: "Please, read the letter to me!" So I had to be the bearer of joy and sorrow, mostly sorrow, and I had to bear it along with all of them, comforting the crying women. They all wished that I would take part in whatever was upsetting them, and I did it gladly and as a matter of course, for it helped strengthen the community spirit among us.

Just as I had to decode and read aloud the newly arrived mail of the illiterates, a whole group of people came to me and asked me to write their fifteen-line letters to their relatives, which were due every four weeks. Then they would put their three little crosses or their name at the bottom. On these writing days I sometimes wrote sixty or eighty letters, long into the night, and was inaugurated in this way into the most horrid family circumstances.

The inmates of Block II were, in some cases, also married. The husbands were often soldiers, and, because their wives were in concentration camps, they filed for divorce, as they were commanded or urged to do by the superior duty station. Then I had to draw up letters of negotiation, answer divorce claims to lawyers, smooth the way for attempts at reconciliation, etc. Yes, I became a real little lawyer in Block II, and my "juridical letters" even seemed to make an impression on the administration of the camp, to whom every letter had to be presented. The overseer who was employed for such cases simply told the inmates of my block: "Go to your block elder, she knows how such letters must be written!" This overseer, Schröers, who must have been a social worker or something of the kind earlier on, was helpful and good to the inmates, even if she was a bit peculiar and spinsterish.[1] She

---

1. Buber-Neumann also mentions an Overseer Schröers but gives no further information on her (*Under Two Dictators*, 281).

never hit an inmate. She wore a blond crown of braids around her head and looked like an older version of a maiden from a German folk tale; only the horrid SS uniform belied this.

When I had to write almost a hundred letters on a given writing day, in addition to performing all the other chores, and then, finally, sat down to write my own letter to loved ones at home, then it often happened that my handwriting was, by that time, no longer very precise. Although I made my best effort to write clearly, the SS at the mail censorship office found fault with my "illegible" script. And it wasn't really illegible but simply, as is the case with everyone who writes a lot, an exhausted script. Yet the often uneducated SS men could not deal with such a script. They confused the dative and accusative forms of "me" in their sentences and had no clue about grammar or orthography. Despite this fact, they sat in the mail censorship office of the concentration camp and were happy to make themselves important by not forwarding as many letters as possible. The inmates simply got their letters back, and, often enough, a beating, a kick, or a notice with an announcement of punishment in addition. I, too, was called one day to the mail censorship office and was handed my letter with the comment that the letter would not be forwarded. And if I did not write in a more orderly fashion the next time, I would be permanently forbidden to write. I dared to respond: "But the letter can easily be read!" This objection was too much, however. I was immediately boxed on the ears twice and crept away like an abused dog. I felt sorry for my poor relatives. I knew that they were waiting, and, although I wrote every month, on one occasion, as I learned after my release, they received not one line from me for three to four months and were already counting me among those who had been made into ashes.

During the last four months of my sojourn there, we were allowed to receive packages. Our joy over this was indescribable. My first package of butter, marmalade, cake, and so on, soon arrived. And how this cake tasted! On the first evening there was already nothing left of it. Half of it was divided out. There were so many among us who never received a package that we luckier ones were glad to divide ours out. This was completely self-evident for most of us. Now, after two years, all of a sudden I didn't have to eat dry bread anymore, I could spread it with butter, with marmalade! I felt like a queen.

Many, many packages arrived for the inmates. Some received two to three a week, especially the Poles. Unfortunately, these packages were often stolen over night. Where were we supposed to store the contents? We didn't have anything that could be locked. Most people took their packages with them into their cots at night and put them at the foot end. But by the next morning they had disappeared from the cots. The relatives had often gone short for the sake of the packages, and for this reason the loss was doubly bitter. But these incidences also show what kinds of people were housed in this concentration camp, as well as how starving the prisoners were.

Naturally, every package was checked by the mail censorship office, and the contents were searched painstakingly. Cakes, bread, and sausages were cut open, often several times, to see if something was hidden inside them. Whatever was not allowed to be sent, like smoking material, alcohol, or coffee, was not distributed. It was painful to have these so longed-for things taken away by the SS and to know that they were preparing enjoyable hours for themselves with these things.

During the last four months, I received some nourishing packages with welcome contents from my mother, siblings, and dear friends. Two books from the honorable Professor Adolf Donders from Münster gave me special pleasure. They were *Stations of the Cross* by Reinhold Schneider,[2] and a book about catacomb Christianity: to be allowed to hold a book in my hands again, I could not grasp it![3] The books were in a package the loyal priest sent to me. As a return address he had written down the address of my relatives. But books were not allowed to be given out. In the mail censorship office, however, were two SS men who had gotten to know me better through my activities in the office of the chief overseer during the last months. At first they did not want to give me the books. I begged them, but then I saw the indecision in their faces, as well as the fear of punishment that could await them if anyone found out that they had delivered books to an inmate. I turned to leave sadly, for I didn't want to embarrass these people too much, who couldn't act any differently. But then one of them called out behind me: "Here, Herbermann, take the muck! But don't get caught with it!" Happy as a child on Christmas morning, I hurried away with my two books and with the rest of what was in the package. What a blessing these two books were! I left them there at my departure, for they were always on a journey from one

---

2. Nanda refers here first to Schneider's book *Der Kreuzweg* (Kolmar: Alsatia, 1942), a short motivational story by the famous Catholic author (see chapter 6, note 1) that was published in book form. As the Schneider scholar Franz Anselm Schmitt reports, Nanda wrote to Schneider's publisher in 1946 to convey the message to the author that his book had been such a salvation to her and others in the concentration camp: "Nauda [*sic*] Herbermann, Editor of the *Grail*, who spent a number of years in a KZ, to the Herder Publishing Company, March 24, 1946: 'Tell Mr. Schneider that his book *The Stations of the Cross* was sent to me in the KZ by Prior Donders, that I always kept it hidden in my straw sack, and that it moved from barracks to barracks, from one inmate to the next. I knew whole sections of it by heart'" (*Reinhold Schneider,* 137).

3. Though Nanda's reference to a "book on catacomb Christianity" is too vague to pin down, the book in question may be *Die Katakomben. Bilder von den Mysterien des Urchristentums* (The catacombs: Images of the mysteries of ancient Christianity), by Emil Bock and Robert Goebel (Stuttgart: Verlag der Christentumsgesellschaft, 1930).

inmate to another, from one barracks to another. The old mother superior, the nuns, the teachers, like-minded people of all sorts—how happy they were! However, we did have to be very careful that the books were not found in the straw sacks! I already knew *Stations of the Cross* by heart in places and hoped optimistically to possess this work again later on. And sure enough, a few days after my release, *Stations of the Cross* by Reinhold Schneider was sent to my house by friends.

Chapter 32

Taking leave of Block II

One afternoon in late fall I was called into the office of the chief overseer.[1] This happened fairly often in regard to various inmates from my barracks. But this time it concerned me. She told me tersely and succinctly that in the future I was to work with her in the office. This was certainly a sizable "promotion" for me—but my prostitutes! It was inexpressibly difficult for me to part from them, and yet it had to be. This new assignment naturally involved my being transferred to Block I, the so-called elite block, in which only political prisoners were located. This happened on the very same day. The next morning I was to report to work with the chief overseer.

To be honest, I was afraid of this new job, which weighed deeply on my soul. A new block elder was assigned to Block II. In the evening, my prostitutes embraced me: "Our mother is going away!" Yes, very mixed feelings dwelled in me, and I, too, could not hold back tears while taking leave of my prostitutes, to whom I had become so close, to whom I clung with sincere, solicitous love. We were so accustomed to one other. "God bless you all" was my silent prayer for them, who had given me their trust, together with whom I had borne great sorrow, whom I had been allowed to bring closer to God and heaven again, and who could only accept an "outsider" with great difficulty.

In the following months I often went back to them, which of course I was not allowed to do, but the joy on both sides made the risk worthwhile. This devotion on the part of the poorest of the poor was something good and beautiful. When they saw me on Camp Street, they waved and called out from far away. Yes, my prostitutes! As long as I live I will keep my heart wide open to you poor and outcast creatures; for I have been able to look deep into your souls, and I know that you alone are not the guilty ones. The state and the general public have often sinned greatly against you!

---

1. This would have been fall 1942.

Now I lived in Block I. I was accepted by the inmates there in a friendly and loving way. In general it was very pleasant that better morals and a higher level of education held sway here. I was assigned by the block elder to a cot on the second level next to Claire, with whom I shared a good companionship. She was a Silesian who had been engaged to a Jew. For this reason she had been brought to the concentration camp. This Claire was completely at the end of her rope, her nerves were shot, and she was overly sensitive as a result of the long incarceration, but she was good at heart. During the last months she, too, worked in the office of the chief overseer.

Chapter 33

In the office of the chief overseer

I began my new assignments with a very heavy heart. And the assignments were quite varied. It was a shame that Chief Overseer Zimmer was transferred out of this camp only a few days after my summons to the office.[1] Though she did have a very heavy hand, she was by far less evil than many others. She was thought of by the prisoners as a curiosity, and she had a fresh, red-cheeked face, a very round body, and was a good fifty years old. I noticed right away in the first few days that extreme tension reigned within the administration of the camp. The commandant, Kögel, that horror-inducing beast, was transferred, and a new commandant, SS Senior Storm Trooper Suhren, not quite as brutal as his predecessor, replaced him.[2] In addition, the infamous demon, Chief Overseer Mandel, and the above-mentioned Chief Overseer Zimmer were summoned to another concentration camp. Chief Overseer Langefeld, who had previously been chief overseer in Ravensbrück, came back to our camp. I was taken over by her. Among the overseers, too, there were suddenly all kinds of transfers. The "most trustworthy," usually the most brutal among them, were commanded to go with Commandant Kögel and Chief Overseers Mandel and Erich to the Jewish camp near Lublin and

---

1. Emma Zimmer worked as a chief overseer in the camp until 1943 when she was fired. Irmgard Heike presents two possible reasons for her firing: either she was thought to be too old to continue her work there (she was fifty-five), or she was held unfit for the job because of her predilection for excessive drinking on the job ("'. . . da es sich ja lediglich um die Bewachung der Häftlinge handelt . . . ,'" 228). Though Nanda has a good impression of Zimmer, Buber-Neumann disagrees. She recounts several episodes during her time as block elder over the Jehovah's Witnesses, when Zimmer, who seemed to have a particular hatred for the Witnesses, abused and bullied them in an extreme way (*Under Two Dictators*, 232). Zimmer was transferred to Auschwitz along with Mandel.
2. Fritz Suhren became commandant of Ravensbrück around November 1942, when Max Kögel was transferred to Majdanek, along with some of his staff, including Chief Overseers Mandel and Erich. Suhren, who had previously served in Sachsenhausen, remained commandant through 1945. He was executed by the French in 1950 (Feig, *Hitler's Death Camps*, 459).

to Auschwitz.[3] The poor, poor people who were delivered into their hands there! Many new faces came into our camp.

On a single day, approximately thirty new overseers arrived in the camp. They had simply been transferred there by the employment office whether they wanted to or not. The chief overseer was horrified by their appearance and their manner and conduct. "Herbermann," she said, "You look cleaner and more pleasant in your inmate's uniform than these women over here." Yes, there was really not much to be said for these new overseers. They introduced themselves to their new "boss" in a disorderly fashion: they had messy hair, as if they had just gotten out of bed, and were eating and making noise and were completely undisciplined. There were young girls of seventeen or eighteen years of age among them, who up until then had been housemaids, factory workers, and so on, and were now extremely unhappy to have to treat poor inmates inhumanely in a concentration camp. A few of these simple girls poured their hearts out to me later and cried bitter tears. I came into contact with them quite often as a result of my work at that time, and some of them came to trust me, for they knew what I had to accomplish and submit to there from five o'clock in the morning until oftentimes ten o'clock in the evening, sometimes even late into the night, and a few times without ever even getting to bed at night.

It can be said without exaggeration that the most capable inmates had to do the main work in the administration of the camp, for they were usually more intelligent than all of the employees and officials of the camp at all. Often, as we worked in the front of the office, our heads would slump forward from overwork, misery, and exhaustion, from hunger and weakness; and sometimes I held in my balled fists the cursed paper on which the camp commandant or his representatives had written down the most horrible punishments for the smallest offenses, if they were offenses at all. If, for example, ten to twenty-five canings were dealt out for two or three stolen potatoes, or food deprivation for three days was ordered for one single stolen turnip (and how good they tasted raw!), or detention was given for the theft of a piece of boracic soap, or hours-long punishment standing, or even confinement in the dark (I knew from experience what that meant!), then a well-justified rage welled up in me again! For the most part, I knew the inmates whom these punishments awaited, and how I would have liked to have spared them!

Yet my typewriter had to click and clack, typing these verdicts and

---

3. By "the Jewish camp near Lublin," Nanda is referring to Majdanek, located right outside the town of Lublin, Poland. According to Germaine Tillion, women inmates from Ravensbrück had been shipped to Majdanek for execution in March 1942 (*Ravensbrück,* 242). Nanda is writing here of fall 1942.

noting them down on the index cards, verdicts announced the next day at the official "Proclamation of Punishments." Today I can confess that, since everything in me bristled against so much injustice and meanness, I simply ripped and threw away some report forms together with the punishment decrees filled out by the commandant. Too often I couldn't do it, since it could have easily attracted attention. Other punishment verdicts I hid, setting them under some files, where they may have lingered until the liberation of this concentration camp. In any case, I dared to do it, and, truly, my heart beat faster and I had sleepless nights because of it. I never spoke with a single person in the camp about it. If I had been betrayed, I would have been beaten to death!

How many inmates were driven to the slaughterhouse, to the block, every week! Poor, unhappy sacrificial lambs! And I had to accompany them into the cell building, the house of horror and death, for the carrying out of this punishment! I walked along next to them crying. Then I was exhausted for the rest of the day. This assignment weighed on and tormented my soul so heavily that I could not find peace any longer at night, all the more so when the chief overseer displayed unpredictable moods aimed particularly at me. She must have felt my silent, and therefore all the more intense, rebellion, and my great contempt for her and her kind. I couldn't "kiss up" and didn't want to, not here. No, it was beneath my dignity! I would rather let myself be treated like a slave by her. I think that she wanted to be rid of me; one day she transferred me to the camp inspector, under whose command the so-called division of labor for the entire camp stood. This was the curious, repulsive man who constantly obliged me to make faces. I now had to work together with him. This, too! To him the inmates were only "filthy pigs," "pieces of sow," "brainless cows," and "old pieces of s——t." Now I had to retain a bit of composure in his presence. And so I forced myself to do that, too.

From now on, only numbers upon numbers swam around my head day and night. I sat at the adding machine, calculating and counting until I was completely exhausted; for it was no easy task to have to account daily, in detail, for the eighteen to nineteen thousand inmates, and for where every single one of them was working, until, at the end, the exact number of inmates of the camp was reached (particularly because this number changed daily through new admittees and departees, through transfers to the sick bay and the detention building, and through flight and death). The horribly puffed-up, hollow simpleton of an inspector didn't take care about anything and couldn't have accomplished this work himself. He only gave his signature. Though I was still sitting next to the chief overseer in the office and still experiencing each day far too much of all the horror committed against all the poor helpless creatures for my tormented mind, at least I didn't need to copy these punishment verdicts personally on the typewriter and note them down onto corresponding index cards. Not having to do this anymore was a great relief to me, as was not having to lead the poor inmates who were destined for canings into the detention building, which was so agonizing for me. Oh, yes, this was a salvation! But still, my present work did not suit me at all either. The year as block elder in Block II had certainly been exhausting and full of sacrifices. But, despite all their wildness, their licentiousness and vulgarity, I must honestly confess that I would much rather have gone back to the prostitutes, among whom I sometimes found a good (if troubled) heart. For how could a heart not harden, not turn to stone here in this hell, among beasts who have not earned the right to be called human beings?

Chapter 34

Comrades

Probably the most comforting thing in Block I was that I found a few inmates there with whom I had a natural affinity. There was the good Mirzel. This young, completely innocent creature, being held here as hostage for her father, was an angel of gentleness and goodness of the heart; I often wondered how she, who was still so young, had remained true to her nature in this horrid environment. Despite physical weakness, she was a strong individual with infinite trust in God and deep inner faith. She prayed a lot. Unfortunately she got very sick and lay in the sick bay for many long weeks, where she yet remained when I was released, and I still don't know today what became of her. On the morning of my release—she had heard about it even in the sick bay, for something so unusual naturally passed through the camp like wildfire—she stood waving, unspeakably sadly, at the window. I would have liked to take her in my arms and carry her back to her good mother in Holland.

And Alfredine, how can things be with you? She had been the secretary of the Borromäus Association somewhere in the Saar region, spent three years in the concentration camp, and was then released, but not to go home.[1] She had to keep working as a civil servant in the office of the camp. Alfredine was as gentle as Mirzel and had wonderful, black eyes that blazed bright with indignation when something unjust and violent occurred in her surroundings. She was very reserved, was only together with Mirzel, Käthe, and me in her few free minutes, and often, when our time on Sunday allowed, we hid ourselves in some very lonely corner, secretly and without being seen, amid cold and snow, and intimately said our Sunday mass by heart.

---

1. Carlo Borromeo was a Catholic saint who had been the archbishop of Milan. The Borromäus Association is short for the Association of St. Karl Borromäus for the Distribution of Good Books, the largest Catholic organization for education of the populace in Germany, founded in 1845 by August Reichenberger in Bonn.

Käthe, "sweetie," as we called you, you too belonged to our group, although as a kitchen inmate you were housed in Kitchen Block III. Employed as a social worker in Krefeld, she was removed from her post and taken into custody for a disparaging comment about the Third Reich. She, too, was in the concentration camp for many long years. She was one of the most faithful followers, a noble person with a pure soul who always remained true to herself, was always friendly, always good, completely anchored in God. On the second-to-last evening before my release, I was together with her again for a short time, and we spoke of home. After her release I received a letter from her from Frankfurt. She, too, had lost all her belongings in air raids and so moved to Jülich. Where can she be today?

And you, dear, brave mother superior of over seventy years of age, you who always squeezed my hand so tightly whenever you saw me and didn't want to let go. How often I was shocked by your appearance. You were doing more poorly everyday, suffering immensely. I often offered up my suffering silently for you, because I realized that the burden you had to bear was simply too much for your old, already completely collapsed shoulders. But you were completely resigned, and in your childlike piety you mastered it, despite all this. A great goodness of heart and serenity illuminated your quiet eyes.

And Maria, you dear, faithful creature! Shortly before my release you sat innocently in the house of death. You were charged with having accepted a piece of margarine from a kitchen inmate. How much homesickness you had for your husband and children who lived in Thorn. You always spoke of them. . . . You were a true comrade, always anxious to relieve another's lot, to stand by others helpfully. Are you sojourning back at home again?

There were also some inmates in Block I who were possessed of a monstrous desire for admiration, who liked to distinguish themselves, so that their damaged and demeaned personalities might somehow come into their own again. They were unhappy with themselves, with any kind of work, and suffered under the sickly delusion that every other inmate wanted to do them wrong. But one has to understand them. They had already been exiled for so long, a few for over ten years already, and they had to bear so much unearned sorrow, so much horrible debasement, for the sake of their beliefs and ideals. And some of them had played an important role in public life before, earlier on, while now they were buried alive.

Our block and barracks elders were good. In particular, the barracks elder Resi showed a touching goodness and strict fairness toward everyone. With her there was no party system, which, unfortunately, was otherwise quite noticeable in Block I: some inmates suffered from it quite a bit. This also disturbed our daily life together. Of course, it can easily be understood that like minds are attracted to one another. There was no betrayal in Block I and there would have been much to betray there. Some people in the block had a masterful understanding of how to organize provisions for themselves, which the rest of us never got close to. We knew about it, and we all had the same hunger and appetite for something better, for sandwiches and so on. Many things were smuggled out of the SS kitchen for these inmates. But we don't want to count it against them, since most of them were in the concentration camp for much longer than we who only spent two or three years there.

I confess that my nerves were also often completely run down as a consequence of many sleepless nights and the work in the office of the chief overseer, which was horribly draining on my soul, and that, despite all attempts to pull myself together, I was sometimes irritated and bad-tempered. Of course I reproached myself then, seriously resolved to not let myself go any more, but this resolve failed at times. Again and again I begged for courage and strength. I had so many worries about my loved ones. And yet I could only recommend them for God's protection over and over everyday. What had our late father[2] written to me shortly before his death:

Why should you fret?
Safe in God's retreat
Are your heart and soul . . .
From his hands,
Whatever they may spend,
Accept it, dear daughter, all whole . . .

Yes, I wanted to accept it all whole and continue to remain patient, brave, and resigned. And with God's grace one really is capable of everything. Here everyone bore a heavy cross; the great difference between fundamental views was only that some bore the cross with Christ, others, however, bore it without him. And those who bore the cross with Christ had it easier, for God himself helped us at it. However, those who bore it without him, and that was the majority of inmates, had it harder than was bearable for human beings. They lapsed into bitterness and complete desperation. Yes, these poorest creatures suffered in the depths of their souls something even worse than any economic and material need, even worse than any horrible, physical mistreatment. In the end, anything can be borne (I experienced this deeply) if one does it for the sake of a great love; but life, especially a life in the concentration camp, cannot be mastered if one does not understand the

2. Nanda's father, Diedrich Ferdinand Herbermann, was a tax collector in Münster and later in Hamm, Westphalia. He was born in Glansdorf on November 8, 1863, and died in Hamm on January 2, 1932. He married twice: his first wife, Maria Anna Laumann, died in April 1902, nine years after their marriage; his second wife, Maria Anna Helene Hülsmann, whom he married in October 1902, was Nanda's mother.

meaning of such horrible suffering, and if strong faith and love no longer burn in one's heart.

I can truly say that I encountered the great boundlessness of God's love hourly behind the bars and fences of the concentration camp. It was as in the desert, where God let the bread of heaven rain down on his children. If it was painful for us to do without the great mercy of the living Eucharist, God could nevertheless be felt in spirit among us. And because I was allowed to experience the whole abundance of God's goodness in this hell, I can only bless these years behind bars. I know deeply that this darkest stretch of my life was not without profound meaning. A current of energy for the future will always flow out of these years of the most tormenting suffering into me and hopefully also into many others. Whoever has been allowed to master such years in God's grace will be able to deal with anything else as well, since he knows to whom he must turn.

Chapter 35

My brother's visit

Personal visits in the camp were something quite extraordinary and rare. The consent of the Central Reich Security Office in Berlin was required for this, and it was only granted with difficulty. I had never counted on a personal visit. And yet I was allowed to experience this startling surprise and pleasure.

In October 1942, I was taken away from work by an overseer who was armed with a pistol and led to the political administration of the camp. What did this mean? What good could have been expected to come out of this? I did not think of a visit; I thought that a telegram (telegrams were not handed out but read aloud to inmates in the political division) would notify me of the death of my long-sick mother or the death of a fallen brother, for my family had not had any news of our youngest brother, who served with the Reich Marines, for many long months.[1] For this reason we were fearful and in constant worry for his life. My thoughts were occupied by such suppositions on the way to the political division, which was located outside the walls of the camp. The overseer was not allowed to tell me what it was about. Perhaps she did not know either, and I did not dare to ask. My heart beating fast, I finally arrived at the room in question. I was received by the SS outside the door. I was shocked when all of a sudden I was standing face to face with my brother Heinz.[2] The memory of this reunion will always remain with me.

My brother was also deeply moved by the excitement and anticipation that preceded his visit, and then by the prisoner's clothing in which he saw me there before his eyes. I can still see today how his chin and all his facial muscles trembled. Still, he controlled himself and told me whatever he could report during such a reunion under the guard of the SS. I myself said nothing. Trembling, I could only bring across my lips a few questions

---

1. Nanda refers here to Heinrich Bernhard Ferdinand.
2. See chapter 28, note 1 for information on Heinz. He married Elizabeth Maria Ruth Klinkert in 1930, and their daughter was named Bianca Maria Monika.

that burned on my soul. I asked after my mother, my brothers, my sisters. For twenty minutes we were allowed to see and speak to each other. He even showed me a few pictures of the family and of his child Monika, whom he loved so much.

Then he encouraged me, gave me hope of a speedy release: "If you are not free by Christmas, then certainly by Easter! We'll leave nothing untried." I can still hear these promising words, which I clung to as if I were drowning. I received new hope in my seemingly hopeless situation. He also told me that he had already come to the gates of the concentration camp in May of this year, but that the commandant had refused a meeting with me. And yet, he had finally managed (coming from the eastern front and finding himself on a duty journey for a few days, which included a few days of leave) to get all the way in to me this time. How profoundly thankful I was to this brother, who wrote to me from the east after his visit: "The best thing about my days of leave was that I got to see and talk to you!"

The twenty minutes were over. We had to take leave of one another. It was difficult and painful, since this was my first encounter with one of my loved ones since my arrest.[3] My brother left the room with a heavy heart, and when the overseer then came to accompany me back, and I left the building with her, there he stood waving at me from the nearby lake, until I had disappeared from his sight. With permission from the overseer, I was allowed to turn around once more, but not to raise my hand for one last greeting. So I could only speak one last farewell with a crying, aching heart. Goodbye to my home, to freedom! Oh, I had to be brave, bear my lot, bear myself up, take my heart in both hands. It was certainly a brave life which was demanded here.

In the following days, various overseers who had seen my brother, and naturally immediately learned who this visitor was, asked me about him, for he had always exerted great forces of attraction on women.

The entire camp took part in such a visit, some in honest compassionate joy, others full of envy. And when I told them, in my joy, that it was apparently still possible that I might be released, they laughed at me. How hurtful that was! Oh, and my heaven came crashing back down on me. Nevertheless, the hopeful and encouraging words of my brother still stood before me, and I still hoped, hoped, hoped despite all!

---

3. Twenty months had elapsed since Nanda's arrest and thus since she had seen any family members.

Chapter 36

Dignified endings . . .

During the first days after the visit of my brother, I was simply of no use for my work, which demanded the most rapt attention. I despised it more than ever. I would have liked to have lain down in a green meadow and dreamed and dreamed. . . . And why should I torment myself here, ruining my health? So that this hellish institution could keep on running nicely and smoothly according to regulations? If these people could have looked inside me and guessed my thoughts I would have been summarily shot without delay. But thoughts were free even in the concentration camp! "Who Can Guess Them?" This song of freedom was one of our most often sung prison songs. Freedom of thought was the only thing left us.

I had to pull myself together, keep on working, but I just couldn't function properly. Halina was an especially loyal helper to me in these days. We frequently substituted for one another and helped one another without attracting attention. Halina was a good comrade. Do you still remember, Halina, how a sympathetic SS man once gave us a few cigarettes? And how we smoked them outside late at night, completely hidden and in secret (although twenty-five lashings stood on a cigarette!), and then thoroughly brushed our teeth so that no one would notice? Are you back at home again with your little boy? After my release I wrote to your son and told him about you. Did he ever receive those lines? You, too, are among those whom I would like to see again on this earth!

And you, stout, little, good-natured, but angry and self-conscious Wanda, I think about you, too! Sometimes during the last months you spread a piece of bread with organized margarine for me, and then sprinkled organized sugar on it for me as well! You had a sister in the same camp who worked in the SS canteen, and sometimes bits of leftovers came down to you. I will never forget that you, as a Pole, still maintained a good camaraderie with us Germans. But we did the same with you all too, right? Do you still remember, Wanda, how you played the "fly on the wall" of the chief overseer once, out of great worry over a fellow inmate, and I was supposed to betray you to her? No, there was no betrayal among us! Rather, one suffered for the other, although at times small frictions and tiffs did crop up among us. But that is unavoidable in any place where ten thousand of the most diverse kinds of people are cooped up together on one single square kilometer, not of their own free choice, but by force.

Marianne, a girl from Vienna, also belonged to our work detail, functioning as one of the two "camp runners," as the inmates were called who had to convey the orders and arrangements of the chief overseer to the camp. She also had to pick up the prisoners from their individual barracks and bring them to punishment reports and announcements, to the political offices, to the records department, and so on. In the last few months of my stay there, she was even allowed to gather together the departees. But there were usually only one or two of those a week at the most. And what significance does that have with an inmate count of approximately twenty thousand, where eighty to a hundred new inmates often arrived weekly?!

You camp runners also had the disturbing assignment of picking up the poor, resistant "guinea pigs" for the SS doctors from their individual barracks. I can still see the lists before me, on which the names and inmate numbers were written. We who worked in the offices up front sat or stood bent over these lists in unobserved moments, our faces full of horror and rage. And then we even saw the lists of those sentenced to death, the list of those who were shot. They were mostly Poles who had been tormented, mistreated, and exploited in the concentration camp for years already, and only after these years of torture did the death sentence ensue from Himmler and his hangmen. Did not all of these pitiable women confront death (which now only meant salvation for them) with unheard-of composure, like old heroes? At their sight I always had to think of the martyrs of our holy Church, and they were truly martyrs of their homeland, their people, their faith. What profound joy, what beautiful resignation these pale, haggard, and care-worn women wore on their sorrowful faces. It was the joy of a better world.

Once I was able to do a last act of kindness for one of the women who was sentenced to death, something that still makes me happy today. The woman in question was a Pole, a mother, who had been languishing in the concentration camp with her daughter for many long years already. Why had this noble woman been sentenced to death? Her husband had been a Polish officer; she didn't know where he was or even if he was alive. This was the case with many women. They knew nothing of their husbands, who had fought for their Polish homeland. They knew just as little of their children, their relatives, who had been brutally kidnapped by the SS and the Gestapo, never to be seen again. In the house of this mother a search had taken place, and weapons had been found. And now, after years of banishment, came the order of Himmler to shoot this mother along with other inmates. There were nine of them who were shot by the SS on this evening.

A young Pole came to me at noon on the same day, begging me: "Nanda, you must help, please, please! Mother and daughter must see each other once more!" The two were naturally housed in different blocks, in order to make their incarceration all the more unbearable. Since an overseer appeared at the same moment, I rashly whispered to the Pole, "Go away quickly! I will think about how I can help and then I'll come to you!" I thought over where I could now bring mother and daughter together so that it would not be noticed and came to the decision that it would best be done on the outermost end of the camp. In any case I had to and wanted to take the risk upon myself. Since I wore the red armband, which gave me the right to walk through the camp alone, this was possible. But woe to me if it were to become known! Twenty-five lashings, six weeks of confinement in the dark, and a year of the punishment block would have been in store for me. Yet in the face of the imminent death of this poor mother and the grief of this even poorer child, I saw it as my human duty. As soon as I had taken care of the pressing work at my typewriter, I went on my way. First I went to the barracks where the mother was and took her, who was so composed, so brave and strong, and so resigned, to the place I had chosen for this last farewell. Here she hugged, kissed, and blessed me, repeating the words again and again, "How can I ever thank you?" I remained mute and could not speak, for my soul was deeply moved. Stuttering, I could only bring forth the words, "Think of me in heaven!"

Then I ran away quickly to get the daughter. She already knew what was happening, for I had been able to get a message to her. She stood and waited. "Hurry, hurry, come to your mother!" The poor child was shaking all over her body: "Oh Nanda, my mamuschka, my mama!" I could not comfort her and cried with her. When we had arrived by her mother, these two good people sank sobbing into each other's arms and embraced one another with an ardor otherwise unknown in life. Then this heroic mother blessed her child again and again, made the sign of the cross on her brow, mouth, and breast: "Be good! May our Father in heaven protect you!" And this mother, who would be in eternity in two hours, comforted her daughter with complete calm and composure. Only a saint could be like that, I thought. What must have gone through this mother's head, having to leave her crying child alone in this horrible world, in the hell of the concentration camp. And at the end she said so sincerely: "If you should ever see your father again, my child, and your siblings" (she named three names), "then tell them that I am always and will always remain with them."

Unfortunately I had to admonish them, for time was running short. It would also have attracted attention in the office if I had remained away any longer. Once more, they embraced and blessings were given. Oh, it was beyond human strength! I couldn't watch it any longer, this heartbreaking pain. And again I thought: "Yes, the kingdom of heaven suffers from violence. And only those who need violence usurp it." God in heaven, what difficult tests you put your creatures through! I took the loudly sobbing child, whom the mother entrusted to me at the end, and brought her quickly back to the block. Poor little Sascha, in this hour your young heart died as well.

Now I went back for the mother, who blessed me and asked me to bless her, and brought her to her block, for the very last time. There stood many of her Polish fellow prisoners, and they took her in their arms. Two more short hours and this brave woman was fetched for death.

I will never be able to forget her. Even today, in remembering these hours of suffering, I am deeply moved and must interrupt my writing with thoughts of her. How she looked after me: "I won't forget you up there!" Those were her last words to me. And she kept her promise, I know that. Little Sascha clung to me with childlike love in the future. Whenever it was possible for me, I snuck over to her everyday for a few minutes in the evening. Through these last commonly experienced minutes with her mother and me, she had become my little Sascha, too, a piece of me. Is she still alive today? And if so, where can she be? Did she find her father, her siblings? Or must she go on tormenting herself through this hard life, abandoned and homeless, she, who already had to suffer too much in her youthful years.

Stefan George speaks in one of his books of "many endings without dignity."[1] In these months, I must use these words again and again in reference to the criminal men of the Third Reich. But an ending in the concentration camp was often full of dignity, more dignified than that of the men who initiated and were guilty of and ordered the endings, even though they made use of the word "dignity" at the most inappropriate moments.

---

1. Stefan George (1868–1933) was a famous German poet who hoped to renew German civilization through the cultivation of a new poetics informed by the French notion of *l'art pour l'art*.

Chapter 37

Jews . . .

When I was delivered to the concentration camp in August 1941 there were still very many old and young Jews there; there were whole barracks filled only with Jews. What these creatures had to be subjected to in terms of vulgarity, torment, perversion, and meanness cannot be described in words. The hate sown in the hearts of readers of the most disgusting of all newspapers ever published in Germany, *Der Stürmer,* published by the obese Gauleiter of Nuremberg, Julius Streicher, had fallen on fertile ground among the SS and overseers here, above all among the administration of the camp, and bore its shocking fruit here in the concentration camp.[1]

Not only were beatings and kicks, to which we were all subjected, committed against these helpless creatures, not only were dogs sicced on them; no, whether old or young, they also had to perform the most difficult of all work. I will never be rid of the image presented to us for weeks on end: old Jews, as old as the hills, straining in front of an old roller, which ought to have been pulled by at least two horses, huffing and puffing, with bare, wounded feet, with bleeding hands, their tired faces care-worn and furrowed with suffering.[2] And these women were for the most part unaccustomed to physical labor. There were filthy rich Jews[3] among them, half-Jews: absolutely everyone was driven into prisons and concentration

---

1. Streicher, the Gauleiter of Franconia, founded *Der Stürmer* in 1923 and continued to edit it until 1945. *Der Stürmer* became renowned worldwide for its horrible anti-Semitism and was particularly infamous for its cartoon depictions of Jews, its pornography, and its sensationalist, fabricated stories of ritual murder. Because of its tabloid-style sensationalism and its shocking tactics, *Der Stürmer* became very popular and influential among the German public, reaching a circulation of 500,000 in 1937. Its lurid visual style provided both a backdrop and an impetus for the Nuremberg Race Laws of 1935 (statistics from Wistrich, *Antisemitism,* 250–52).
2. This roller is still in the camp and is shown in many photographs from the Nazi era.
3. Herbermann's regrettable terminology here reveals an unexamined anti-Semitism, typical of her society, despite the sympathy for the plight of Jews also expressed here. See the introduction for a discussion of Christian anti-Semitism.

camps in those fateful years because of their "non-Aryan descent." A few of them were converts. I like to think back to a Frau Professor R., who, despite her advanced age, was still beautiful and had wonderful, dark, shining eyes. I was able to converse with her a few times about spiritual matters. She was Austrian, and her spouse was not unknown in cultural circles. She, too, had already lived for years in complete uncertainty about her husband and children. She never complained and was never cross, but bore her horrible fate with exemplary spiritual greatness.

In the course of the year 1942 came the order from Himmler that the camp had to be "cleansed" of Jews. Then the large Jewish transports began. The torment of uncertainty, the fear of what was to come stood in the eyes of these people. Yes, what became of them? They were loaded into cattle cars amid the insults and growls of the SS, these poor people, martyred and persecuted to death, who so wanted to die, simply in order to not have to bear this life any longer, for it was beneath all human dignity. Did not they, too, by nature and by virtue of the Creator, have the right to a bearable life on earth? From what I know, they were all shipped at that time to Lublin and Auschwitz, where large Jewish camps were located. I hardly believe that one of them is still alive.

Chapter 38

Sick transports . . .

I never quite made head or tail of these sick transports, which began all of a sudden in 1942.[1] In the concentration camp one could, if one kept one's eyes open, often catch a glimpse behind the scenes, but to get to the bottom of everything was still impossible for me, despite my job in the office of the chief overseer, where many things were revealed to me. It is clear, however, that hundreds of prisoners, chosen by the SS garrison doctors and the commandant, were transported from the camp to some kind of institute, where they were probably first abused as guinea pigs and then given lethal injections or murdered in the gas chambers.

It was always upsetting when such a transport was put together again, a motley assortment from every block. Many of my prostitutes from Block II were among them. Usually the inmates in question were physically ill and infirm or weak and therefore could not be used for full work duty. Why should they be nourished with potatoes and turnips or stinking cabbage in addition! Away with them! The sorts of people who fell victim to these transports cannot be described. Murder, murder in this realm as well, mass murder in every possible form! I am convinced that the majority of the people whose lives were taken in this way could have lived for twenty more years and then some and could also have accomplished something, for the majority of them had performed hard labor up to the horrible day of their transport out! The people in question were not only sick with tuberculosis or prostitutes infected with syphilis. No, there were also healthy people among

---

1. Nanda's suspicions about the so-called sick transports were correct. In 1942 the prisoners who were condemned to death were sent to institutions (such as Bernburg) that were involved in the euthanasia program, or to Auschwitz (Gutman, *Encyclopedia of the Holocaust*, 1227). Other methods for killing prisoners included shooting them in the neck and giving them phenol injections. In early 1945, a gas chamber was established at Ravensbrück, in which over two thousand people were put to death (1227). These sick transports, which, despite their name, often carried perfectly healthy persons, were also called "transports noirs" (Tillion, *Ravensbrück*, 74).

them, such people who, as a consequence of the unbearable existence they were forced to live out here, perhaps had an attack of the heart or nerves once a month, brought on by all the torment and privation and excitement put upon us daily by the commandant and SS guards. There were inmates among these doomed individuals who had lived and worked side by side with us for years, who had never had an attack, but whose bodies were weak and not particularly robust.

The screaming at the crack of dawn during the loading of these doomed individuals, this fear of death, when all of a sudden at two or three in the morning the command was given that various inmates had to report for transport, people who previously suspected nothing, but now suddenly learned with horrifying certainty what awaited them—this screaming still rings in my ears today. The poor people at the Möhnetal Dam must have screamed in a similar way in 1944 when, after the bombing of the dam, the water mass roared over their towns and villages with a speed of sixty kilometers per hour, and the uncannily high waves, which they attempted to flee, engulfed them.[2] And how they were loaded up! As with the Jews on the cattle cars, insults like "you rotten pigs" or "infected rabble" were shouted at them as a last farewell! That was the background music to their trip toward a lonely death. One can only understand the world according to what one experiences. After all that my eyes had to look at in dread during these years, I understand the final cigarette and cognac of the man who is sentenced to death.

Why are people so horrible and vengeful toward one another? Wherein lies the sad secret of why people are so inhumane toward one another? Poor brain, it cannot let these tormenting questions rest in the face of all the horror done by people unto people here! Why, why, why? Oh, there is no other key to this sinister riddle other than the one that lays hidden in the depths of God's omniscience.

---

2. In May 1943, the RAF targeted three dams on the Ruhr River: the Möhne, the Eder, and the Sorpe. The Möhnetal Dam held 140 million tons of water for industrial and household use and to generate electricity. When the RAF bombed the Möhne on May 16–17, at least 1,200 German civilians died as the waters rushed over the destroyed dam, drowning people who were caught asleep in their beds (statistics from Snyder, *Historical Guide to World War II*, 598–99).

Chapter 39

Heydrich murdered!

Heydrich, Heinrich Himmler's deputy, had been murdered in a village in Czechoslovakia.[1] The perpetrator was unknown. What did the Geheime Staatspolizei and the SS do? The village was set on fire and the ground was razed, while all male and female villagers were arrested and taken into custody. One day, then, the entire female population of this place was delivered to the Ravensbrück Concentration Camp. The eldest villager was almost eighty years old. This happened at the time when I was still block elder in Block II. We in our barracks had already learned that new admittees had arrived. We heard a wild noise. What could possibly be going on out there? Other admittees came silently and without a sound. What could this shrieking mean? Then one of the camp runners came to me with this assignment: "You are to come up to the front immediately; I have to get all the other block elders as well. You are to help control the new admittees who are resisting the orders of the SS! Bring the barracks elders with you!" So there were finally some admittees who did not let themselves be intimidated, who dared not to bow down to the power of the SS! I was curious about the "new ones," who were, in my eyes, extremely courageous.

---

1. Reinhard Heydrich (1904–42) was the head of the Reich's Central Security Office and the chief architect of the Nazis' plan to exterminate European Jewry. Heydrich was the first to order the concentration of Jews in ghettos and the mass deportations of Jews out of Germany and Austria. He also organized the Wannsee Conference in 1942, where top Nazis laid out plans for the "Final Solution." In 1941 Heydrich became the Deputy Reich's Protector of Bohemia and Moravia and moved to Prague to speed along the process of deportation and extermination there. In May 1942, Heydrich was riding in an open car (flouting security measures) in the Czech village of Lidice when two Czech agents threw a bomb under the car and began shooting at Heydrich. Heydrich ultimately died of his wounds on June 4, 1942. As Nanda describes, the Nazis took extreme measures of retribution for Heydrich's assassination. They executed all the men of Lidice and deported all the town's women, having burned down the entire village. The killings extended well beyond the bounds of Lidice to Prague and Berlin as well.

When we block elders arrived in front of the office of the chief overseer with our barracks elders, many women were lying on their bundles on the ground, cursing and crying. They lashed out whenever the SS guards got close to them, allowed nothing to be told them, and did not follow the commands to go into the office in order to be entered onto the long, long lists of inmates who found themselves in the concentration camp. We inmates quietly came up to them and consolingly led them one at a time into the office. Despite a great expenditure of understanding and goodness, it was not easy to appease them. Didn't they have the right to defend themselves against this arbitrary arrest? We were successful in appeasing them to a certain extent, but a small portion of them kept on raging.

Now they had to undress themselves completely, then they went into the delousing cabin, then into the bath. I still remember well how they refused to take off their clothes and underthings, how ashamed they were to stand there completely naked before us and before all of the guard personnel, and before the disgusting SS doctor, who had come in, too. I felt this shame profoundly along with them, and tried to comfort them with the fact that we had all experienced the same thing. Much was required to quiet these crying women. Almost all of them wore a necklace with a Madonna on it beneath their clothes. They clung to these medallions as they undressed and did not want to give them up. They were then brutally ripped from their necks. And the crying and sobbing recommenced again and again, especially when the heads of some of them were shorn. The commandant blustered about with his brutal voice in the midst of this, threatening detention and other punishments.

When we learned during the following days what these newly delivered women had already been through and experienced, how they had all been ruthlessly taken from their houses, away from their husbands and children, and loaded up, going from one prison to another, not knowing where they were and if they were even still alive, a wave of rage went through the entire camp. Yet we were all equally helpless and powerless, could only comfort one another and help each other to bear up, and keep on asking God to make us strong enough for this fate and to stand by us in his almighty power.

Chapter 40

Little black-haired Gypsy girl . . .

And when you have buried everywhere
Free thought, individuality—
When no one has a dream anymore,
The flood closes in tremulously.

—HERMANN STEHR

These verses of Hermann Stehr often went through my head.[1] No, they no longer had any dreams, the authorities and powers of the Third Reich. They only knew murder, horror, power, greed, oppression, and deprivation of the rights of those who had fallen victim to their power. They were no longer human beings.

I, too, like so many others, feared that I would completely break down, physically and mentally. I had reached the point where every evening I wished that I would not have to live through a new morning. But morning after morning the sinister camp siren sounded shrilly over our barracks. And our parole was always, again and again: down from the cot, down from the sacks, filled so miserably with straw or meager wood shavings; a thoughtful, deep breath; and then a new, long, cruel day to be borne again. What would it bring? Who of us would be led away into the house of horror today? Who would get a caning? Who would get the death injection? Who would no longer lie among us during the next night?

---

1. Hermann Stehr (1864–1940) was a German author of novels, novellas, and poetry, notable for the deep current of religious mysticism that runs through his work. Because Stehr's work was sanctioned by the Nazis—Stehr himself even held a post in the *Reichsschrifttumskammer* (the Reich's chamber of writing)—it is somewhat odd that Nanda uses his poem as an epigram here.

Yes, my thoughts wandered fearfully in this way every new morning. They accompanied the wonderful, tranquil sunrise, which should have brightened even our darkness, should have warmed us through, since it could not be forcibly kept from us.

In the camp there was a sick, lovely little Gypsy girl. Sometimes, when I dared to make a forbidden visit to the sick in the sick bay, I liked to stand at her grievous sick bed for a few seconds as well and look into this young, sorrowful, beautiful, and harmonious little face. She lay there like a little, black Madonna with unfathomable eyes shaded by extremely long lashes.[2] She was always content, she always smiled at me. She lay in a huge hall, together with many other sick people, bed upon bed, row upon row. The air was miserable. No invalid could heal in there.

One day my little Gypsy was dead, too. She had probably also been given the death injection. All of us who had been especially fond of this child assumed this was the case. This time I could not find out for certain. Aside from a few young inmates, an older Pole also worked as a nurse in Sick Bay II. She sacrificed herself in a touching manner for her fellow prisoners and did them numerous little acts of kindness, especially in their extremely lonely and tormenting hours of death. She had (no one knew how) an entire little Madonna in her possession, which she held in high esteem. And she told me, beaming, how the poor, dying creatures became quieter at the sight of this Madonna, and prayed with her silently.

Now, I knew from experience that the dead bodies were usually stuck into coffins or boxes as quickly as possible, and I really wanted to see my little Gypsy once more. Cautiously, I crept around the sick bay. Just don't get caught! I held a little wreath of forget-me-nots hidden under my apron, which I wanted to bring the dead child as a last salutation. Inmates had brought these flowers back from outside labor, with permission of a friendly overseer, for the service room of the block director. I quickly bound together the little wreath, as I had often done as a child with my siblings in the meadow. I bound my tears into the wreath as well. I thought this little wreath would look especially good on the little black-haired head. And even if she died in the concentration camp, she would have a little wreath of flowers. I succeeded with my intentions. The old inmate's nurse, with whom I got on well, probably suspected my desires. She also knew how very attached I had been to this child. When she saw me going secretly back and forth in front of the sick bay, she waved to me; I scurried quickly inside, and saw the still-open box in the corridor. There lay my little, black-haired friend, naked,

2. Belief in the "black Madonna" is a tradition dating back to the twelfth century. There are both a famous sanctuary in Czestochowa, Poland, and a shrine in Vilna (ca. 1500) to the black Madonna.

completely naked, without any pillow. Even in death she had nothing upon which to lay her young, but already so tired head! Yet, you shall have this wreath, you, my homeless, abandoned, locked-up, black-haired little bird. And it fit well. Secretly I made the sign of the cross, prayed an Ave Maria, and sped away, deeply moved. The brutal garrison doctor entered the sick bay with two overseers at exactly that moment. But the old nurse, always on her guard, quickly shut the corpse box, which was picked up within the hour and brought to the crematorium.

Chapter 41

It was enough to drive one mad . . .

It is a good thing that one has yearnings. I, too, had to have something during these dark years I could yearn for. It was so horrible, day after day, month after month, in rain, cold, and snow, under the burning sun, hungry and thirsty, waiting, always just waiting for salvation. One lay there as if on a huge pillow into which one slowly sank deeper and deeper. The cold was so extreme that our noses almost froze shut, and even tears, which hung in our eyelashes, would freeze if we didn't constantly open and shut our eyelids. Our feet and whole bodies were so stiff that we could no longer move. All around there were comrades-in-suffering, also waiting and staring up to heaven. Many, so many, gave up and waited no more.[1] But how should you understand it, you who weren't there! Such a thing cannot be described. Sometimes I wished that someone would come and beat me over the head with a board so hard that all thought, all of this tormenting thought, would cease. But no one performed this beneficial act on me. Mentally and spiritually I had to go on bearing this ordeal. It was really enough to drive one mad.

And my fellow prisoners! How they crept along with their often staggering, emaciated, and mistreated bodies! How many times did one of those entrusted to me in Block II stand before me: "Nanda, I can't stand it anymore; I'm going to end it!" From my own aching heart I tried to give them some courage again, to hold them up, to prevent them from suicide. But this encouragement often became difficult for me. And when I didn't succeed in dissuading them of their intentions, then I sacrificed my few hours of sleep and prayed, watched, and listened to see that one of the poor creatures didn't secretly escape through the barracks window in order to make a fast end

---

1. Some prisoners "gave up" actively and threw themselves against the electrified barbed wire fences, committing suicide. Others simply gave up the will to live and were identified by other prisoners as "Schmuckstück," a German term meaning literally a piece of jewelry. This term is the equivalent of "muselmann," a word used in other camps to refer to an inmate who is near death from hunger, exhaustion, and despair.

to her life on the electrically charged barbed wire, which had happened so many times.

Once very late, around midnight, I raced after Erna and caught her just in time, one could say a few meters from death. She lashed out, raged and screamed at me: "Leave me in peace! Even you cannot save me! I don't want to live anymore!" Then I spoke with her very calmly, full of understanding and sympathy, I cried with her, and I was so happy when, after a difficult inner struggle, she did decide to return to the barracks with me, on my arm. From this night on we two had a secret together, of which no one else knew. For suicide attempts there was a punishment of the hardest confinement in the dark, which lasted for weeks. This Erna was over forty years old and had already been locked up for over fifteen years. She was very difficult to keep under control, and no longer believed in anything.

Here a strong faith, in connection with a profound trust in God, remained the only thing that could hold us and bear us up. But whosoever did not possess this faith, or had lost it here, had lost absolutely everything and remained in the claws of despair, without hope, apathetic, indifferent, given over to insanity.

Chapter 42

Hope for salvation

It was February 1, 1943. Again I was called away from work by an overseer, and again I was taken, trembling and faint-hearted, out to the feared political division. I had no idea what awaited me. What was happening today? Oh, God, stand by me! This fear is dreadful. How many things could happen to me and how horrible they could be!

When I had arrived at Political Director Herr Borchard's, I reported according to regulations in rigid posture like a Prussian soldier (horrible when women must play soldiers!): "Inmate Herbermann, #6582." But the political director nodded at me benevolently. My fear receded then. It may be said in defense of this political director (who had come by way of God knows what unfortunate circumstances into the SS and then, as political director, to the concentration camp) that he was always good and friendly to the prisoners and that he really didn't belong in this society at all. He was always businesslike, never used a vulgar word, never beat an inmate, but rather helped if he could. Yes, people like this did exist, and in the administration of the camp to boot; but for this reason it is not astonishing that this Herr Borchard did not get along well with the commandant and the inspector and the rest of the administration, and that obstacles were laid in his path wherever they could be. I only wish that this man may be spared a heavy lot. All the prisoners gladly dealt with him over personal matters.

Herr Borchard now disclosed to me that a telegram had come from the Reichsführer with the inquiry as to what I "propose to do in the case of a possible release, and how I would conduct myself in the future in relation to the Jesuit priest Muckermann." Herr Borchard also commented that this was something quite unusual, and that an inquiry regarding an inmate rarely came from Himmler. He thought that I could count on being released in the next few weeks for certain. I was ecstatic and could hardly collect myself on account of my joy and blissful excitement. Would this life, this hell, really come to an end for me soon? Would I really be able to see my loved ones and my home again?! I couldn't grasp it.

Now I received a pencil and paper and had to sit at the desk in Herr Borchard's room and deliver up a statement to be sent to Berlin telegraphically that very day. The legal adviser, SS man Jacobi, also a proper man who did not see the prisoners as fair game or as mere cattle, also came in. The two men talked over my case with me again, advised me to explain various things. I began to compose my statement. I probably don't need to mention that I explained that I would of course be ready to take on any kind of work. Oh, I would have broken stones and carried coal outside for freedom; for freedom no price was too high for me.

When I was finished with my statement, I showed it to Herr Borchard and Herr Jacobi, who approved of it. The whole thing was then dictated on the typewriter, and I signed this so decisive piece of writing with my name. By now I had flushed over and over again from pure excitement and joy. Herr Borchard said: "But now you look much different than before, when you first came in here." And both gave me the assurance once more that I could certainly count on my release within the next fourteen days. To be allowed to have such confidence, this was a happiness beyond compare. The overseer with whom I had to work at that time, Overseer Laurenzen, came to take me away. This overseer, with whom I got on by and large, was very young, and for that reason still quite unsteady; in addition, she possessed an overwhelming amount of ambition to be something special. Unfortunately, she became a leader in the division of labor very early on, with power over the entire camp organization, something that (characteristically) had only a negative influence on her. To me she was generally humane (though often moody), and she let me work independently. She often dealt out kicks, but to my knowledge had never delivered canings. She was constantly in a feud with Chief Overseer Langefeld. These two hated each other very much. This made my work extraordinarily hard, and this hate among the overseers often made my life in the office of the chief overseer one of torment, since each one wanted me to betray the other. Yes, even inmates were abused for this purpose, and unfortunately some of them let themselves be easily bribed by nice words and fawning for this purpose.

This Overseer Laurenzen now picked me up. She had waited for me for a long time because of the urgent work I needed to accomplish and had rung at Herr Borchard's door a number of times to inquire about what was keeping me so long. Now she had gotten curious, and, glowing, I explained to her what had happened. She was not happy for me, but immediately objected: "I won't let you go! Who will do your work?" She wanted to make an application for me to keep working for her as a civil employee in the camp after my release, which sometimes happened with released inmates, since intelligent workforces were lacking everywhere. But I never would have agreed to it. I honestly toiled in the camp, and I performed some essential work, but to let myself be caught again was out of the question for me. "Frau Overseer," I explained, "Another inmate will be found who can do the work just as well, perhaps even better than I can!"

Naturally, my fellow inmates were also very interested in what had gone on in the political division. The good and selfless were honestly happy for me, and waited with me day after day for the hour of freedom. But many did begrudge me my hope and my great and justified prospect of freedom. "Why should you get out sooner than us? Just don't put on airs! Some of us have been here much longer than you: do you think you're an exception?" Oh, that hurt and made a deep impression on me. But they were all so unhappy and so despairing that they only thought of themselves, and such a thing as happiness for others no longer existed for them.

Unhappy they were in life, and unhappy in death. My profound depression and hopelessness, at times even after this event, naturally did not disappear with their objections. But despite everything I held my confidence high during the first fourteen days. Oh, perhaps a new life would really begin for me, a resurrection from the dead would truly await. Such a tormenting impatience gripped me that today I don't like to think back to those weeks of waiting, when I simply could not summon up any more energy. My strength was used up. Now, when the gates were supposed to open for me, I really only perceived for the first time that I had lived through these years of the most onerous incarceration only through the utmost expenditure of energy.

I couldn't sleep at night, dreamt with open eyes of freedom, of my loved ones; I imagined my past life, my future, and made plans. Was salvation really before me? I was lonely in these weeks before my release, more lonely than ever before, since I was now the only one among the eighteen or nineteen thousand inmates of the camp who suspected that freedom was waving at her. What goes through one's mind in such circumstances! I fixed my eyes firmly on my future, built plans, built everything from the bottom up in my mind. Yes, I built castles in the air, as everyone who has been robbed of their freedom would probably do in such a situation of waiting, which truly wears one down.

I had to pull myself together at work, in my dealings with my fellow prisoners, and under the SS guards. And I had to be proper, very proper. I couldn't do anything incautious that could attract punishment. I observed my every move, in order to avoid building a wall between myself and that enticing freedom, waving at me from afar.

Chapter 43

How did Himmler's telegram
come about?

My brothers and friends had, as I already mentioned, left no stone unturned in their attempt to get me set free. My oldest brother went through many difficult appeals for me, sending petitions to Berlin; and my brother Clemens went to Berlin and contacted lawyers there, who were in his opinion qualified to achieve something for me. But I had already been told during the interrogations in Münster: "Stay off our throats with the damned lawyers!" Together, five brothers, all of whom wore the clothing of the German army, made petitions, as did our dear old mother. But all efforts were for naught; nothing helped. During my incarceration I of course heard absolutely nothing of these efforts on the part of my brothers and friends.

Now, however, my brother Heinz, who had told me during his visit to the concentration camp that he would achieve something, had assured me that I would be freed, if not by Christmas, then certainly by Easter. He had met someone in Berlin who exercised great influence with the all-powerful Himmler. He, too, made many inroads, was untiring, made use of all his best abilities and all his ingenuity, and he was able to make it all the way to Himmler's adjutant, who promised him that he would have my file sent to him from the Central Reich Security Office, the head agency in charge of all Gestapo headquarters. Himmler himself supposedly looked at my file, according to statements his adjutant made to my brother. In any case, his telegram was proof of this. I am eternally grateful to all of my brothers for this loyalty and action for me. Through the many petitions attached to my file, they all helped pave my way to freedom.

Chapter 44

The last weeks

It is not hard to imagine that I now lived in constant expectation, day and night. If my fellow prisoners had taken almost all hope away from me, especially after the first fourteen days had passed (during which the question of my release was, after all, supposed to have been decided), then the political director always gave me hope whenever he occasionally appeared at our office. When the circumstances and those present allowed, he nodded at me confidently: "Herbermann, it will turn out all right for certain! Be patient!" Oh, yes, patience . . . patience is probably the most difficult and seasoned of all virtues, and how easily a broken heart, too often disappointed, falls back into impatience!

These last weeks of my life as an inmate are still as clear to me as the first ones, especially the dark and tormenting nights of having to wait for the decision. When would I learn my fate? Since Saturday was the actual release day, I waited week after week for Saturday. Some people in the office were feverish with anxiety along with me. The Overseer Gallinat, who sat together with Chief Overseer Langefeld next door, came to my table sometimes and said: "If you are released, I'll bring you to the train."[1] Every released inmate was accompanied to the train station by a guard, since we didn't know the way, and the camp lay far out from the town, which was so picturesquely located. This Overseer Gallinat was a strange one, as they say, somewhat eccentric and more unpredictable than any other overseer with whom I had contact in the camp. Her character had apparently never fully developed, and she had no ideals, which could have evened out her temperament. This explained her care-worn, gaunt, bitter face. When she began to rage, to scream, to beat, her voice cracked and she sounded like

---

1. Buber-Neumann refers to a Gallinat who was the second chief overseer, beside Langefeld, in Ravensbrück at this time. While Langefeld was in charge of the camp's internal affairs, Gallinat was, according to Buber-Neumann, in charge of outside camp affairs (*Under Two Dictators*, 263).

a fury. One minute she was friendly, the next she was suddenly mean, so mean and nasty that once, after she had beaten some inmates terribly, a few prisoners could no longer contain themselves and attacked her, screaming, "German whore!" after her. I don't know if this word could be applied to Overseer Gallinat; for as far as I could observe, she lived in seclusion (in contrast to many other overseers, who for the most part were quite morally and ethically depraved). Since it could not be ascertained which inmates had attacked and insulted the overseer, and they did not voluntarily report themselves, there was a camp-wide punishment again: standing punishment and food deprivation. For me, food deprivation was not the worst thing, for my stomach could take in almost nothing anymore. But the standing punishment, hour after hour, was horribly difficult for me. After I had performed heavy outdoor labor, I suffered constantly from bad back pains. These back pains had increased so much during the last months that after I had sat for a long time, I often could no longer lift myself up from my writing chair and crept around like an old woman. I'm still weighed down by this suffering today. In the doctors' opinion, it is a disease of the dorsal vertebrae.

I still want to mention two good inmates with whom I came to-gether day after day during the last months. They were Jehovah's Witnesses, both white-haired grannies of almost seventy years of age. They had left their husbands and children, ended up in the concentration camp for their "beliefs," and had lived a pathetic but heroic life here for over a decade now. They were always gentle and friendly. The work of these two consisted of cleaning the offices of the chief overseer, the inspection room of the overseers, the corridors, office toilets, and so on.

For curiosity's sake, I frequently talked with them about their "beliefs." There must have been something to it that held them so tightly to their views, since everyday they only would have needed to sign a form with a statement of their withdrawal from the sect of the Jehovah's Witnesses in order to escape from this hell. These preprinted certificates lay in piles of hundreds in the office of the chief overseer and never, ever diminished. Rarely had a Jehovah's Witness signed such a form. I can personally only remember two cases, two young Dutch women who signed their statement of withdrawal. As much as I have to say against their views and their beliefs, they remained steady in their outlooks, they relinquished nothing, and they voluntarily endured superhuman things even at a very advanced age. Somehow they were primitive, and their outlooks didn't hold pace at all with life in the restless world outside. Yet, while they were versed in the Scriptures, they didn't give my objections to various passages in their Bible any currency, and they were obstinate about it in addition, so that it was impossible to debate with them objectively.

But their disposition remained cheerful, and there were few inmates in the camp who were so pleasantly disposed as these Jehovah's Witnesses. They were animated by a trust in God that could move mountains. In their barracks there were no arguments, no envy, no grudges, not even the disgraceful betrayal of inmates to one another. One of the grannies, who came from Swabia, was so congenial and had such a fresh, good-natured old-lady's countenance and bright, lively eyes, which could still shine in a dear and cheerful way despite all the horror. When she saw me, she called me "Nannerle!"[2] Her comrade was, in contrast to her, quite sickly and deteriorating; the long incarceration had taken all her strength away. But she, too, had this wonderful deportment, although one noticed that a profound grief consumed her. Once I found her sitting crying in a hidden corner, praying to herself: "Oh, God, help me! Help my children!" I was so sorry for this lonesome granny. She couldn't be helped. Still, that evening I gave her a sizable piece of cake from a package that had just arrived, for she constantly suffered from great hunger. Then her sad furrowed brow cleared up somewhat, at least for a moment.

I must mention something else here as well, which may sound unbelievable to the ears of the uninitiated. An overseer (I don't want to say her name) had discovered during the last weeks of my stay in the camp that I sometimes composed poems and was somewhat skilled in the use of a pen. She was totally clumsy at it and had not even properly mastered German grammar. It must have been unpleasant enough for her as a married woman (or had all self-respect vanished in the camp?) to approach me and ask me to draw up her love letters to one of the leading men in the camp, to compose "love poems" for him, and to introduce myself in this way into their unpleasant and despicable relationship. Soon, however, she was coming to me and demanding my help with all kinds of large and small assignments brought about by this indefensible love story. Although everything in me resisted writing letters and poems of this kind, I finally had to give in in order to avoid subjecting myself to new acts of violence and to her caprice.

Here I was able to look into a moral abyss which could not have been more abject and depraved, even among the prostitutes in Block II. Disgust often overcame me and made me shake when I heard certain things. I, as an inmate, was supposed to play the love-letter-writer to one of the most evil monsters in the entire concentration camp, to a man who made use of only the most vulgar curse words in relation to the inmates, so that even the most out-and-out prostitutes, accustomed to the crudest of words, shrunk from him!

And wasn't this overseer at all ashamed in front of me as a prisoner,

---

2. "Nannerle" is the diminutive form of Nanda's name, typical for the southern German region of Swabia, where this granny was from.

since I was now forced to look so deeply into the filth of her truly dirty life? No, I would not have been petty, had the love in question been great, pure, and unrequited. But in this case everything, absolutely everything, was founded on the most repulsive sexuality. Yet I had to put a good face on a bad job, and so I wrote these letters as a slave inmate. Nevertheless, I never touched erotic or suggestive things in drawing up these letters. I told this shameless overseer that whatever she felt was missing in these letters, she should add to them herself; my conscience would not allow me to answer some of the points made in the letters from this man. Naturally I had to pay for these objections through mean treatment and persecution during work. But I took it, in addition to so much else. There was no other way for me. I had certainly learned in my bitter school of suffering to bear patiently whatever the will of the Lord imposed upon me; but to weigh down my conscience with vulgarity and vileness, I would never give myself up to that, even after ten years of incarceration. Perhaps this overseer did finally grasp this fundamental attitude of mine in the end.

Oh, when would I finally be allowed out of this hell of depravity, out of such an environment, into purer, fresher air, into the freedom of God's wide world? Four whole weeks of anxious waiting had already gone by since Himmler's telegram. It was already the first of March, and still the decision about me had not come down. Life became more unbearable to me with every passing day.

Then, on a Saturday, I received a letter from my eldest brother, dated March 6, which was stranger than ever before, but out of which spoke a very certain confidence. The parts of the letter (I smuggled it out as documentation when I was released) relating to my possible release had been scratched out with a sharp object. But with the help of three inmates, I was able to decode these parts anyway. I had been well trained under the Gestapo and SS in respect to this. The following sentences were scratched out: "You can rejoice with us. Fate was well-disposed to us . . . If you need any clothing for the trip, please let us know what. . . . Finally we received good news from Berlin." My heart beat wildly. Freedom, freedom, how this hope filled me all over again!

I received another letter, equally as confident, from the east, from my brother in Berlin. The parts not scratched out, but rather badly erased, filled me with a newly justified hope to be released soon. Oh, you blessed, tormenting, exhausting hope for freedom! To see my sick mother again, my dear siblings, my good friends. I pictured it all. I would enjoy the vast, beautiful earth anew, have flowers in bloom, see the halls of my home again, as well as my Münster, beloved above all else!

One morning I had noticed a little flower between the boards of our barracks, which had stretched its bold nose between the laths. It was as if it wanted to be on the lookout on behalf of the entire kingdom of flowers to see if the SS was still enacting its horrors in this area, and if the poor inmates were still overfilling the camp, or if the moment had already come when the love of nature would be allowed to make its appearance here as well. When had I last experienced a flower growing and observed it with melancholy for this long? It had been from the barred window of the prison in Münster: an inconspicuous, pathetic little flower in a crack in the prison wall. I had observed it with such attentiveness! And had . . . envied it! It was free after all, like every single one of God's creatures should be, and it was allowed to and could bloom, even in the most hidden of places. And now I would really be able to take real pleasure in flowers again!

And how wonderful it would be to be allowed to open a door with a lock again on one's own, to sit in a soft armchair again, and at a cheerfully set table. Could I properly conduct myself with a fork and knife at all anymore? Hadn't I completely forgotten how in these years? With an unappetizing wooden spoon we bolted down our even more unappetizing and stinking midday meals. When I smelled the stench that arose from these buckets of food as soon as they were opened, I often had to think of the time when, as a child at my grandparents' during vacation, I had seen how food was prepared for pigs. How often we sent the food back to the kitchen so that everyone would not get sick, and then kept on starving.

But how skillfully other inmates could peel their potatoes with the stem of the wooden spoon! I could never muster the manual dexterity to do this. The skins always stuck to my wooden spoon, and I had to remove them again and again in order to be able to keep peeling with the dull spoon at all.

Now all this self-denial, going without, and improvisation was to end all of a sudden? I was to be allowed to live again, in a cultivated and refined manner? To sleep in a bed made up in white? To be truly warm in my bed and not have to freeze day and night? Oh, how I wanted thankfully to enjoy all this, which had been so self-evident before, and never again to be insulted, beaten, or tormented! Never again to have to stand at attention before an SS guard who was often only eighteen or twenty years old! Never again to be afraid of being thrown into confinement in the dark, never to have to stand for roll call again, or to stand for punishment. Never to have to go barefoot! Never more, never more, to be beaten and tormented so innocently, and to always be allowed to live among good, dear people! To have a house again, a home! Oh, God, how beautiful that had to be!

And I could finally attend church again, hear holy mass, which I had done without for so long—yes, even a high mass in the beautiful Münster Cathedral with organ accompaniment and choir singing, and, above all, to take part in the graceful strength of the sacraments, which had been denied us here so completely in our profound suffering, even in death!

And to be allowed to feel the love of being surrounded by dear, concerned people, who belonged together, to be asked if one has any wishes, when one feels troubled or sick. How spectacular that all must be! Oh, it wasn't possible for me to imagine all this happiness, and yet it stood before me, day after day, night after night, hour after hour, until finally, finally the longed for morning of freedom dawned.

Chapter 45

March 19, 1943

On the evening of March 18 (I had had a lot to do yet in the office) the political director, Herr Borchard, came to me at my desk and asked, "Herbermann, where does your brother live in Berlin?" I answered this question, but found it very peculiar. Did this possibly have something to do with my release? I didn't dare ask a question because there were various overseers in the room, and this question could have been badly misinterpreted. Asking questions did not befit an inmate. Inmates were only to answer when they were asked something and to obey. Their rights went no further.

When Herr Borchard went out the door then, smiling at me, it seemed to me as if he would gladly have told me more. I snuck up behind him unnoticed, and the darkness that had already set in was very opportune for my purposes. There stood Herr Borchard and asked, "So, what is it?" Now I had the courage to verbalize the question that was tormenting me: "Have you heard any news? Will I be released and when?" "Yes, you'll be released!" was the blissful answer. "Oh, do tell me when it will be, Herr Borchard," I begged him so sincerely. "But I can't tell you that. Soon, soon!"

The position of prisoner forbade me from pressing Herr Borchard any further. I knew well that he was not allowed to tell me, that he had already told me too much. And I give him credit for this humanity yet today. My heart was beating wildly, and I could only take care of the rest of my work by expending all my energy. Home, home! Everything was racing through my poor head. I went into the block where almost all of the inmates already lay in a deep slumber. But Claire, my cot neighbor, woke up. I reported to her what Herr Borchard had said. She said, "Oh, what does that all mean? It's still nothing certain! You'll still probably have to wait for weeks or months!" Finally we both came to the conclusion that it would not be tomorrow, but perhaps on Saturday, although it was highly likely that it would not be until April 20, Hitler's birthday (people due to be released had already been held back until then for some time now, so that their release would look like a large, generous gesture on that day). But it was all only melodrama! Finally we wished each other good night, and Claire, overtired from her exhausting work, sunk into a deep sleep, while I was still tossing and turning and couldn't find peace. Oh, if only it were the last of all the tormenting 777 nights of my long incarceration!

When I sat in the office again at five the next morning, pulling myself together with all my power to get anything done at all, I felt how Chief Overseer Langefeld and Overseer Gallinat scrutinized me when they appeared around six o'clock. A few of the other overseers did the same. I suspected: soon, soon they will tell you! And truly! At seven o'clock the overseer came to me at the typewriter: "Herbermann, what crime have you committed this time?" I was astonished, dumbfounded at that moment. "Crime, Frau Overseer, I haven't committed any crimes!" The sky crashed down on me at this moment. And when she saw me so upset and disappointed, she spoke those liberating words: "No, you haven't committed any crimes! Put your work down! You are released!"

A racket and romp now rose up in the office. But I stood there exactly as I had in the hour of my arrest, frozen into a statue, and simply could not comprehend this blissful fact all at once. Only when my fellow inmates, who worked together with me in the same room, surrounded me, hugged me, and cried loudly—only then did my first liberating tears come, too.

And a deeply moving farewell began, together with heartfelt wishes on all sides. And again and again I heard: "If only I could go with you!" My heart was breaking with grief. They all had to stay; I alone was allowed to go. That, too, was so very difficult.

But we were not left all that much time for this effusion of feelings. An overseer had already come in and told me threateningly: "You already know well that from the moment in which you have learned of your release onward, you are not allowed to speak to another inmate. Otherwise you could still be charged to stay here." And, directing herself to the other inmates, she ordered: "March! Get to work."

A twenty-year-old, simple girl with shining red hair, a dear, shy thing, was released at the same time as I was on this morning. As she told me, she already had a year of prison behind her for intimate acquaintance with a Pole, and had then come into the concentration camp for about a year. She, too, had received canings, and her hair had been shorn a number of times. Her curly hair was now approximately five centimeters long again. She looked like Struwwelpeter.[1] Later she also told me that she had worked in the country and had gotten along well with the Poles who had been

---

1. Struwwelpeter is a reference to an illustrated children's book, beloved in Germany. The book was published in 1845 by Heinrich Hoffmann, a physician who wrote it as a morality tale for disobedient children. Struwwelpeter is a little boy who refuses to have his hair or nails

occupied there, but that nothing had ever occurred between them. Poor, beaten, violated creature!

We two happy beings now stood next to each other in front of the office of the chief overseer, as was so common in the case of releases, and waited for an overseer, who soon showed up to accompany us to the so-called effects division, where we could receive our own clothes again. As we went across Camp Street, the work roll call, which occurred every morning after the roll-call count, was already over, and the many columns were moving out toward their hard labor.

If someone was released, the whole camp knew about it after five minutes. When my prostitutes ran into us on Camp Street, despite all prohibitions there were hellos, calls, waving, and wishes, so that the overseer who was accompanying us said: "They've all gone crazy today!" No, they had not gone crazy, they were just devoted, these outcast and pitiable children of human society, on whose lives the sun probably never shone again. This mute farewell from them, to whom I was not allowed to say one more dear word, was painful for me. They had been entrusted to my care for a long time; I knew their need, their spiritual poverty, their desertion, and their deepest despair. "Nanda, take us with you! Write to us soon!" Oh, how gladly I would have taken them all with me, kidnapped them from the hell of this concentration camp, and given them over to respectable, good, humane treatment, where they would have had the opportunity to rebuild their botched lives. I also did write to them a few times, but whether my lines ever reached them I will never know.

Happiness and pain and profound sadness tormented me during these last hours of my stay in the concentration camp. Before we went into the effects division, we had to go to the sick bay with the overseer for an examination by one of the SS doctors. This was not a pleasant matter, since one was often subjected to one last vulgarity by these parasites and murderers of humanity. But in the face of the consciousness of the freedom that stood before us we put up with this as well. After the examination, which had been the task of a "gynecological specialist," for heart and lungs were not taken into account, we had to sign something saying that we "had been released from the camp in good health" and that we would in the future lay "claims of no kind upon the state" in regard to possible sicknesses, which arose all too often as a consequence of such years. But what inmate would not sign that in such an hour? Only to get out, even if one's body became sick and ailing later after such a dog's life. What did that matter to us in this hour! I remember a few cases where a declaration of release arrived from the Central

---

cut. Dressed by his mother in normal clothes, he looks exceedingly bizarre with long hair that sticks straight up and out and fingernails longer than his fingers.

Reich Security Office in Berlin, but the inmate in question had been gravely ill for a long time, even on death's door. Yet even she blissfully signed to the effect that she had been released from the concentration camp "in good health." How unscrupulously the Third Reich proceeded even here!

In the effects division I got back some of the items of clothing I had brought with me when I was delivered to the camp. My watch and other pieces of jewelry were also handed over to me. I began to put on my own underthings. What a joy that was, to be allowed to move about again in clean underthings and one's own clothing! To be able to wear proper, leather shoes on my feet, injured from going barefoot and from the bad wooden clogs. And no more striped inmate's clothing! The kind of feeling called forth by such an hour cannot be described, it can only be experienced!

When I was finished with dressing and had packed the rest of my things in my suitcase, I told the overseer that my fur coat and my tall leather boots were still missing. In that moment she became fresh, showed me an index card with my name on it, on which the items of clothing I had brought with me were detailed one by one. Fur coat and boots were not cited there. The overseer became hateful toward me and claimed that I had never worn a fur coat or boots, and that I possessed only the audacity to attempt to get richer through my claim. But in the magnificent consciousness that I was a free person again and could defend myself, I replied to her quietly: "If you do not bring me my fur coat and boots immediately, I will apply directly to the commandant. I will not leave the camp without this property of mine. And you can bet your life on the fact that I will leave the camp yet today, and with my fur coat and boots!" For she had even threatened me that I should prepare myself for another year in the concentration camp because of my "impudent claims." But I knew one thing that steeled my courage in these minutes: no commandant and no overseer would ever dare detain someone whom Himmler had released. When I stood by my claim with complete decisiveness, the overseer's certainty disappeared noticeably, and soon she disappeared as well. The second inmate to be released stood there ready in her pretty Hessian peasant dress like a maiden from fairyland and waited. She was aghast at what was happening in the last hours of my stay in the camp. But nothing more could disturb us in this hell.

After about a quarter hour, the overseer came back with a fur coat and the boots. "Are these your rags?" "Yes, those are my things!" Now she tried to be friendlier to me, since she had grown very uncertain, perhaps out of fear that I could still report what she had allowed to happen. But I was silent and did not respond to this false friendliness. Now I was no longer Inmate Herbermann #6582; instead I wore my own clothes, and my self-confidence, which had been repressed for so long, was coming back, too.

Then we went back to the political division again, where we had to sign various forms. On one of these forms it was printed that the released inmate was never allowed to talk about camp life, the setup of the camp, camp punishments, and other events. We were bound to strict silence. This in itself is proof of what went on there. Every person imprisoned in a penitentiary can tell about what he has experienced; and no one who was released from any kind of prison in Germany ever had to sign something like this before the Nazi domination. If it came out that a released inmate had let out something about the events in the KZ, that inmate would be immediately transported back to the camp by the Gestapo and would receive fifty to a hundred lashes. This horrible knowledge held back all released inmates from reporting about their experiences in the KZ.

Back at the office of Herr Borchard, we talked together for another few minutes alone.

"How happy I am that you are getting out of here, Fräulein Herbermann! You did not belong here. I would gladly go with you; for this is not the place for me either. When you are back in Münster, think sometimes of poor Borchard, who must live on in this horror."

This confession of an honest man, which I have made every effort to repeat word for word, impressed me deeply and occupied my thoughts quite often after my release. He stretched out both hands to me. I will never forget this Herr Borchard. Then he took me to my earlier block director, Overseer Gode, who had told him that she would like to say goodbye to me. She, who was just as unhappy as Herr Borchard in her position, looked at me with affection: "Herbermann, you earned it!" And the tears ran down her kind, motherly face. She had stood by me in the most difficult hours. Back then, when I was taken away to the house of death, she had dared to stick up for me with Commandant Kögel, the beast in person, which took great courage. This overseer was good, like no other with whom I came into contact in my long incarceration. "If some day other times come to pass," she said, "then you'll have to visit me in Bremen." She did not belong in a concentration camp. She suffered in spirit quite terribly from the horrors and injustices committed upon helpless women here.

Now I had taken my leave from these two noble people, into whose hearts I had been allowed to look and whom I will always think of with thanks, and all of the formalities had been settled. We still had two hours of time before the departure of our train. We were brought by an overseer into the infamous cell building, where we spent our last two hours in a room that was, however, quite bright. And again the most difficult part of my life, that period of confinement in the dark, rose up in me, alive again in this place. Oh, those eight days and eight nights of boundless torment, indescribable horror, and complete isolation.

But away with such thoughts! In a short time we would be liberated.

234

I wanted to be happy in this hour and be thankful for all the tangible mercy I had experienced during these years. But then the groaning of the poorest creatures reached my ears all over again and I could not be truly happy. I imagined them, lying like animals in their cells, pathetic, freezing, filled with fear, beaten to a pulp. I heard the crazy ones raging and singing—singing in a heartbreaking way. Yes, this was my last impression, and I took it with me into freedom, trembling. Poor, poor creatures! All this is still burning in my soul today and will never stop burning.

In order to create a diversion for myself and to see myself as a person again, I took a little hand mirror from my bag and observed myself for a long time; I hardly recognized myself. My comrade asked me if she might also be allowed to look into the mirror once. And when she inspected her shorn head, she began to cry bitterly. "What will my mother say?" "She will love you just as much as before, perhaps even more so!" I answered, and she was comforted. Then she confessed to me shyly that she did not have enough travel money to be able to pay for the trip at all. In the course of the years some money had been sent to me, which was good for absolutely nothing in the camp (though at the top of all our notepaper it said: "Anything can be bought in the camp"), so I gave to this child from my heart so that she could get back to her mother as soon as possible.

Finally Overseer Gallinat came, who had always said that she wanted to accompany me to the train station in the case of my release. And she kept her promise, which held little value for me. I would so like to have taken my first step into freedom alone, completely alone. For anyone can find the way toward freedom. One needed and wanted no company for this, particularly none of this kind.

I found her presence bothersome and encumbering in this hour, on the morning of March 19, 1943, on the Feast of St. Joseph, to whom I had prayed ardently everyday throughout this difficult time.[2]

---

2. St. Joseph, the husband of the Virgin Mary and the father of Jesus Christ, is considered the patron saint of the universal church by Catholics.

Chapter 46

Freedom! Freedom!

After I had passed the gatekeeper of the camp and turned my back forever on the sinister walls, which were higher than a house, I took the deepest breath of my entire life, and looked back again, for the very last time. My eyes skimmed over the walls, up and down, and for a long time, for a very long time, I could not break free from this sight, which brought back everything that I had experienced once again. Lord God, I praise you! Just as the first constraint is the last gasp for a free spirit, so the first gasp of a newly granted freedom is like rising from the dead, the beginning of a *vita nuova*, a new life. And in this moment I experienced, in the blessed circumstance of my freedom, something completely new and different in the meaning of the word "life."

Being locked up! What feelings this had awakened in me! It was this horrible feeling that paralyzed me body and soul, which often could have driven me to fits of rage, and even to despair, with my rash temperament. But I knew that rage and despair didn't help at all. Then I had to call on reason, which so many people had completely lost in this situation, and resign myself to the unavoidable. And even in my imprisonment I had great wealth in my faith and my trust in God, and with God's mercy I preserved them even through the most despairing hours. I understood the meaning of suffering. Only in this way could I be silent and resigned, even if the torment of my situation had often crept all the way into my dreams. For weeks I did not sleep at all in the concentration camp. And when I finally did find sleep, then dreams sought me out in order to torment me, to prick at me, to unbalance me. Then, in the early morning, unfathomable melancholy and sadness about my lost freedom lay over my heart, which had been so grievously tested. But now I had this freedom again, this exquisite gift from heaven, and could not yet quite figure out how to get used to it.

Chapter 47

Going home . . .

After about one hour we arrived at the train station in Fürstenberg and bought our tickets. I telegraphed my sister-in-law in Berlin. Everyone gaped at us, since the overseer was with us, and one could tell from looking at her where she came from. And my little red-haired, shorn companion, who was not wearing a hat, also drew many stares. The Fürstenbergers knew already: these people could only be released inmates from the concentration camp.

Finally the train came, and we climbed into the upholstered cars! What a feeling! Life! Life! The red-haired girl sat happily next to me. I had invited her to do so for the journey to Berlin. But the express train went much too slowly for us, much too slowly. In the twentieth century, an airplane really ought to stand ready for such occasions, I thought to myself.

The sun shone warmly and pleasantly on this day, the sky was a deep blue, and not even a gentle breeze stirred. From the compartment window, I saw the first signs of spring. That something like this still existed in the world! In the wide, blue space above us I glimpsed a bird, then another one, and observed their flight for a long while. Now they fluttered above a lake, then again over a small forest. Yes, you birds, you have the most spectacular thing life has to offer, freedom! How many poor people, horribly robbed of their freedom in prisons, penitentiaries, and concentration camps, envy you. I felt sadness all over again for all my fellow prisoners, whom I had had to leave behind in hell that morning.

At one small station, a young woman with a child boarded and came into our compartment. How long had it been since I had seen a child?! Again and again I had to look at it and violently hold back my tears. For so long I had not played with or spoken to a child, had had no little creature in my arms, as I had so often in earlier years with the families of my siblings. But now I was to have that again as well.

Finally we were in Berlin, where my brother Heinz, whom I had thought to be in the east, welcomed me on the platform. He was in Berlin on a duty journey and had learned of my release and my arrival in Berlin through my telegram, which I had sent to his wife from the post office in Fürstenberg. He greeted me, deeply moved and in a brotherly fashion.

Then we brought my little companion to the right platform, as she had to change trains in Berlin and could not properly find her way alone in this tumult, and I was happy to be able to show a fellow inmate one last act of kindness.

I now spent two harmonious days in Berlin, together with my loved ones, who surrounded me with much care and goodness. My brother, as well as my sister-in-law and my oldest sister,[1] who lived in Berlin, showered me with love, which I could hardly bear; for I was no longer accustomed to it. First I had to learn to bear it again, since I had been all too distanced from love. I loved them all more than ever, they who had suffered so much on my account.

I had sent communication of my release by telegraph from Berlin to my mother in Soest and my oldest brother in Münster and had told them the time of my arrival in Münster. How astonished I was when I arrived in Hamm late in the evening to see my loved ones at the train station, laden with flowers: my sick mother, my oldest brother, my little sister, my sister-in-law, her parents and brother, and my two oldest nephews! Such a reunion cannot be described. We were so very happy. Now we all had each other back again, something which, at times, we had no longer believed would happen. They had probably been counting on getting my ashes, which the relatives of an inmate who had died in the concentration camp could have sent to them for a fee of five marks.

A table was set festively at the home of the parents of my sister-in-law Annalies, exactly as I had imagined it at certain times, asking myself whether I would ever experience it again.[2] And still, everything seemed like a dream to me. I could not yet grasp reality and glowed with excitement and joy.

That same night, I went on to Münster with my mother, my oldest brother, and my nephews. Now I didn't have to greet my beloved home from a great and painful distance, but was allowed to see it and experience it again. The wife of my brother was waiting at the train station. My entire large family (at least everyone who could be there) took part in my return home.

During this night walk to my brother's apartment, I asked him why we weren't going to my own apartment. This question was visibly painful for my relatives. After they were silent for a time, my brother disclosed to me

---

1. Nanda refers here to Anna Maria Agnes Herbermann (b. 1894) who was a nun serving in Berlin and as a missionary.
2. Annalies Drees was married to Nanda's brother Clemens. They married in 1933 and were the parents of four children: Annaliese, Hélène, Niklas, and Peter.

that my apartment had been confiscated in 1941 and that strangers were now living there. And I had furnished this home of mine so very personally, had acquired piece after piece of furniture through my own hard work. This news, which I had not reckoned with at all, struck me bitterly, very bitterly indeed. But I bravely accepted this disappointment in the blissful consciousness of freedom. My relatives had carefully and nicely set up a large room in their apartment for me, for which I was very thankful. When we laid ourselves down to rest early in the morning, I felt that I was boundlessly wealthy, and I knew that I had now really returned home.

Chapter 48

The Gestapo yet again

During my release, I had been told by the political division of the concentration camp that I was to register with the Geheime Staatspolizei immediately upon my arrival in Münster. So on March 22, 1943, according to this order, I made my last, difficult journey to Gutenbergstraße, to the building in which I had been subjected to so many terrifying interrogations and had lived through so many hours of torment.

Downstairs at the porter's, I had to sign my name and indicate to whom I wished to speak and what matter it concerned. Then the exact minute of my arrival was noted down and afterward the exact minute of my departure. How careful these gentlemen and underlings of Himmler were at that time, how uncertain of themselves they must have been, if they felt the need to meet their orders with such exactness! I climbed up the many steps and knocked on the door of the room that was so well known to me. When I entered, Herr Dehm called out to me: "Here's our Nanda, back again!" I was astonished by this impudence and answered icily: "To you I am not 'Nanda,' but 'Fräulein Herbermann' as usual!" Then he wanted to know why I was being so cold, since I was, after all, free again. "Oh," I said, "don't you remember, Herr Dehm, how you in particular told me during the last interrogation, that, after all these interrogations, which you had spent so much precious time on, you were none the wiser than on the first day? And that I then replied to you that you could never get any wiser through me, even if you interrogated me and locked me up for a hundred years, that I would never play the informer! Perhaps you no longer know how you answered me, but I have not forgotten it in any case: 'You'll be put where you belong. I'll take care of that!' And you certainly 'took care' of that."

The conversation went back and forth on that morning. They even dared to ask me questions about the organization and procedures in the concentration camp, which was probably meant to be a trap. But I remained silent. If anyone in Germany was completely in the know as far as concentration camps, then it was the gentlemen of the Gestapo and SS, and of course those people who had themselves suffered and lived in need in the concentration camps. The large majority of others knew and heard hardly anything more detailed about it.

Various officials and employees came in, probably out of pure curiosity to see a released inmate for once. And it was on this day, too, that they told me that the warrant for my arrest had said: "Until one year after the end of the war."

At the very end, when I was all ready to go, an SS senior storm trooper came in and greeted me in the most friendly manner, although I had never seen him before. He said, clapping me on the shoulder (and I winced under this touch), "We could really use a woman like you here. What do you think about that? You know the bishop and all the priests here!" Aha, the friendliness was for this reason! Now I was supposed to play the spy for them in addition! He urged me to leave the Church, to leave "all that confessional junk" behind me, then I would be a "made woman." I could not grasp the fact that they would dare to make such an offer to me, of whom they knew well enough that I would never be disloyal to my flag. At the same moment I said goodbye with the words: "I went to the camp Catholic, and I came out even more Catholic." I could no longer breathe in there.

Chapter 49

Epilogue

After this morning, it was especially comforting that I was allowed to experience a reunion with my fatherly priest friend Prof. Dr. Donders on the afternoon of that very same day. So many noble friends were no longer among the living when I returned home. . . . I could only linger at their graves, which have since been smashed in air raids. But the oldest and most trusted of all of them, who had been consumed with worry and had borne my fate with me deeply from a distance, at least I was allowed to meet him again on this earth, for which I praise God's goodness still today. This reunion was one of the most profound joys for me. On Sunday, April 4, this noble priest held a high mass of thanks for my newly recovered freedom in the Münster Cathedral, now so terribly destroyed.[1] On August 9, 1944, God called home his never-tiring servant, who was completely consumed by worries and suffering, into eternal peace.

When we have been separated for a long time from everything that belongs to us, from relatives and friends, from all our possessions, from our dear habits, inclinations, and duties, and from the activities we are accustomed to performing daily; namely, when brutal violence has taken us away from them, how the desire grows with every hour to take back that which we have done bitterly without for so long, to seize possession of it again—how we enjoy to the fullest these first heartbeats of freedom! You are free, free, you have back what belongs to you! My heart felt this exultantly.

When this overwhelming moment of freedom and newly acquired possession comes, however, when we sense warmly the first sunbeam of newly granted happiness and our hands and heart stretch out toward them impatiently, how suddenly all excitement, all overpowering feelings, can disappear again. How does that happen? Was the joy excessive? Were we

---

1. Münster had been heavily targeted by the RAF and then by the U.S. military for air raids from 1939 on. By the end of the war, the inner city of Münster, including the area where the cathedral is located, was 90 percent destroyed.

ungrateful? Was the expectation exaggerated? Among us in the concentration camp, it was the case that the fantastic dreams, which we gave ourselves up to in the longing for freedom, really were exaggerated. Probably everyone who has been locked up for many years, especially those prisoners who have been martyred, naturally exaggerates the true concept of real freedom. God knows, freedom is certainly the most precious gift of natural life—and yet one should not create a fantasy image of a reality in which one no longer lives oneself, when one is instead bound at the hands and the feet, bound at the spirit and the soul. In our brooding misery, the most modest maid or the simplest factory worker seemed like a queen to us: in comparison to our situation, they passed as almost the ideal of freedom. They did not wear inmates' clothing, they did not have shorn heads, they were not constantly accompanied by the SS, overseers, and dogs, were not surrounded by this horror, this torment every hour, but could move around freely, breathe freely.

In the first period of my newly recovered freedom, my own personality tormented me. But who can fathom a heart which, after a long period of suffering, after a death-like existence, must accustom itself once more to love, to joy, to a world filled with beauty! I could no longer express my joy outwardly, I had simply unlearned it. Just as great pain is usually mute and is suffered through silently, great joy and great happiness are borne similarly after profound suffering. Does not the Creator of all happiness and all joy also speak to our souls in silence? And we do understand him in such moments. And so joy and gratefulness do best to rise up to their Creator during these hours in silent thanks. And how much constancy and how much mercy did I have to thank God for! No, he does not desert his own. I was allowed to experience myself that "Need is never greater than the helper," as the second strophe of the song I hummed so often during these years so aptly says:

"Trust, my soul, trust securely in the Lord,
Commend all to him, he will so gladly aid.
Do not fawn, soon the morning will dawn,
And a new spring will follow winter's last yawn.
In any storm, whatever your need,
He will e'er shelter you—your loyal God.

Trust, my soul, trust securely in the Lord,
Commend all to him, he will so gladly aid.
If all should break, us God won't forsake,
To be greater than the helper, need can't fake.
Eternally true, Savior in need,
Please save our souls as well, you loyal God."

Chapter 50

A final word

Tears as you have now cried them,
A people has ne'er cried;
In such wretched chains of death,
A people was ne'er tied.

—ERNST VON WILDENBRUCH[1]

The grounds for my arrest are given as follows on the red warrant I have in my hands:

"According to the results of the findings of the state police, she endangers, through her conduct, the stability and security of the people and the state, in that she does egregious harm to the interests of the Reich through her subversive activities and collaboration with one of the most critical and harsh opponents of the National Socialist state. Signed by Heydrich."

This document also belongs in this book, as simple proof of the monstrous irresponsibility with which the Gestapo works. I explained at the beginning of my remarks why I was arrested and what alone led to my arrest. The Gestapo's grounds, which do not at all correspond to the facts, are a completely made-up indictment against me, who remained loyal to a human being and emigrant even across the boundaries of Germany. Loyalty and silence were my only crimes.

Why am I now publishing this book, which is truly written with my lifeblood? I mean to portray the life demanded of an inmate of the Geheime Staatspolizei and the SS during the Third Reich in prisons and concentration

---

1. Ernst von Wildenbruch (1845–1909) was a German popular author, known particularly for his plays and poetry, which were often marked by a nationalistic spirit, characteristic of the period around German unification during which he wrote.

camps so objectively and in a manner true to life that the reader can gain a clear picture of this life in hell.

But I have a second and more essential goal in mind with the publication of these remarks: the entire German people is now being held responsible by many parties for the horrible and abominable things that occurred in the concentration camps. This is not right. I don't want to pass judgment here or bring anyone to justice; but it would be good if everyone who has read this book would look inside himself and seriously search his conscience.

Those who do not have blood on their hands might use whatever strength is still available to them to work along with us, who have experienced and suffered this horror on our own bodies and in our own souls, so that our Germany may be revived with honor, and we may finally take shelter and be at home there again, so that a fatherland may exist for us again, for us who have wandered around for the last twelve years, homeless and constantly persecuted and spied upon in our own fatherland. And we will try to make amends for the horror and depravity, for the murder and atrocious injustice committed by Germans unto Germans and unto hundreds of thousands of innocent foreigners. We, the survivors, have this holy obligation, as well as the obligation to atone before God and the world. One thing remains true, and the world will also learn to understand it after our time of atonement: the German people may not and cannot be simply equated with these Nazi criminals.

I would like to close this book with this excerpt from an article by Ernst Wiechert,[2] which appeared in the *Hannover'schen Kurier* on October 2, 1945:

> Now we stand before the deserted house and see the eternal stars shining over the wreckage of the earth or hear the rain rush down on the graves of the dead and on the grave of an era. More alone than any people has ever been alone on this earth, and more stigmatized than any people has ever been stigmatized.
>
> Remember the bird in the fairy tale, who comes once every thousand years to break a granule from the diamond mine. Remember what stands before you and that, in the history of the world, there has never been a greater task than your task to revive the blood of a people, and to wipe away the shame from the face of an entire people. Do not believe in the

---

2. Ernst Wiechert (1887–1950) was a German author who advocated resistance to National Socialism in his writings and lectures. For this he spent a brief period in a concentration camp in 1938, an experience he later recorded in his well-known book *Der Totenwald* (The forest of the dead) (Zurich: Rascher, 1946). Though his books were widely read in Germany in the period immediately following World War II, Wiechert eventually emigrated to Switzerland in 1948 out of frustration at the Germans' failure to break with the past.

thousand-year-old lie that shame was wiped away with blood, but in the recent truth that shame can only be wiped away with honor, with penitence, with metamorphosis, with the words of the lost son: "Father, I have sinned, henceforth I want to sin no more."

Do not complain that we will go barefoot, that we will go hungry, that the judge will stand over us day and night. Look into the eyes of destiny, like the martyrs of the camps did.

Is it not a splendid lot which has fallen to us, and can we not go about it with happy hearts? And here, at this point, let me ask one more thing of you, the last thing and perhaps the most difficult. In the time which is to come, there will perhaps be a few among those who have sinned for twelve long years, not among the hangmen and murderers, but among those who cried "Hosanna," whose blind eyes will open; and if you believe that their hearts have changed, do not repel them. We have all erred and it does not befit us to judge.

When we have all become so chastened and sensible then God, too, will bless us again with the time when we Germans can go before the lands of the world, respected and accepted, with our old, beautiful song, which has hardly ever sounded in Germany during the last twelve years:

"Oh Germany, highly honored,
You holy land of faith!"

Note

The names of inmates, with the exception of those about whom I only had positive things to report, have all been changed. The names of the commandants, the other administrators of the concentration camp, and the overseers have all been retained whenever I mention them.

Afterword

Ravensbrück Now

Today a Soviet tank stands by the entrance to Ravensbrück, a staunch reminder of the liberation of the camp by the Red Army on April 30, 1945. Just beyond the tank, on the left, stand several homes, pleasant in mien though now in disrepair, which once housed Nazi officers and their families. An exception to the general tumbledown look of these buildings is one undergoing significant renovation to become an accommodation for former prisoners revisiting the site of their suffering and memories. These are primarily members of the *Lagergemeinschaft* (Camp Organization), an association of survivors of Ravensbrück that holds regular meetings here at the camp memorial.

On the right spreads out the lake, its present-day tranquillity belying the purpose it served from 1943 to 1945 as a repository for ashes from the crematorium. Startlingly close, across the lake, one sees the spire of the Protestant church in Fürstenberg, the outline of stores and homes. Could the residents of the town have been oblivious to the plight of the prisoners and the stench of the ovens? Schwedt See, the lake that figures prominently in so many Ravensbrück memoirs, is today dominated by a statue high on a pedestal, which was created by sculptor Will Lammers and dedicated on September 12, 1959.

The former commandant's headquarters and home, a large and impressive building just to the left of the road, comes next into view. This building now serves as the museum and offices of the camp, although it has done so only since the 1980s when the Soviet army turned it over to the camp administration for that purpose. Extensive, thoughtful, and compelling exhibits in this building detail, among other things, the lives of twenty-six specific prisoners: their country of origin, the "offense" that resulted in their imprisonment, and their life after surviving the camp. Also available is information regarding the daily lives of inmates, their work, their resistance, their small gifts to one another. Several black binders of articles and bibliographies provide yet more information. An informal English-language guide to the camp, prepared by Professor Jack Morrison of Shippensburg University, Pennsylvania, is also available. For a period of time near the end of her imprisonment, Herbermann worked in this building.

Another one of the few surviving original buildings is the infamous cell block where special punishments were meted out; Herbermann was once imprisoned here. This structure, which served as the camp museum from 1959 to 1984, is a two-level building in which the second floor, upon which one enters, has been sliced open through the middle from one end to the other; such a cut allowed the guard to view both levels of cells at once. Still firmly implanted in the floor are the metal rings to which the omnipresent SS guard dogs were chained. Today, the cell block contains the bookstore, which provides brochures, posters, videos, and books in several languages about Ravensbrück. Downstairs, three cells have been set up to show the three types of punishment meted out here:

1. Three-day punishment—the inmate was provided with a bed, toilet, stool, heat, and window.
2. Forty-two-day punishment—the inmate was provided with a bed, stool, toilet, but no window so the cell was in darkness.
3. "Standing punishment"—the prisoner was provided no furnishing, no window, and no time limitation; most prisoners died under these circumstances.

A nearby cell contains the "beating block," a slatted wooden frame over which women were strapped to be beaten; a leather truncheon hangs on the wall. The upstairs cells have been transformed into memorial rooms for countries from which prisoners were deported to Ravensbrück. Each country was given the opportunity to create its own memorial; some are information oriented, with documents, photographs, and the names of the women; others are more artistic and symbolic, with sculptures and other works of art. Just outside the entrance is "the shooting passage," a narrow space between two walls where executions were carried out.

Between the cell block and the lake stand the crematorium, a memorial rose garden, and a sculpture on the site of the former gas chambers (which were used late in the war). When the Red Army arrived at the camp in April 1945, approximately three thousand women had been left behind, too sick to march out of the camp or flee. Many of these women subsequently died, despite the efforts of care providers, and were buried in a mass grave, over which a rose garden has been planted. According to Olena Wojtowycz, a Ukrainian Ravensbrück inmate, "The ill-fated women remaining in Ravensbrück to the end of the war were never set free. Instead, all those captured by the Red Army were sent to the East. Ukrainians, Belorusians, and Russians in particular (considered by Stalin to be traitors), found themselves again in prison-camps, only now the camps were part of the Gulag archipelago" (Wojtowycz, *Ravensbrück*, n.p.).

Behind the former commandant's headquarters is the place where roll call took place daily, and the foundations of the buildings that used to house the showers (for arriving prisoners) and the kitchen. The Red Army remained housed at Ravensbrück until 1993. They tore down the wooden barracks, or blocks, which used to stretch away from this square and built stone structures for barracks in their place. Still remaining in this area is an original Nazi building that was the laundry for the Nazi soldiers and in which a second gas chamber was installed but never used.

On the fiftieth anniversary of the liberation of the camp, a reunion was held for all surviving prisoners who wished to attend. Many of the exhibitions currently in place were created for this occasion. Much refurbishing of the camp was done as well, although large areas still remain closed to the general public, deemed unsafe. Rather astonishing is the fact that these returning prisoners wished to have a roll call daily; astonishing because reading the memoirs of survivors such as Germaine Tillion, Sylvia Salvesen, and Wanda Poltawska, it is clear that the roll call is remembered as a singular ordeal. A visit to the camp today, though it has changed much since 1945, gives a visceral sense of the environment, if not the ordeal, which the women who were imprisoned and died there experienced.

Suggestions for Further Reading

Other Memoirs Written by Former Prisoners of Ravensbrück

We have been able to identify twelve memoirs, written by women about significant time they spent in Ravensbrück, which have been translated from various languages into English or were originally written in English. Few of these are easily available, and searches through out-of-print book search services have proved fruitless. They must be sought out instead through interlibrary loan, and a few are in the permanent collection of the United States Holocaust Memorial Museum, which is not a circulating collection. Because these memoirs are so difficult to locate, we include here a brief synopsis of each, with an emphasis on the similarities and differences between each and Herbermann's memoir. We refer readers to the bibliography for a list of other Ravensbrück memoirs, in their original languages, and for mention of anthologies of brief reminiscences by former prisoners.

Geneviève de Gaulle Anthonioz, *The Dawn of Hope: A Memoir of Ravensbrück* (1998)

Translated from the French. This slender memoir was written by the niece of General Charles de Gaulle; she was Christian and a member of the French resistance movement. Arrested in July 1943, she spent six months in Fresnes Prison in France and was deported to Ravensbrück in February 1944. She was assigned #27372. She waited until age seventy-eight to write her memoir, which might be better termed a meditation. Anthonioz summons remarkably sharp images from her long days of solitary confinement in the cell block. Her account of Ravensbrück shares much in common with that of Herbermann, including her reference to the camp as an "abyss," the sustenance she drew on from spirituality, her longing for books, her description of her early release, as well as references to Gypsies, Jehovah's Witnesses, and the victims of "medical experiments." Since her return to France, Anthonioz has devoted herself to working with the homeless.

Sara Tuvel Bernstein, *The Seamstress: A Memoir of Survival* **(1997)**

Written in English. Bernstein spent only four months in Ravensbrück, from September 1944 to January 1945. She was Romanian by birth, Jewish, and was conscripted by the Hungarian National Guard into a labor camp near Budapest; from there, she was shipped with her sister and two close friends to Ravensbrück. Assigned the number 85803, Bernstein, at twenty-six, was the oldest of the four and quickly established herself as their guardian. "Having a sister, a cousin, or a friend in the camp with you was sometimes the only thing that gave you the courage to go on; each lived solely for the other" (243). All four were assigned to a work detail unloading vegetables from arriving ships all day; such a work assignment gave access to extra food, a key to survival. Bernstein recounts the arrival of countless Jewish women from Auschwitz in January 1945. She also describes the process by which these new arrivals and other Jewish women in the camp, including Bernstein and her trio, were sent to the infamous huge tent, put up when all blocks were overflowing. Conditions there were execrable, making her long for the "luxury" of their former barracks.

Shortly thereafter, the four were deported to Dachau; one of the friends died enroute. The other three were eventually liberated by American soldiers. Thinking back on her experiences in Ravensbrück as she departed, Bernstein wrote: "We had been in Ravensbrück for four months by calendar time. There are other kinds of time, however; immeasurable time, when the days and nights fall into a vast, black wasteland as deep and wide as the immensity of space. Such was the nature of time in Ravensbrück" (244).

Margarete Buber-Neumann, *Under Two Dictators* **(1949)**

Translated from the German. Buber-Neumann was a German Communist who had taken up residence in Moscow with her second husband, Heinz Neumann. There, she was initially arrested on June 19, 1938, and sent to a Russian prison camp in Siberia. In August 1940, the Russians turned her over to the Germans and she was sent to Ravensbrück, arriving about a year prior to Herbermann. Her prisoner number was 4208. (Buber-Neumann's memoir lists August 1941, as the date of her arrival in Ravensbrück, but this must be a printing error. Her prisoner number is lower than Herbermann's, suggesting earlier arrival. In addition, she states that upon her release in April 1945 that she had been imprisoned there for five years. Further evidence for the 1940 date appears in Tillion's memoir, where she cites 1940 as the date of Buber-Neumann's arrival in Ravensbrück [Tillion, xix].) Buber-Neumann was a careful observer of details and her account is especially valuable for information about the admittance procedures at the camp, for her description of time spent in the Jehovah's Witnesses block (Block III), and for information about the other Communists in the camp and the occasional conflicts among them. She describes both an aviary and strolling peacocks glimpsed as she arrived! She devotes considerable space to an account of her strong and sustaining friendship with Milena Jesenska, a journalist who had an intense romantic relationship with writer Franz Kafka, and who was also a political prisoner in Ravensbrück; Jesenska died in May 1944 in the camp.

Like Herbermann, Buber-Neumann was sent to Block II, the asocials' block, to serve as block elder; she spent two months there about a year prior to Herbermann's arrival. Buber-Neumann describes her initial impressions of Block II: "When I entered the hut there was a tremendous noise going on and the place stank like a monkey's cage . . . all eyes turned to me. I felt as though I were naked in a cage of wild animals" (196–97). However, like Herbermann, Buber-Neumann recognized that these women were "victims of society in one way or another" (198) and she expressed disgust at the selection of prisoners from Block II for the Mauthausen brothel. Overall, Buber-Neumann's descriptions of Block II confirm those of Herbermann.

Another convergence of Herbermann and Buber-Neumann occurred in the office of the chief overseer, Frau Langefeld. Both women were summoned to work in this office in the autumn of 1942, though neither mentions the other in her memoir. Both describe their effort to hide or destroy reports of "misbehavior" in order to spare their fellow prisoners from punishment. Both women experienced punishment in the cell block firsthand.

Charlotte Delbo, *Auschwitz and After* (1995)

Translated from the French; parts of the manuscript were completed in the late 1940s. A relatively small slice of Delbo's memoir is devoted to the sixteen months she spent in Ravensbrück, from January 1944 to April 23, 1945. Delbo's journey to Ravensbrück began in March 1942, when she was arrested by the French police in Paris for her involvement in the underground; Delbo was not Jewish. Taken with her husband Georges Dudach to a Gestapo prison, Delbo was eventually deported to Auschwitz; her husband was executed by firing squad before her departure. After a year in Auschwitz, Delbo and seven other French women were inexplicably taken by passenger train to Berlin and then beyond to Ravensbrück. Her brief descriptions of the camp are episodic rather than linear: the Gypsies in the camp; how she acquired a copy of and memorized Molière's *Le Misanthrope* ("To lose one's memory is to lose oneself," wrote Delbo); how she escaped a selection and then a roundup for a labor transport; and how she was rescued by the Swedish Red Cross. Delbo's memoir is, somewhat paradoxically, at its most horrifying when it is most spare. Poetry is interspersed throughout the poetic prose. *Auschwitz and After* is actually a trilogy: *None of Us Will Return* was written in 1946, but like Wanda Poltawska's memoir, was stored away in a drawer until its publication in 1965; *Useless Knowledge,* much of which was written in the late 1940s, followed in 1970 and the accounts of Ravensbrück are included here; and the final volume, *The Measure of Our Days,* appeared shortly thereafter. Delbo died of cancer in 1985.

Denise Dufournier, *Ravensbrück: The Women's Camp of Death* (1948)

Translated from the French; original manuscript was completed in September 1945. Dufournier was arrested in June 1943 for her involvement in an underground organization she calls La Comète, dedicated to rescuing downed American and British airmen, caring for them, and returning them to England. After four months of solitary confinement in France, she was deported to Ravensbrück in January 1944, arriving in the same month as Delbo, and was assigned prisoner #27389 upon arrival. Dufournier provides us a spirited and exacting account of life in the camp in the latter days of its existence as overcrowding, and then a relaxing of discipline, took hold.

Like Germaine Tillion, she maneuvers to get herself *verfügbar* status, that is, "available" for work rather than already assigned to a particular work squad. She describes in some detail the various subterfuges used by inmates to avoid work. She also describes the infamous sand detail, in which prisoners shoveled sand all day, with no apparent purpose, as well as work details in factories and on the painting squad, the means of survival for Dufournier until her release to the Red Cross in the closing days of the war. Her account of her year-and-a-half stay is also laced with references to the prostitutes and the lesbians in the camp; she gives a robust description of the varying roles of the "Jules," women who dressed in trousers and tweed jackets, despite the "dress codes," and who sometimes carved a "cow's cross" into their foreheads with a knife to attest to their fidelity (92).

Dufournier confirms other memoirs that recount the transition the Jugendlager Uckermarck made from youth camp to extermination camp. She depicts the *Revier,* or sick bay, in horrifying terms. Finally, throughout her memoir, she relates to her readers the strong camaraderie that existed among the French prisoners and their gallows humor. (For example, they referred to the large buildings storing items stolen from arriving prisoners as the "Galeries Lafayette," after a famous Parisian department store.) Despite disputes that occasionally arose among the women of different nationalities, Dufournier asserts: "Amongst us all, however, the living and the dead, there existed a fraternity stronger than anything on earth; it was as if we belonged to an immense community, outside the human race, situated on a mysterious planet, where the macabre, the ridiculous, the grotesque rubbed shoulders and intermingled in a fantastic and irrational chaos" (130–31). This is a fitting summary of all depictions of Ravensbrück.

Gemma Gluck, *My Story* (1961)

Written in English. Gluck, the daughter of a Jewish mother and a Christian father, both Italian immigrants to America in the late nineteenth century, was the sister of Fiorello La Guardia, mayor of New York City during World War II. Gluck, and her husband, Herman Gluck, a Hungarian Jew, were living in Budapest in 1944 when they were both arrested on June 7. The arrest was apparently a retaliation for an anti-Nazi speech made by Gluck's brother to a gathering of Polish Jews in New York City, although by the spring of 1944, Eichmann had arrived in Budapest to make yet another country *judenrein,* or "free of Jews." Herman Gluck was sent to Mauthausen, Gemma to Ravensbrück, where she was assigned prisoner #44139 and sent to Block II, Herbermann's block (Herbermann had been released a year earlier). Gluck's memoir includes accounts of the varieties of nationalities in the camp, famous people imprisoned there, Jehovah's Witnesses, Christmas celebrations in 1944, punishments, the "rabbits," and the building of the gas chamber in November 1944. She dedicated her memoir to "the martyred women of Ravensbrück, the thousands who perished and the few who survived. Their valiant resistance to the Nazis preserved the image of human dignity in a time of inhuman brutality" (n.p.).

Micheline Maurel, *An Ordinary Camp* (1958)

Translated from the French. Maurel was deported from France to Ravensbrück in August 1943. She was assigned #22410 and, after spending the requisite time in quarantine, was sent on to a Ravensbrück subcamp, Neubrandenburg, located near the Baltic Sea. Here, she was put to work as a slave in an airplane factory. In her final chapter, she writes movingly of the difficulty she had adapting to life after the war. Speaking to her friends who perished in the camp, she says: "And yet, how can I be happy now, my poor comrades . . . ? I feel that there is a staggering sum of suffering to be made up. I am torn by that suffering. I feel the camp around me. . . . The real me . . . remains seated back there because she can no longer walk, holding out her empty bowl" (141).

Wanda Poltawska, *And I Am Afraid of My Dreams* (1989)

Translated from the Polish; first published in Poland in 1964. Poltawska was a Polish Catholic, arrested in Lublin on February 17, 1941, for her work in the Polish resistance movement; she arrived in Ravensbrück on September

23, 1941. (Note that this closely parallels Herbermann's arrest on February 4, 1941, and arrival in the camp on August 1, 1941.) Poltawska was prisoner #7709. Her experience as a "rabbit" (in Polish, *kroliky*) informs her entire memoir: the surgery, the recovery, the revolt of the other "rabbits," and her strong solidarity with the other Polish women. Poltawska began writing her memoir as soon as she returned home, in the summer of 1945, in an effort to stop the nightmares of camp life she had whenever she fell asleep; she then left the manuscript in a drawer until January 1961.

Her book is remarkable in several respects. Her memory of events is vivid and intense and she summons lurid details about her surroundings, her emotions, and other people, especially their cruelties. She recounts her close friendship, one of a protective nature, with another Polish woman, Krysia; Poltawska determines that they will both survive and they do. Her account is one of many where a strong relationship within the camp was a means of remaining motivated to live. Poltawska also supplies information on women being asked to "volunteer" for service in brothels, and a description of the infamous Overseer Dorothea Binz. Poltawska gives us yet another, very candid description of Block II: "Block II. I go cold at the mere thought of it . . . those women . . . the block where we first understood the full hideousness of that odd word 'elel'—LL—the initials of lesbian love" (57, ellipses hers).

Sylvia Salvesen, *Forgive—But Do Not Forget* (1958)

Translated from the Norwegian. Salvesen, a member of elite Norwegian society and wife of the physician to the king of Norway, was arrested by the Gestapo in Norway in September 1942, for her work in the underground. After a ten-month imprisonment near Oslo, she was transported to Germany and consigned to Ravensbrück as prisoner #20837. She lived among the Jehovah's Witnesses for two months and describes them as kindly, trustworthy, and clean, as they are depicted in other memoirs. Salvesen almost immediately goes to work in the sick bay and devotes herself to identifying, locating, and caring for all other Norwegian prisoners. She also managed to smuggle out several letters, which did indeed reach the outside world and helped bring packages and rescue efforts. Salvesen's memoir bears resemblance to Herbermann's (though their imprisonments did not overlap) in that both women drew sustenance from their spirituality.

Elisabeth Sommer-Lefkovits, *Are You Here in This Hell, Too? Memories of Troubled Times, 1944–45* (1995)

Translated from the German. Sommer-Lefkovits was a Slovakian Jew who was arrested in late November 1944, for supplying partisans with medications; she was a trained pharmacist. She was deported to Ravensbrück the same month, accompanied by her sons, Paul, age fourteen, and Ivan, age seven. In the introduction to the book, Elaine Feinstein says: "This is in many ways a unique memoir. It is the only firsthand account I know of a mother's efforts to preserve the life of her child in the full horror of the Camps" (9). After three months in Ravensbrück, Sommer-Lefkovits was sent on a death march to Bergen-Belsen with Ivan; Paul had been sent to the men's camp at Ravensbrück and did not survive. Describing her sufferings, Sommer-Lefkovits says: "I was never religious but had always believed in God. But how can anyone continue to believe in God when He manifestly allowed such terrible atrocities to happen?" (53). In contrast to Herbermann, and like Elie Wiesel, Sommer-Lefkovits lost her faith as a result of the atrocities she experienced.

Corrie ten Boom, *The Hiding Place* (1971)

Ten Boom is widely known for sheltering Jews in her family home in Haarlem, Holland. A secret room, well concealed beyond the watch shop in the front of the house that continued to serve customers, was "the hiding place." Arrested by the Gestapo with other members of her family in their home in February 1944, ten Boom arrived with her sister Betsy in Ravensbrück, which she describes as "a vast scar on the green German landscape," in the fall of 1944. She was assigned prisoner #66730, and she and Betsy spent the first few days in the infamous huge tent, built when barracks space ran out. Eventually, they were assigned to Block XXVIII and to work in the Siemens factory, then on a potato detail, and then to knit socks. Betsy's health failed from the beginning of their imprisonment and she died in December. Ten Boom's account of her stay is suffused with her Christian faith and the comfort she and her sister found in their beliefs; in this regard, the account is comparable to that of Herbermann. Ten Boom was released for an unknown reason on New Year's Day 1945, and, alone, made her way back to Holland.

Germaine Tillion, *Ravensbrück* (1975)

Translated from the French; originally published in 1973. Tillion was arrested in Paris on August 13, 1942, for her work in the French resistance and arrived in Ravensbrück on October 23, 1943, almost exactly seven months after Herbermann had been released. Betrayed by a priest, Tillion was intensively interrogated by the Gestapo and eventually charged with espionage. She was part of the *Nacht und Nebel* (night and fog) deportations from France, a term that gave Alain Resnais the title for his famous early documentary on the death camps, made in the 1950s.

One might say that Tillion's memoir is somewhat of a sociological study of Ravensbrück. From the beginning, Tillion took upon herself the task of studying the camp, seeking out and secretly recording information, and conspiring to expose as much as she could after the war. When she was liberated, she carried out in her pocket a roll of film with photos of the maimed legs of the Polish women who had undergone operations. Tillion divided her book into three sections:

Part I

Tillion termed this section "an eyewitness account," as it was based on secret notes she took from 1942 to 1945. This section is full of facts and figures such as the number of arriving prisoners, the mortality rates, the number of factories and commandos using prisoner labor, the ratio of guards to prisoners, and changes wrought by Himmler's visit to the camp.

Part II

Written between 1947 and 1953, this section is called "an historical study," and it traces the fates of one convoy of French women to the camp— those who survived, those who died, those who were exterminated in the Jugendlager Uckermarck, a youth camp on the perimeter of Ravensbrück that was eventually used as a killing center.

Part III

Termed "Some Remaining Questions," this part of the memoir was written at a later date. Some of it was interpolated into the earlier text, evidence that Tillion kept on questioning and revising.

In 1944, in the camp, Tillion gathered her comrades together and told them: "Understanding one's situation is exhilarating in itself, perhaps because awareness of a burden is one way of overcoming it, perhaps also because awareness and comprehension are the more profound vocations of the human species, and one of the goals of humanity's place on the evolutionary scale" (164). In order to achieve such understanding of her situation, Tillion sought daily the status of *verfügbar* or "available" (rather than "assigned" to a work detail) in the camp. This enabled her to avoid work detail and hence to be free to observe and research, recording her notes in code. She bemoans the difficulty of obtaining accurate information in her introduction: "[I]n the case of the Ravensbrück concentration camp: the memoranda, the lists, the orders, the letters—most had disappeared" (vii). Nonetheless, Tillion's memoir stands as a testimony to the Nazi twin pursuits of profit and extermination in the camp system and to her own indomitable spirit to carry on research in the face of tremendous danger and suffering.

Bibliography

Primary Sources—Ravensbrück Memoirs and Other First-Person Accounts

For annotation of several of these entries, see Suggestions for Further Reading.

Andreas-Friedrich, Ruth. *Battleground Berlin: Diaries, 1945–1948.* Trans. Anna Boerresen. New York: Paragon House, 1990.

———. *Berlin Underground, 1938–1945.* Trans. Barrows Mussey. New York: Henry Holt, 1947.

Anthonioz, Geneviève de Gaulle. *The Dawn of Hope: A Memoir of Ravensbrück.* Trans. Richard Seaver. New York: Arcade, 1999.

Bernadac, Christian. *Camp for Women: Ravensbrück.* Geneva: Ferni, 1978.

Bernstein, Sara Tuvel. *The Seamstress: A Memoir of Survival.* New York: G. P. Putnam's Sons, 1997.

Boom, Corrie ten. *The Hiding Place.* New York: Bantam, 1974.

Buber-Neumann, Margarete. *Under Two Dictators.* Trans. Edward Fitzgerald. London: Victor Gollancz, 1949.

Delbo, Charlotte. *Auschwitz and After.* Trans. Rosette C. Lamont. New Haven: Yale University Press, 1995.

Dufournier, Denise. *Ravensbrück: The Women's Camp of Death.* London: George Allen and Unwin, 1948.

Gluck, Gemma. *My Story.* New York: David McKay, 1961.

Herbermann, Nanda. *Der Gesegnete Abgrund. Schutzhäftling Nr. 6582 im Frauenkonzentrationslager Ravensbrück.* Nuremberg: Glock und Lutz Verlag, 1946.

———. *Der Gesegnete Abgrund. Schutzhäftling Nr. 6582 im Frauenkonzentrationslager Ravensbrück.* Ed. Elisabeth Prégardier. Annweiler/Essen: Plöger Verlag, 2000.

———. *Was Liebe Erträgt.* Celle: Verlagsbuchhandlung Joseph Giesel, 1949.

Klüger, Ruth. *Weiter leben: eine Jugend.* Göttingen: Wallstein, 1992.

Lobel, Anita. *No Pretty Pictures: A Child of War.* New York: Greenwillow Books, 1998.

Maurel, Micheline. *An Ordinary Camp.* Trans. Margaret S. Summers. New York: Simon and Schuster, 1958.

Mayerhofer, Emma. *Ravensbrück: Was geht das mich an.* Wien: Österreichische Lagerge-meinschaft Ravensbrück, 1976.

Meyer, Walter. *Tomorrow Will Be Better: Surviving Nazi Germany.* Columbia: University of Missouri Press, 1999.

Millu, Liana. *Smoke over Birkenau.* Trans. Lynn Sharon Schwartz. Evanston, IL: North-western University Press, 1997.

Müller, Charlotte. *Die Klempnerkolonne in Ravensbrück: Erinnerungen des Häftlings Nr. 10787.* Berlin: Dietz, 1981.

Nelken, Halina. *And Yet, I Am Here!* Amherst: University of Massachusetts Press, 1999.

Neray, Ruth Bindefeld. *Death by Design.* Toronto: Childe Thursday, 1992.

Poltawska, Wanda. *And I Am Afraid of My Dreams.* Trans. Mary Craig. New York: Hippocrene Books, 1989.

Saint-Clair, Simone. *Ravensbrück: L'enfer des femmes.* Paris: Fayard, 1945.

Salvesen, Sylvia. *Forgive—But Do Not Forget.* Trans. Evelyn Ramsden. London: Hutchin-son, 1958.

Sommer-Lefkovits, Elisabeth, *Are You Here in This Hell, Too? Memories of Troubled Times, 1944–1945.* Trans. Marjorie Harris. London: Menard Press, 1995.

Symonowicz, Wanda, ed. *Beyond Human Endurance: The Ravensbrück Women Tell Their Stories.* Trans. Doris Ronowicz. Warsaw: Interpress Publishers, 1970.

Tillion, Germaine. *Ravensbrück.* Trans. Gerald Satterwhite. New York: Anchor Press, 1975.

Vermehren, Isa. *Reise durch den letzten Akt. Ravensbrück, Buchenwald, Dachau: eine Frau berichtet.* Reinbek bei Hamburg: Rowohlt Taschenbuch Verlag, 1979. Originally published: Hamburg: Christian Wegner Verlag, 1946.

Wojtowycz, Olena Wityk. *Ravensbrück: The Largest Women's Concentration Camp in Germany.* Chicago: Ukrainian Institute of Modern Art, 1992.

Secondary Sources

Aziz, Philippe. *Doctors of Death.* Trans. Eduard Bizub and Philip Haentzler. Vol. 3. Geneva: Ferni, 1976.

Baskin, Judith. *Women of the Word: Jewish Women and Jewish Writing.* Detroit: Wayne State University Press, 1996.

Baumel, Judith. *Double Jeopardy: Gender and the Holocaust.* Portland, OR: Valentine Mitchell, 1998.

———. "Social Interaction among Jewish Women in Crisis during the Holocaust." *Gender and History* 7.1 (1995): 64–84.

Bendremer, Jutta. *Women Surviving the Holocaust: In Spite of the Horror.* Lewiston: E. Mellen Press, 1997.

Benz, Wolfgang, and Walter H. Pehle, eds. *Lexikon des deutschen Widerstandes.* Frankfurt am Main: S. Fischer Verlag, 1994.

Bergen, Doris L. *Twisted Cross: The German Christian Movement in the Third Reich.* Chapel Hill: University of North Carolina Press, 1996.

Bernadac, Christian. *Women's Kommandos.* Geneva: Ferni, 1978.

Bos, Pascale. "Women and the Holocaust: Analyzing Gender Difference." In *Experi-*

ence and Expression: Women and the Holocaust, ed. Elizabeth R. Baer and Myrna Goldenberg. Forthcoming, 2001.

Brenner, Rachel. *Writing as Resistance: Four Women Confronting the Holocaust.* University Park: Pennsylvania State University Press, 1997.

Bridenthal, Renate, Atina Grossmann, and Marion Kaplan. *When Biology Became Destiny: Women in Weimar and Nazi Germany.* New York: Monthly Review Press, 1984.

Bromberger, Barbara, et al. *Schwestern, vergeßt uns nicht. Frauen im Konzentrationslager: Moringen, Lichtenburg, Ravensbrück 1933–1945. Katalog zur Ausstellung: Frauen im Konzentrationslager.* Frankfurt am Main: Verlag für Akademische Schriften, 1988.

Buchanan, Tom, and Martin Conway. *Political Catholicism in Europe, 1918–1965.* New York: Oxford University Press, 1996.

Buchmann, Erika. *Die Frauen von Ravensbrück.* Berlin: Kongress-Verlag, 1961.

Burke, Tim. *Lifebuoy Men, Lux Women: Commodification, Consumption and Cleanliness in Modern Zimbabwe.* Durham: Duke University Press, 1996.

Bynum, Caroline Walker. *Holy Feast and Holy Fast: The Religious Significance of Food to Medieval Women.* Berkeley: University of California Press, 1987.

Carlton, Erin. *Thinking Fascism: Sapphic Modernism and Fascist Modernity.* Palo Alto: Stanford University Press, 1998.

Cochrane, Arthur C. *The Church's Confession under Hitler.* Pittsburgh: Pickwick Press, 1976.

Cole, Diana. "A Sudden Spate of Women's Holocaust Memoirs." *Lilith* 18.1 (1993): 26–28.

Conway, J. S. "Between Cross and Swastika: The Position of German Catholicism." In *A Mosaic of Victims: Non-Jews Persecuted and Murdered by the Nazis,* ed. Michael Berenbaum, 179–87. New York: New York University Press, 1990.

———. *The Nazi Persecution of the Churches, 1933–45.* New York: Basic Books, 1968.

Cosner, Sharon, and Victoria Cosner. *Women under the Third Reich: A Biographical Dictionary.* New York: Greenwood, 1998.

DeSilva, Cara. *In Memory's Kitchen: A Legacy from the Women of Terezin.* Northvale, NJ: Jason Aronson, 1996.

Dietrich, Donald. *Catholic Citizens in the Third Reich: Psycho-Social Principles and Moral Reasoning.* New Brunswick, NJ: Transaction, 1988.

———. "Catholic Resistance in the Third Reich." *Holocaust and Genocide Studies* 3.2 (1998): 171–86.

———. "Catholic Resistance to Racist Eugenics." In *Germans against Nazism: Nonconformity, Opposition and Resistance in the Third Reich,* ed. Francis R. Nicosia and Lawrence D. Stokes, 137–55. New York: Berg, 1990.

Dobkowski, Michael. "A Deafening Silence: A Reconsideration of Christianity and the Holocaust." *Dimensions: A Journal of Holocaust Studies* 12.2 (1998): 23–24.

Dworkin, Andrea. "The Unremembered: Searching for Women at the Holocaust Memorial Museum." *Ms.* 5 (November/December 1994): 52–58.

Ezrahi, Sidra. *By Words Alone: The Holocaust in Literature.* Chicago: University of Chicago Press, 1980.

Fehrenbach, Heide. *Cinema in Democratizing Germany: Reconstructing National Identity after Hitler.* Chapel Hill: University of North Carolina Press, 1995.

Feig, Konnilyn G. *Hitler's Death Camps: The Sanity of Madness.* New York: Holmes and Meier, 1981.

Felstiner, Mary Lowenthal. *To Paint Her Life: Charlotte Salomon in the Nazi Era.* New York: Harper's, 1994.

Fine, Ellen S. "Women Writers and the Holocaust: Strategies for Survival." In *Reflections of the Holocaust in Art and Literature,* ed. Randolph L. Braham, 79–95. New York: Columbia University Press, 1990.

Fishman, Ellen. "Why Women Are Writing Holocaust Memoirs Now." *Lilith* 15.2 (1990): 6–7, 29.

Fonseca, Isabel. *Bury Me Standing: The Gypsies and Their Journey.* New York: Vintage, 1995.

Frevert, Ute. *Women in German History: From Bourgeois Emancipation to Sexual Liberation.* Providence, RI: Berg, 1989.

Friedländer, Saul. *Nazi Germany and the Jews, Volume 1: The Years of Persecution, 1933–1939.* New York: Harper Perennial, 1997.

Fuchs, Esther, ed. *Women and the Holocaust: Narrative and Representation.* Lanham, MD: University Press of America, 1999.

Füllberg-Stolberg, Claus, Martina Jung, Renate Riebe, and Martina Scheitenberger, eds. *Frauen in Konzentrationslagern Bergen-Belsen, Ravensbrück.* Bremen: Edition Temmen, 1994.

Gallin, Mother Mary Alice. *German Resistance to . . . Hitler: Ethical and Religious Factors.* Washington, DC: Catholic University Press, 1961.

Gardner, William. "Catholic Resistance in Occupied Countries." Privately printed, 1942.

Gellately, Robert. *The Gestapo and German Society: Enforcing Racial Policy, 1933–1945.* Oxford: Clarendon Press, 1990.

Gill, Anton. *The Journey Back from Hell: An Oral History: Conversations with Concentration Camp Survivors.* New York: Morrow, 1988.

Goldenberg, Myrna. "Choices, Risks, and Conscience." *Belles Lettres* 10 (Winter 1993–94): 42–45.

———. "Different Horrors, Same Hell: Women Remembering the Holocaust." In *Thinking the Unthinkable: Meanings of the Holocaust,* ed. Roger S. Gottlieb, 150–66. Mahwah, NJ: Paulist Press, 1990.

———. "Food Talk: Gendered Responses to Hunger in the Concentration Camps." In *Experience and Expression: Women and the Holocaust,* ed. Elizabeth R. Baer and Myrna Goldenberg. Forthcoming, 2001.

———. " 'From a World Beyond': Women in the Holocaust." *Feminist Studies* 22.3 (Fall 1996): 667–87.

———. "Lessons Learned from Gentle Heroism: Women's Holocaust Narratives." *Annals of the American Academy of Political and Social Science* 548 (November 1996): 78–93.

———. "Testimony, Narrative, and Nightmare: The Experiences of Jewish Women in the Holocaust." In *Active Voices: Women in Jewish Culture,* ed. Maurice Sacks, 94–106. Urbana: University of Illinois Press, 1995.

Griech-Polelle, Beth. "A Pure Conscience Is Good Enough: Bishop von Galen, the Nazis, and the Question of Resistance." Ph.D. diss., Rutgers University, 1999.

Grossmann, Atina. "The New Woman and the Rationalization of Sexuality in Weimar Germany." In *Powers of Desire,* ed. Ann Snitow et al., 153–71. New York: Monthly Review Press, 1983.

———. *Reforming Sex: The German Movement for Birth Control and Abortion Reform, 1920–1950.* New York: Oxford, 1995.

Gurewitsch, Brana, ed. *Mothers, Sisters, Resisters: Oral Histories of Women Who Survived the Holocaust.* Tuscaloosa: University of Alabama Press, 1998.

Gutman, Israel, ed. *Encyclopedia of the Holocaust.* New York: Macmillan, 1990.

Halio, Jay, and Ben Siegel, eds. *Daughters of Valor: Contemporary Jewish American Women Writers.* Newark: University of Delaware Press, 1997.

Heike, Irmgard. "'. . . da es sich ja lediglich um die Bewachung der Häftlinge handelt . . .': Lagerverwaltung und Bewachungspersonal." In *Frauen in Konzentrationslagern Bergen-Belsen, Ravensbrück,* ed. Claus Füllberg-Stolberg et al., 221–40. Bremen: Edition Temmen, 1994.

Heineman, Elizabeth. "The Hour of the Woman: Memories of Germany's 'Crisis Years' and West German National Identity." *American Historical Review* 101.2 (April 1996): 354–95.

Heinemann, Marlene E. *Gender and Destiny: Women Writers and the Holocaust.* New York: Greenwood, 1986.

Herbermann, Charles G., ed. *The Catholic Encyclopedia.* 15 vols. New York: Robert Appleton, 1912.

Herbermann, Nanda. "Frauenliteratur." *Der Gral* 3.30 (December 1935): 135.

——. "Zu unserem Kunstwerk." *Der Gral* 1.29 (October 1934): 41–42.

Herzog, Monika. *Drawings of Ravensbrück: ". . . hope, which lives in us eternally."* Fürstenburg: Mahn- und Gedenkstätte Ravensbrück, 1993.

Higgonet, Margaret, Jane Jenson, Sonya Michel, and Margaret Collins Weitz, eds. *Behind the Lines: Gender and the Two World Wars.* New Haven: Yale University Press, 1987.

Hoffmann, Peter. *German Resistance to Hitler.* Cambridge, MA: Harvard University Press, 1988.

Horowitz, Sara R. "Memory and Testimony of Women Survivors of Nazi Genocide." In *Women of the Word: Jewish Women and Jewish Writing,* ed. Judith Baskin, 258–82. Detroit: Wayne State University Press, 1996.

——. "'The Pin With Which to Stick Yourself': The Holocaust in Jewish American Women's Writing." In *Daughters of Valor: Contemporary Jewish American Women Writers,* ed. Jay Halio and Ben Siegel, 141–59. Newark: University of Delaware Press, 1997.

Huyssen, Andreas. "Mass Culture as Woman: Modernism's Other." In *After the Great Divide: Modernism, Mass Culture, Postmodernism.* Bloomington: Indiana University Press, 1986.

Jacobeit, Sigrid, ed. "Ich grüße Euch als freier Mensch." *Quellenedition zur Befreiung des Frauen-Konzentrationslagers Ravensbrück im April 1945. Schriftenreihe der Stiftung Brandenburgische Gedenkstätten Band Nr. 6.* Fürstenberg: Stiftung Brandenburg Gedenkstätten und Edition Hentrich, 1995.

Jacobeit, Sigrid, and Grit Philipp, eds. *Forschungsschwerpunkt Ravensbrück. Beiträge zur Geschichte des Frauen-Konzentrationslagers.* Berlin: Edition Hentrich, 1997.

Jacobeit, Sigrid, and Lieselotte Thoms-Heinrich. *Kreuzweg Ravensbrück. Lebensbilder antifaschistischer Widerstandskämpferinnen.* Leipzig: Verlag für die Frau Leipzig, 1987.

Jacobeit, Sigrid, ed., with help from Elisabeth Brümann-Güdter. *Ravensbrückerinnen. Schriftenreihe der Stiftung Brandenburgische Gedenkstätten Band Nr. 4.* Fürstenberg: Stiftung Brandenburgische Gedenkstätten and Edition Hentrich, 1995.

Katz, Esther, and Joan Ringelheim, eds. *Proceedings of the Conference: Women Surviving the Holocaust.* New York: Institute for Research in History, 1983.

Kaufman, Doris. "Ein 'Warner gegen die Mächte der Finsternis'. Pater Friedrich Muckermanns Kampf gegen Bolschewismus und Nationalsozialismus in Münster 1924–1934." In *Überwältigte Vergangenheit—Erinnerungsscherben, Faschismus und Nachkriegszeit in Münster i.W.,* ed. H. G. Thien, H. Wienold, and S. Preuß, 13–28. Münster: Verlag Westfälisches Dampfboot, 1984.

Keegan, John, ed. *The Times Atlas of the Second World War.* New York: Harper and Row, 1989.

Kiedrzynska, Wanda. *Ravensbrück: kobiecy obóz koncentracyjny.* Warsaw: Ksazka i Wiedza, 1961.

Klier, Freya. *Die Kaninchen von Ravensbrück. Medizinische Versuche an Frauen in der NS-Zeit.* München: Knaur, 1994.

Koonz, Claudia. *Mothers in the Fatherland: Women, the Family and Nazi Politics.* New York: St. Martin's, 1987.

Krause, Martina, ed. *Ravensbrück Memorial Museum: An Overview.* Oranienburg: Stiftung Brandenburgische Gedenkstätten, 1996.

Kremer, Lillian. "The Holocaust and the Witnessing Imagination." In *Violence, Silence, and Anger: Women's Writing as Transgression,* ed. Deirdre Lashgari, 231–46. Charlottesville: University Press of Virginia, 1995.

———. "Holocaust Writing." *The Oxford Companion to Women's Writing in the United States,* 395–97. New York: Oxford University Press, 1994.

———. "Holocaust-Wrought Women: Portraits by Four American Writers." *Studies in American Jewish Literature* 11.2 (Fall 1992): 150–61.

———. *Women's Holocaust Writing: Memory and Imagination.* Lincoln: University of Nebraska Press, 1999.

Laska, Vera. *Women in the Resistance and in the Holocaust: The Voices of Eyewitnesses.* Westport, CT: Greenwood, 1983.

Levi, Primo. Foreword to *Smoke over Birkenau,* by Liana Millu. Evanston, IL: Northwestern University Press, 1991.

Lewy, Guenter. *The Catholic Church and Nazi Germany.* New York: McGraw Hill, 1964.

Linden, R. Ruth. *Making Stories, Making Selves: Feminist Reflections on the Holocaust.* Columbus: Ohio State University Press, 1993.

Litschke, E. "National Memorial of Ravensbrück—Museum." Rostock: Ostsee-Druck, n.d.

Litschke, E., and K. Schlaefer, eds. *Der Zellenbau Ravensbrück: The Cell Block of Ravensbrück Women's Concentration Camp.* Fürstenberg-on-Havel: Ravensbrück National Memorial, 1987.

Littell, Franklin H. *The Crucifixion of the Jews.* New York: Harper and Row, 1975.

Lorenz, Dagmar. *Keepers of the Motherland: German Texts by Jewish Women Writers.* Lincoln: University of Nebraska Press, 1997.

Magnus, Shulamith. "'Out of the Ghetto': Integrating the Study of Jewish Women into the Study of the 'The Jews.'" *Judaism* 39.1 (1990): 28–36.

Mariaux, W. *The Persecution of the Catholic Church in the Third Reich: Facts and Documents.* New York: Longmans Green, 1942.

Marrus, Michael R. *The Holocaust in History.* Hanover, NH: University Press of New England, 1987.

Martin, Elaine, ed. *Gender, Patriarchy and Fascism in the Third Reich: The Response of*

Women Writers. Detroit: Wayne State University Press, 1993.

Milton, Sybil. "Women and the Holocaust: The Case of German and German-Jewish Women." In *When Biology Became Destiny: Women in Weimar and Nazi Germany,* ed. Renate Bridenthal, Atina Grossmann, and Marion Kaplan, 297–333. New York: Monthly Review Press, 1984.

Morrison, Jack G. "For Women Only: The Ravensbrück Concentration Camp." *Proteus* 12.2 (Fall 1995): 51–55.

Muckermann, Friedrich. *Der Gral* 12.28 (September 1934): 576.

———. "Pompa diaboli." *Der Gral* 9.28 (June 1934): 385–89.

Nicosia, Francis R., and Lawrence D. Stokes, eds. *Germans against Nazism: Nonconformity, Opposition and Resistance in the Third Reich.* Oxford: Berg, 1990.

Noakes, J., and G. Pridham, eds. *Nazism, 1919–1945: A History in Documents and Eyewitness Accounts.* 3 vols. New York: Schocken, 1990.

Noyce, Wilfred. *They Survived: A Study of the Will to Live.* New York: E. P. Dutton, 1993.

Ofer, Dalia, and Lenore Weitzman, eds. *Women in the Holocaust.* New Haven: Yale University Press, 1998.

Owings, Alison. *Frauen: German Women Recall the Third Reich.* New Brunswick, NJ: Rutgers University Press, 1993.

Paul, Christa. *Zwangsprostitution: Staatlich errichtete Bordelle im Nationalsozialismus.* Berlin: Edition Hentrich, 1994.

Paul, Gerhard, and Klaus-Michael Mallmann, eds. *Die Gestapo. Mythos und Realität.* With a foreword by Peter Steinbach. Darmstadt: Wissenschaftliche Buchgesellschaft, 1995.

Petro, Patrice. *Joyless Streets: Women and Melodramatic Representation in Weimar Germany.* Princeton: Princeton University Press, 1989.

Peukert, Detlev J. K. *Inside Nazi Germany: Conformity, Opposition, and Racism in Everyday Life.* Trans. Richard Deveson. New Haven: Yale University Press, 1987.

Phayer, Michael. "The German Catholic Church after the Holocaust." *Holocaust and Genocide Studies* 10.2 (Fall 1996): 151–67.

———. *Protestant and Catholic Women in Nazi Germany.* Detroit: Wayne State University Press, 1990.

Phayer, Michael, and Eva Fleischner. *Cries in the Night: Women Who Challenged the Holocaust.* Kansas City: Sheed and Ward, 1997.

Rabinbach, Anson, and Jack Zipes, eds. *Germans and Jews since the Holocaust: The Changing Situation in West Germany.* New York: Holmes and Meier, 1986.

Remmler, Karen. "Gender Identities and the Remembrance of the Holocaust." *Women in German Yearbook* 10 (1994): 167–87.

Ringelheim, Joan. "Thoughts about Women and the Holocaust." In *Thinking the Unthinkable: Meanings of the Holocaust,* ed. Roger S. Gottlieb, 141–49. Mahwah, NJ: Paulist Press, 1990.

———. "The Unethical and the Unspeakable: Women and the Holocaust." *Simon Wiesenthal Center Annual I* (1984): 69–87.

———. "Women and the Holocaust: A Reconsideration of Research." *Signs: Journal of Women in Culture and Society* 10.4 (1985): 741–61.

———. "Women and the Holocaust: A Reconsideration of Research." In *Jewish Women in Historical Perspective,* ed. Judith R. Baskin, 243–64. Detroit: Wayne State University Press, 1991.

————. "Women and the Holocaust: A Reconsideration of Research." In *Different Voices: Women and the Holocaust*, ed. Carol Rittner and John K. Roth, 373–405. New York: Paragon House, 1993.

Rittner, Carol, and John K. Roth. *Different Voices: Women and the Holocaust.* New York: Paragon House, 1993.

Ritvo, Roger A., and Diane M. Plotkin. *Sisters in Sorrow: Voices of Care in the Holocaust.* College Station: Texas A & M University Press, 1998.

Roth, John K., and Richard L. Rubenstein. *Approaches to Auschwitz: The Holocaust and Its Legacy.* Atlanta: John Knox Press, 1987.

Saidel, Rochelle. "Ravensbrück Women's Concentration Camp: Before and After Liberation." In *Remembrance, Repentance, Reconciliation: Studies in the Shoah*, ed. Douglas F. Tobler, 165–75. Vol. 21. New York: University Press of America, 1998.

Schmitt, Franz Anselm, ed. *Reinhold Schneider. Leben und Werk in Dokumenten.* Olten: Walter-Verlag AG, 1969.

Schoenfeld, Gabriel. "Auschwitz and the Professors." *Commentary* (June 1998): 42–46.

Scholder, Klaus. *The Churches and the Third Reich.* 2 vols. Trans. John Bowden. Philadelphia: Fortress Press, 1988.

Schoppmann, Claudia. *Days of Masquerade: Life Stories of Lesbians during the Third Reich.* New York: Columbia University Press, 1996.

Schulz, Christa. "Weibliche Häftlinge aus Ravensbrück in Bordellen der Männerkonzentrationslager." In *Frauen in Konzentrationslagern Bergen-Belsen, Ravensbrück*, ed. Claus Füllberg-Stolberg et al., 135–46. Bremen: Edition Temmen, 1994.

Schwertfeger, Ruth. *Women of Theresienstadt: Voices from a Concentration Camp.* Oxford: Berg, 1989.

Snyder, Dr. Louis L. *Encyclopedia of the Third Reich.* New York: Paragon House, 1989.

————. *Louis L. Snyder's Historical Guide to World War II.* Westport, CT: Greenwood, 1982.

Steward, John S. *Sieg des Glaubens: Geheime Gestapo-Berichte über den Widerstand der Kirchen.* Zurich: IM Thomas Verlag, 1946.

Tec, Nechama. *When Light Pierced the Darkness: Christian Rescue of Jews in Nazi-Occupied Poland.* Oxford: Oxford University Press, 1986.

Terras, Victor, ed. *Handbook of Russian Literature.* New Haven: Yale University Press, 1985.

Thomas, Theodore N. *Women against Hitler: Christian Resistance in the Third Reich.* Westport, CT: Praeger, 1995.

von Ankum, Katharina. *Women in the Metropolis: Gender and Modernity in Weimar Culture.* Berkeley: University of California Press, 1997.

von Lang, Jochen. *Die Gestapo. Instrument des Terrors.* Munich: Wilhelm Heyne Verlag, 1990.

Wagner, Christa. *Geboren am See der Tränen.* Berlin: Militärverlag der Deutschen Demokratischen Republik, 1987.

Weiss, John. *Ideology of Death: Why the Holocaust Happened in Germany.* Chicago: Ivan R. Dee, 1996.

Wistrich, Robert S. *Antisemitism: The Longest Hatred.* New York: Pantheon, 1991.

————. *Who's Who in Nazi Germany.* New York: Routledge, 1995.

Young, James. *Writing and Rewriting the Holocaust: Narrative and the Consequences of Interpretation.* Bloomington: Indiana University Press, 1988.

Zahn, Gordon C. *German Catholics and Hitler's Wars: A Study in Social Control.* New York: Sheed and Ward, 1962.

Zörner, G., ed. *Frauen-KZ Ravensbrück.* Berlin: Deutscher Verlag der Wissenschaften, 1977.

Index